History and Drama

History and Drama

—

The Pan-European Tradition

Edited by
Joachim Küpper, Jan Mosch and Elena Penskaya

DE GRUYTER

This book is published in cooperation with the project DramaNet, funded by the European Research Council

Early Modern European Drama and the Cultural Net

European Research Council
Established by the European Commission

ISBN 978-3-11-073644-1
e-ISBN (PDF) 978-3-11-060427-6
e-ISBN (EPUB) 978-3-11-060436-8

This work is licensed under the Creative Commons Attribution-NonCommercial-NoDerivatives 4.0 License. For details go to https://creativecommons.org/licenses/by-nc-nd/4.0/.

Library of Congress Control Number: 2018956629

Bibliografic information published by the Deutsche Nationalbibliothek
The Deutsche Nationalbibliothek lists this publication in the Deutschen Nationalbibliografie; detailed bibliografic data are available on the Internet at http://dnb.dnb.de.

© 2020 Joachim Küpper, Jan Mosch and Elena Penskaya, published by Walter de Gruyter GmbH, Berlin/Boston
This volume is text- and page-identical with the hardback published in 2019.
Cover image: photodeedooo/iStock/Thinkstock
Typesetting: Integra Software Services Pvt. Ltd.
Printing and binding: CPI books GmbH, Leck

www.degruyter.com

Acknowledgments

This collection arose from the conference "History and Drama: The Pan-European Tradition," which was held at Freie Universität Berlin on 26 and 27 October 2016. Organized within the framework of the European Research Council Advanced Grant project "Early Modern European Drama and the Cultural Net" (DramaNet), it brought together experts on early modern literature and culture who teach in Russia, the United States, Austria, and Germany. The essays in this volume are either extended versions of papers presented on that occassion or have been written in response to the scholarly discussion that took place in that forum.

The editors would like to express their gratitude to all participants for the engaging conversations, both during the formal and the informal parts of the conference, and to Jaša Drnovšek and Tatiana Korneeva for their careful planning of the event.

Furthermore, our thanks go to Agnes Kloocke for resolving any and all organizational issues during the conference and the preparation of this volume, and to Orla Mulholland for her meticulous copy-editing of the texts therein.

We appreciate the care that Ulrike Krauß, Gabrielle Cornefert, and the production team at de Gruyter put into this book project, and their time and generosity in answering our questions.

The conference and this collection were made possible through funding from the European Research Council, whose invaluable support of international collaboration and outstanding research in the Humanities we gratefully acknowledge.

Joachim Küpper, Jan Mosch, and Elena Penskaya

Contents

Acknowledgments —— V

Jan Mosch
Introduction —— 1

Joachim Küpper
Literature and Historiography in Aristotle and in Modern Times —— 28

Blair Hoxby
History, Myth, and Early Modern Drama —— 38

Gaia Gubbini
King Arthur in Medieval French Literature: History and Fiction, the Sense of the Tragic, and the Role of Dreams in *La Mort le Roi Artu* —— 42

Susanne Friede
When History Does Not Fit into Drama: Some Thoughts on the Absence of King Arthur in Early Modern Plays —— 56

Julia V. Ivanova
Machiavelli's Soteriology and the Humanist Quattrocento Dialogue —— 60

Pavel V. Sokolov
Lucretia without Poniard: Pieter Corneliszoon Hooft's *Geeraerdt van Velsen* between Livy and Tacitus —— 72

Ekaterina Boltunova
The Historical Writing of Catherine II: Dynasty and Self-Fashioning in *The Chesme Palace* (*Chesmenskii Dvorets*) —— 86

Kirsten Dickhaut
History – Drama – Mythology —— 96

Elena N. Penskaya
Fielding's Farces: Travestying the Historiosophical Discourse —— 101

Olga Kuptsova
Ostrovsky's Experience of the Creation of the European Theatrical Canon and Russian Stage Practice: Personal Preferences and General Trends —— 112

Natalia V. Sarana
The *Bildungsdrama* and Alexander Ostrovsky's Plays —— 121

Gautam Chakrabarti
"Sail[ing] on the Pathless Deep": Michael Madhusudan Datta's Dramatic Entanglements —— 129

Toni Bernhart and Janina Janke
The Crystallization of Early Modern European Drama in the Folk-Theater Tradition in Tyrol: The Marienberg *Griseldis* from 1713, Staged in 2016 —— 147

DS Mayfield
Rhetorical Ventriloquism in Application —— 160

Notes on Contributors —— 193

Index —— 199

Jan Mosch
Introduction

Historiography and literature are verbal representations of actions and events that either have happened or could happen in the human lifeworld. As such, they possess an uncanny 'family resemblance' that has impelled theorists since Antiquity to define the limits of the two 'sister arts.' Historiographical texts, from one point of view, are liable to veer towards fiction. This is the case, for example, when biographies describe the mental states of their protagonists[1] or when factographical texts venture into "virtual history," whose ancient precedent is the so-called Alexander digression in Livy's *Ab Urbe Condita*. Defending Livy's discussion of what *would have* happened if Alexander *had* waged war on Rome against charges of inconsequentiality, Ruth Morello has observed how such fictional devices continue to be perceived as a threat to positivist history: "Orthodox historians have tended to dislike attempts to think counterfactually about the past, on the grounds that 'virtual history' offers little more than entertainment and degenerates too easily into banal trivialities."[2]

Literature, on the other hand, frequently borrows its subject matter from history – be it historical persons, events, places, or social realities – and thus encroaches upon the domain of historiography. As a result, the development of the two discourses is entangled and often competitive. Sixteenth-century Britain may serve as a case in point. At the time, historians like Polydore Vergil and John Stow were discrediting the hitherto popular stories regarding the mythological origins of various peoples,[3] particularly the theory of the Trojan diaspora that saw Aeneas' descendants found both Rome and Britain.[4] One might plausibly hypothesize that

---

[1] Cf. Carolyn G. Heilbrun. "Is Biography Fiction? [With a response by Joan M. Weimer.]" *Soundings: An Interdisciplinary Journal* 76 (1993), pp. 295–314. Heilbrun relates the question to the polysemy of the word "fiction," but seems in general agreement with Roland Barthes' quip that any form of biography produces "a novel that dare not speak its name" (p. 295; Cf. Barthes. "Réponses." *Tel Quel* 47 (1971), p. 92.)
[2] Ruth Morello. "Livy's Alexander Digression (9.17–19): Counterfactuals and Apologetics." *The Journal of Roman Studies* 92 (2002), pp. 62–85, p. 62.
[3] That the material was popular does not, of course, mean that it was universally regarded as credible. When Polydore Vergil insists that these stories were once believed to the letter, this ought to be seen as part of the construal of the 'gullible' Middle Ages by a Renaissance thinker. Regarding the Arthurian tradition, Gaia Gubbini's article in this volume argues that medieval writers were predominantly incredulous of the monarch's historical existence.
[4] Arthur Alfaix Assis observes a "boom in humanistic historiography" in the sixteenth century, noting how metahistoriographical texts, the *artes historicae*, became popular in post-Tridentine

the absence of King Arthur from the Shakespearean stage[5] – despite the considerable creative and commercial appeal that this legend must have exerted – is connected to an attempt to match the humanists' emphasis on the veracity of their accounts. Mythologically speaking, King Arthur was the dynastic link between Aeneas and the ruling Tudor family. The early Tudors still tried to exploit this notion for political gain: Henry VII's older son was christened Arthur. He died, however, before he could succeed his father, and as a consequence, England saw the reign of King Henry VIII, not the return of the "once and future king" promised in the Arthurian material. Combined with the humanists' acerbic source criticism and the established use of history for the discussion of good governance,[6] this apparent triumph of contingency over mythologized providence seems to have favored a demand for stage productions that, poetic license notwithstanding, purported to make the 'actual' past present: "Think, when we talk of horses, that you see them/Printing their proud hoofs i' th' receiving earth,/For 'tis your thoughts that now must deck our kings,/Carry them here and there, jumping o'er times."[7]

The argument that such transtemporal leaps constitute "a form of naivety" on part of the early modern authors, i.e. a mere "metaphysics of presence" that has long been deconstructed, has been rejected by Jean-Christophe Mayer,[8] who suggests adapting Paul Ricoeur's concept of *lieutenance* – the idea that narratives stand in for, or take the place of, the inaccessible past – for the study of history

---

Catholic Europe, too. In this context, the author discusses Jean Bodin, whose *Method for the Easy Comprehension of History* (1566) did away with the idea of the Trojan lineage of Europe as well: *What Is History For?: Johann Gustav Droysen and the Functions of Historiography*. New York: Berghahn, 2014, spec. p. 32.

5 The absence of King Arthur from virtually the entire early modern dramatic canon is a curious and multifarious phenomenon. For a deeper discussion, cf. the article by Susanne Friede in this volume.

6 Jessica Winston has demonstrated the influence that the *Mirror for Magistrates* (1559), a compendium of poems with historical subjects, exercised on the first English tragedies, arguing that the playwrights "were not interested in the specific period of English history presented in the *Mirror*, but liked the way that history functioned in the book: admonishing magistrates and facilitating political discussion" ("National History to Foreign Calamity: *A Mirror for Magistrates* and Early English Tragedy." *Shakespeare's Histories and Counter-Histories*, edited by Dermot Cavanagh, Stuart Hampton-Reeves, and Stephen Longstaffe. Manchester: Manchester University Press, 2006. – For a survey of the genealogy and the ideologically divergent functions of the English history plays, see also the other papers in that volume.)

7 Shakespeare, *Henry V*, Pro.27–30. – William Shakespeare's plays are quoted from *The Norton Shakespeare*, edited by Stephen Greenblatt et al. New York: Norton, 1998.

8 Jean-Christophe Mayer. "The Decline of the Chronicle and Shakespeare's History Plays." *Shakespeare's English Histories and their Afterlives*, edited by Peter Holland. Cambridge: Cambridge University Press, 2010, pp. 12–23, pp. 18–19.

plays. In line with the playwrights' own ideology, such an approach would ultimately make literature a conduit to the past, a form of access that is more immediate than the one provided by the historians' tracts. A comparable subversion of the boundaries of the invented and the empirical currently occurs in fiction studies,[9] where compositionalism – the view that texts can be *both* factographical and fictional – has found some traction.[10]

If, in summary, there is no consensus on the respective epistemological and ontological achievements and limits of historiography and literature,[11] we propose that in order to move forward we must look back to the entwined development of the two kinds of writing. Since Antiquity, the two discourses have been bound up in productive processes of exchange but have also tried to prove their respective relevance by 'othering' the neighboring formation, marking it as mendacious or philosophically irrelevant. This introduction will present a brief historical sketch of that discursive entanglement, followed by an overview of the papers of the present volume, which aims to analyze the specific potentials of history in literature.

One might object that the alleged proximity of historiography and literature is a phenomenon that did not become relevant until the eighteenth century, when the novel started to engender its "reality effect" (Roland Barthes) through minute topographical and social descriptions. Editorial fiction thrived at the same time; the locus classicus for this phenomenon would seem to be Daniel Defoe's

---

[9] For a comprehensive overview, cf. Jean-Marie Schaeffer. "Fictional vs. Factual Narration." *The Living Handbook of Narratology*, edited by Peter Hühn et al. Hamburg: Hamburg University. http://www.lhn.uni-hamburg.de/article/fictional-vs-factual-narration. Accessed 18 April 2018. See also Irina O. Rajewski and Anne Enderwitz. "Einleitung." *Fiktion im Vergleich der Künste und Medien*. Berlin: de Gruyter, 2016, pp. 1–18. The authors address, among other aspects, the "Napoleon problem" (p. 2) – the question whether a historical character in a text is best described as fictitious/fictional/real/pseudo-real, etc.
[10] See, for example, Eva-Maria Konrad. "Signposts of Factuality: On Genuine Assertions in Fictional Literature." *Art and Belief*, edited by Ema Sullivan-Bissett, Helen Bradley, and Paul Noordhof. Oxford: Oxford University Press, 2017, pp. 42–62.
[11] This highlights, of course, the general difficulty of defining literature. A diachronic overview of literary theory is provided by the essays in *Mimesis, Repräsentation, Imagination*, edited by Jörg Schönert und Ulrike Zeuch. Berlin: de Gruyter, 2004. – Joachim Küpper has argued that literature is characterized by its rhetorical mode (e.g. lack of referentiality, code elasticity, and the reader's associative 'roaming' in a secondary world): "Was ist Literatur?" *Zeitschrift für Ästhetik und Allgemeine Kunstwissenschaft* 45 (2001), pp. 187–215. In the following, it will be assumed that the theoretical attempts to sequester literature and historiography from each other result from the anxiety that their specific codes or modes be misconstrued, e.g. a fictional text be read as factographical and vice versa, which endangers the text's specific values – and the reader's cultural capital.

Robinson Crusoe (1719), which (in its first edition) poses as a work of historiography, i.e. an actual castaway's journal that has been prepared for publication by an anonymous editor[12]: "The Editor believes the thing to be a just History of Fact; neither is there any appearance of fiction in it."[13]

It is certainly true that realist literature challenged readers in new ways to distinguish between fact and fiction; in the case of *Crusoe*, the reader is required to recognize that the editor is another character in the text and that his opinion on the veracity of the account does not elevate its referential status in the empirical world. Although ludic in nature, the inclusion of this conceit can be seen as an improper change of the terms of the implicit 'pact' between readers and writers. Eva-Maria Konrad, for one, has sought to demonstrate that editorial fiction cannot guard itself against charges of dishonesty simply by taking recourse to Philip Sidney's succinct statement that "the Poet, he nothing affirms, and therefore never lieth."[14]

Nevertheless, the rivalry between historiography and literature is much older than editorial fiction or the reality effect. The more pertinent point seems to be that both kinds of text share an anthropocentric bias as products of human culture and consciousness. Aristotle famously defines poetry as an imitative art whose "objects of representation [mimesis]" are "living persons," or, literally, "men doing or experiencing something."[15] The subject matter of historiography is not at all dissimilar; any distinction must therefore rely on the ontological status or referentiality of what is verbally mediated in each case: "The difference between a historian and a poet is not that one writes in prose and the other in verse – indeed the writings of Herodotus could be put into verse and yet would still be a kind of history, whether written in metre or not. The real difference is this, that one tells what happened and the other what might happen."[16]

---

12 In keeping with this fictitious historiographical approach, the full title reads: *The Life and Strange Surprizing Adventures of Robinson Crusoe of York, Mariner: Who lived Eight and Twenty Years, all alone in an un-inhabited Island on the Coast of America, near the Mouth of the Great River of Oroonoque; Having been cast on Shore by Shipwreck, wherein all the Men perished but himself. With An Account how he was at last as strangely deliver'd by Pirates. Written by Himself.*
13 [Daniel Defoe.] "The Preface." *The Life and Strange Surprizing Adventures...* London: W. Taylor, 1719.
14 Cf. Eva-Maria Konrad. "'The Poet, he nothing affirms, and therefore never lieth'?: An Analysis of Editorial Fiction." *Diegesis* 4 (2015), pp. 1–17. http://nbn-resolving.de/urn:nbn:de:hbz:468-20150519-150018-3. Accessed 18 April 2018.
15 Aristotle. *Poetics. Aristotle in 23 Volumes*, vol. 23, translated by William H. Fyfe. Cambridge: Harvard University Press, 1932, 1447a. The literal translation is suggested by Fyfe in n. 1.
16 Ibid., 1451a–1451b.

It seems that the distinction is fairly unproblematic for Aristotle, who uses a similar argument at the beginning of the *Poetics* when he contrasts Homer's poems and Empedocles' hexametric rendering of physiological knowledge: "But Homer and Empedocles have nothing in common except the metre, so that it would be proper to call the one a poet and the other not a poet but a scientist."[17] For future centuries, however, the crucial question turned out to be whether such a distinction is possible at all times, at least on part of the recipient. One might object here again that the rhetorical mode of certain genres such as the medieval annals or lyrical poetry is obvious. Hayden White, for one, has contended that the elliptical style of the annals (as opposed to the chronicles and narrative history) is indicative of a pre-modern attitude towards history – a worldview hardly concerned with cause and effect or human agency,[18] which puts it at a farther remove from the aesthetic unity ascribed to works of literature. However, even in the examples quoted by White, the focus of the annals is typically on the weather, the harvest, or political developments such as raids and the royal succession. There is, in other words, an anthropocentric bias to this kind of history-writing, a focus on the survival of a community of people. In a similar vein, lyrical poetry has latterly become the focus of narratological analysis and is increasingly read as a narrative genre that mediates a "temporal sequentiality of events."[19] It is therefore no exaggerated conclusion that the distinction between factography and fiction is always precarious without appropriate context. A modern reader who happens upon the following excerpt of the *Annals of Saint Gall* might be forgiven for thinking that they were dealing with a poem that uses rhetorical devices (anaphora), visual poetry (empty lines), and intertextual references (the biblical account of the Deluge) to articulate a vision of the world's spiritual emptiness and destruction:

> 709. Hard winter. Duke Gottfried died.
> 710. Hard year and deficient in crops.
> 711.
> 712. Flood everywhere.[20]

---

[17] Ibid., 1477b.
[18] Hayden White. *The Content of the Form: Narrative Discourse and Historical Representation.* Baltimore: Johns Hopkins University Press, 1987, p. 6.
[19] Cf., for example, Peter Hühn and Jens Kiefer. *The Narratological Analysis of Lyric Poetry: Studies in English Poetry from the 16th to the 20th Century*, translated by Alastair Matthews. Berlin: de Gruyter, 2011.
[20] Anon., *Annals of Saint Gall*, quoted in White, *Content of the Form*, pp. 6–7.

This mock interpretation is, to be sure, fanciful, but it accentuates Aristotle's important observation that there is no inherent formal criterion for the distinction of factographical and fictional texts. One ancient text to problematize this situation is the second-century treatise *The Way to Write History* by Lucian of Samosata, which remarks that "it is a great, a superlative weakness, this inability to distinguish history from poetry."[21] The author maintains that history-writing, like "talking, seeing, or eating," is too often regarded as requiring no instruction – and that the verification of facts is therefore neglected in favor of popular embellishments.[22] In particular, this Second Sophist criticizes the use of eulogies, arguing that what many historians "seem not to know is that poetry and history offer different wares, and have their separate rules. Poetry enjoys unrestricted freedom; it has but one law – the poet's fancy."[23] As a result, flying horses or the gods are suitable subjects for poetry, or so Lucian argues; prose historiography, on the other hand, should never employ fictitious elements lest it become "nothing but poetry without the wings; the exalted tones are missing; and imposition of other kinds without the assistance of metre is only the more easily detected."[24]

Under Lucian's satirical gaze, then, historiography must keep its distance from literature so as not to turn grotesquely androgynous: "What, [should we] bedizen history, like her sister, with tale and eulogy and their attendant exaggerations? [You might] as well take some mighty athlete with muscles of steel, rig him up with purple drapery and meretricious ornament, rouge and powder his cheeks."[25] The use of a gendered, i.e. hierarchical, image, much like Lucian's scorn of historiography as a natural talent, betrays his attention to history as a skill – not just *epistêmê*, but also *technê* – of the educated elite. A *pepaideuménos* himself, the learned man speaks up against any embellishments that might turn historiography into a popular form; he warns that the "vulgar may very likely extend their favour to this; but the select (whose judgement you disregard) will get a good deal of entertainment out of your heterogeneous, disjointed, fragmentary stuff."[26]

---

21 Henry W. and Francis G. Fowler, editors. *The Way to Write History. The Works of Lucian of Samosata*. Oxford: Clarendon Press, 1905, pp. 109–136, p. 113.
22 The treatise alleges that it is a common vice among contemporary historians merely to write down whatever comes into their mind; Peter von Möllendorff reads this as a parody of enthusiasm. Cf. "Frigid Enthusiasts: Lucian on Writing History." *The Cambridge Classical Journal* 47 (2001), pp. 117–140. Ultimately, Lucian's critical portrayal of *enthousiasmós* among historians is another aspect of his argument that history must keep its distance from poetry.
23 Lucian, *The Way to Write History*, p. 113.
24 Ibid.
25 Ibid.
26 Ibid., p. 115.

As Lucian's treatise makes clear, the anxiety that provoked many critics to insist upon a strict sequestering of historiography and literature from each other is only partly motivated by epistemological concerns. What is at stake is, on the one hand, certainly a paradigm of knowledge: since literature is not bound by the standards of empirical truth, a positivist model of history must presuppose a discernible distance of historiography and literature. On the other hand, however, the ability to recognize the specific codes of the two forms is turned into cultural capital; to distinguish between the objectivizing impetus of science and the defamiliarizing technique of art[27] becomes a marker of learning. The case of Heinrich Schliemann, who controversially[28] claimed to have excavated the 'Homeric' town of Troy, is lodged in cultural memory precisely for what Schliemann celebrated as his insightful subversion of this distinction: "Trusting to the data of the Iliad, the exactness of which I used to believe in as in the Gospel itself, I imagined that *Hissarlik* [...] was the Pergamus [i.e. the citadel] of the city."[29]

Claims to the truth are a commonplace of early modern metahistoriographical and metafictional tracts. Arguing that "the historians' law is that a writer should neither dare to say a falsehood, nor shrink from telling a truth," Polydore Vergil's *English History* (1533) paraphrases earlier accounts of English origins with the hardly concealed intention that they be recognized as falsehoods:

> So then, it is written in that book, of whatever quality it may be, that Brutus was the son of Silvius, the agreed son of Aeneas' son Ascanius, and when he had traveled through Greece and conquered Aquitaine, by the instruction of Diana he sailed to Britain and killed off the giants, who possessed the island at the time, when they speedily flocked together under arms to drive off the newcomers. Then he occupied the island and named it Britain after himself, and so Brutus was the father of the British nation and empire.[30]

Stating that writers like Livy and Dionysius of Halicarnassus do not mention this Brutus, Polydore Vergil leaves it up to his readers (whose erudition he has praised

---

27 The allusion is, of course, to Viktor Shklovsky's essay "Art as Device" (1917).
28 The controversy persists to this day because the claim that Schliemann found 'Homer's Troy' is arguably false; what he did find was a stratum of the town which Homer used as the setting of the narrative. But the process of fictionalization is unilateral; a fictional text cannot be used to make referential claims about the empirical world. On topography and the reality effect, cf. the essay by Joachim Küpper below.
29 Heinrich Schliemann. *Troy and its Remains: A Narrative of Researches and Discoveries Made on the Site of Ilium, and in the Trojan Plain*, translated by anon., edited by Philip Smith. London: John Murray, 1875, p. 17.
30 Book 1, §19. – Quotations from Polydore Vergil are based on the *Anglica Historia (1555 Version)*, edited by Dana F. Sutton. *The Philological Museum*. The Shakespeare Institute of the University of Birmingham. http://www.philological.bham.ac.uk/polverg/. Accessed 18 April 2018.

in an initial *captatio benevolentiae*) to tell fact from fiction, adding only that it is an ancient custom to aggrandize one's tribal lineage:

> [...] many peoples have dared to trace their ancestry even to the gods, as Roman authors took the lead in doing, so that the beginnings of their nation and its cities would be more dignified and blesset, and those things, though they were taken from poetic fictions rather than incorrupt records of things done, have nonetheless been taken for the truth.[31]

In his *Survey of London* (1598), the historian and antiquarian John Stow follows in Polydore Vergil's footsteps when he explains that mythological, i.e. fictional, historiography had legitimate reasons among the ancients, but is not the appropriate frame for his own work:

> As the Roman writers, to glorify the city of Rome, derive the original thereof from gods and demi-gods, by the Trojan progeny, so Geoffrey of Monmouth, the Welsh historian, deduceth the foundation of this famous city of London, for the greater glory thereof, and emulation of Rome, from the very same original. For he reporteth that Brute, lineally descended from the demi-god Aeneas, the son of Venus, [...] built this city near unto the river now called Thames, and named it Troynovant, or Trenovant. But herein, as Livy, the most famous historiographer of the Romans, writeth, antiquity is pardonable, and hath an especial privilege, by interlacing divine matters with human, to make the first foundation of cities more honourable, more sacred, and, as it were, of greater majesty.[32]

While these historians do not speak up against poetry per se, they use it ostentatiously as a foil for their own labors so that their emphatic truth claims threaten the legitimation of literature: why deal with what is invented or feigned if other discourses deal with what is real? Even though the humanists' source criticism was only one mosaic piece in the general debate about the mendacity of literature (and the concomitant controversy about the instructive and corruptive qualities of theater), early modern historiography challenged literature to define its own achievements. Literary theory responded by citing the ancient authority of Aristotle. Philip Sidney's *Defence of Poesy* (c. 1579, published 1595) is typical in arguing that literature is valuable (more so than historiography, in fact) because it re-presents what is real in some higher, idealized form – and thus feeds back into empirical reality by edifying and reforming its audience:

> But now it may be alleged that if this imagining of matters be so fit for the imagination, then must the historian needs surpass, who brings you images of true matters, such as indeed were done, and not such as fantastically or falsely may be suggested to have been done. Truly, Aristotle himself, in his discourse of poesy, plainly determineth this question,

---

[31] Ibid.
[32] John Stow. *A Survey of London*, edited by William J. Thoms. London: Whittaker, 1842, p. 1.

saying that poetry is *philosophoteron* and *spoudaioteron*, that is to say, it is more philosophical and more studiously serious than history. His reason is, because poesy dealeth with *katholou*, that is to say with the universal consideration, and the history with *kathekaston*, the particular. [...]

For, indeed, if the question were whether it were better to have a particular act truly or falsely set down, there is no doubt which is to be chosen, no more than whether you had rather have Vespasian's picture right as he was, or, at the painter's pleasure, nothing resembling. But if the question be for your own use and learning, whether it be better to have it set down as it should be or as it was, then certainly is more doctrinable the feigned Cyrus in Xenophon than the true Cyrus in Justin.[33]

Sidney's argument is astute. Anticipating the ethical objection that truth is of a higher value than falsehoods, he concedes the point, but proceeds to introduce a comparison between different media: paintings, i.e. mimetic media,[34] should conform with their external reality; literature, by contrast, i.e. a medium that is both mimetic and fictional, may depart from reality in order to teach a specific lesson (which we must imagine as true on a higher plane, that of reason). From a critical perspective, one might add that Sidney's appropriation of Aristotle is probably a misinterpretation. Aristotle does indeed concede that a poet may both invent his material and draw on history for inspiration so long as the criterion of verisimilitude is observed: "Even supposing he [the poet] represents what has actually happened, he is none the less a poet, for there is nothing to prevent some actual occurrences being the sort of thing that would probably or inevitably happen, and it is in virtue of that that he is their 'maker.'"[35] However, current readings of Aristotle doubt that he is the detractor of historiography[36] that Sidney and other champions of literature make him out to be; moreover, it has been argued that poetic universality can only claim the, as it were, limited universality of human interactions[37] (as opposed to natural laws or the universal

---

33 Philip Sidney. *The Defence of Poesy. The Major Works*, edited by Katherine Duncan-Jones. Oxford: Oxford University Press, 2002, pp. 212–251, pp. 223–224.
34 Cf. Joachim Küpper. "Mimesis und Fiktion in der Literatur, Bildenden Kunst und Musik." *Zeitschrift für Ästhetik und Allgemeine Kunstwissenschaft* 53 (2008), pp. 169–190.
35 Aristotle, *Poetics*, 1451b.
36 Cf. Thornton C. Lockwood. "Aristotle on the (Alleged) Inferiority of History to Poetry." *Reading Aristotle: Argument and Exposition*, edited by William Wians and Ron Polansky. Leiden: Brill, 2017, pp. 315–333.
37 Cf. Malcolm Heath. "The Universality of Poetry in Aristotle's *Poetics*." *The Classical Quarterly* 41 (1991), pp. 389–402. – Heath argues that for Aristotle, poetry deals with what is universal under certain circumstances. It would make no sense to describe Achilles as the kind of person who is likely to cause the death of his friend; it makes very good sense, however, to describe Achil-

applicability of mathematics) and that the classification of literature as philosophical must therefore be taken *cum grano salis*.[38] Ultimately, as Joachim Küpper argues below,[39] there is a clear motive for Aristotle's emphasis on the universalizing traits of verisimilitude; the ninth chapter of the *Poetics* is not so much a celebration of literature vis-à-vis history as it is an attempt to delineate its function in such a way that it will not consist of futile inventions.

Of course, misinterpretations have creative potential,[40] and one may concede that Sidney's argument for the supremacy of literature is in keeping with the early modern tradition across Europe. Frequently, writers would choose a historical topic with the express intention to introduce a metafictional and metahistorical discussion. The prologue to *Wallenstein's Camp* (1798) by Friedrich Schiller, for example, argues that historiographical writing cannot adequately represent the character of Wallenstein because historians are too deeply entangled in the particular ideologies of the Thirty Years' War. Art is suggested as a counter-discourse, dealing – in keeping with Schiller's poetological postulates – with what is universalized as human nature:

> Confused by party hate and party favor
> Perception of his character is varied
> But now art will contrive to bring him nearer
> To both your eyes and hearts as only human.
> For art, which limits and unites all things,
> Will always trace back each extreme to nature,
> Will see a man caught in the stress of life
> And lay the blame for more than half his guilt
> On the misfortune of unlucky stars.[41]

Truth – though truth grounded in credibility, in verisimilitude – became the commodity of the playwrights: "Such as give/Their money out of hope they may believe,/May here find truth too."[42]

---

les as the kind of person who, under the conditions of the Trojan War as laid out in, for example, the *Iliad*, acts in such a way that the death of his friend is likely or even necessary (pp. 389–390).
38 Silvia Carli. "Poetry Is More Philosophical Than History: Aristotle on Mimesis and Form." *The Review of Metaphysics* 64 (2010), pp. 303–336.
39 Cf. the first essay in this volume.
40 Cf. Cristina Savettieri. "The Agency of Errors: Hamartia and its (Mis)interpretations in the Italian Cinquecento." *Poetics and Politics: Net Structures and Agencies in Early Modern Drama*, edited by Toni Bernhart et al. Berlin: de Gruyter, 2018, pp. 149–168.
41 Friedrich Schiller. "Prologue." *Wallenstein. The Robbers, Wallenstein*, edited by Francis J. Lamport. London: Penguin, 1979, pp. 163–170.
42 Shakespeare, *Henry VIII*, Pro.7–9.

The individual poetics of different authors notwithstanding, the main argument supported by Sidney remains largely intact in early modern times. One final example may suffice. In *Gondibert* (1651), a work loosely based on Paul the Deacon's *Historia Langobardorum*, William Davenant tries to revive the Homeric epic by blending it with the five-act structure of English Renaissance drama. Tellingly, he includes a long preface in which he justifies his choice of subject, arguing that the remote setting of his work would preserve him from any misguided insistence upon the historical accuracy of his version by those who

> know not the requisites of a Poem, nor how much pleasure they lose (and even the pleasures of Heroick Poesie are not unprofitable) who take away the liberty of a Poet, and fetter his feet in the shackles of an Historian: For why should a Poet doubt in Story to mend the intrigues of Fortune by more delightfull conveyances of probable fictions, because austere Historians have enter'd into bond to truth? an obligation which were in Poets, as foolish and unnecessary as is the bondage of false Martyrs, who lye in chains for a mistaken opinion: but by this I would imply, that Truth narrative and past, is the Idol of Historians (who worship a dead thing) and truth operative, and by effects continually alive, is the Mistress of Poets, who hath not her existence in matter, but in reason.

Davenant's differentiation between two kinds of truth – past and operative – clearly relies upon the Aristotelian distinction between historiographical and philosophical texts, while his strategy to "mend [...] Fortune" shows that Davenant makes an (in hindsight, doomed) attempt to resist the model of historical contingency peddled in the English history plays by reactivating both the ancient form of epic and Aristotle's strictures about the verisimilar, non-particular matters of poetry. Historical truth is denigrated as a form of capture – "shackles," "bond," "bondage," "chains" – whereas literature emerges as the locus of freedom qua the universal principle of reason.

The idea that literature might be equal to historiography when it comes to representing the past has gained support in poststructuralist theory and postmodernist narratives. From Clifford Geertz' "thick description" to Hayden White's emphasis on the "tropics of discourse" to the New Historicist conflation of text and context, textualist approaches to culture and the past have become the leading theoretical paradigm within only a few decades. Hayden White, in particular, has argued that the hegemony of modern narrative historiography corresponds to a need for closure that temporal reality as such (what in Shakespeare's most cogent exploration of nihilism, *Macbeth*, is called the "petty pace" of "tomorrow, and tomorrow, and tomorrow")[43] can never satisfy. Narrative history thus materializes

---

[43] Shakespeare, *Macbeth*, 5.5.19–20.

as a libidinous, wish-fulfilling genre that is perilously close to fictional literature: "The demand for closure in the historical story is a demand, I suggest, for moral meaning, a demand that sequences of real events be assessed as to their significance as elements of a *moral* drama."[44]

In line with its general distrust of authority and a singular truth, postmodernism has reacted to White's critique of history in that subset of historical novels that Linda Hutcheon called historiographic metafiction. According to Hutcheon's definition, these novels propagate a textualist view of the past, one that makes historiography and fiction virtually indistinguishable: "Since the [historical] documents become signs of events, which the historian transmutes into facts, as in historiographic metafiction, the lesson here is that the past once existed, but that our historical knowledge of it is semiotically transmitted."[45]

The critique of academic history has spawned an analytical impulse to read literature as referential. A recent volume edited by David Konstan and Kurt A. Raaflaub, *Epic and History* (2009), has surveyed the epic as a quasi-historiographical form, a space both of invention and memory. In his chapter on "Traditional History in South Slavic Oral Epic," John Miles Foley maintains that oral epic encodes a form of "traditionally constituted history," by which he refers to a "historical model" that contests "the perspective of modern, textualized history" and that "may come into conflict with outsiders who claim a different truth" but that also "boasts an immediacy, adaptability, and continuity that conventional history cannot match."[46] Raymond F. Person, a scholar of religion, has built on Foley's model of history to discuss biblical historiography.[47] Drawing on the psychologist Keith Oatley's claim that "fiction can be twice as true as fact" because it supplements "truth as empirical correspondence" with "truth as

---

44 White, *Content of the Form*, p. 24.
45 Linda Hutcheon. *A Poetics of Postmodernism: History, Theory, Fiction*. New York: Routledge, 1988, pp. 122–123.
46 John Miles Foley. "Traditional History in South Slavic Oral Epic." *Epic and History*, edited by David Konstan and Kurt A. Raaflaub. Boston: Wiley-Blackwell, 2009, pp. 347–361, pp. 355–356.
47 One might note in passing that the nineteenth-century controversy about Schliemann's discoveries was also a debate about the historiographical referentiality of the Bible (and, by extension, the veracity of its revelatory content). As David Gange and Rachel Bryant Davies have shown, Schliemann's remark about his trust in the *Iliad* as though it were the gospel is not a rhetorical hyperbole; for Schliemann and his contemporaries, the theory of Homeric Troy encompassed the historical existence of Biblical cities like Sodom and Gomorrah as well. Cf. "Troy." *Cities of God: The Bible and Archaeology in Nineteenth-Century Britain*, edited by David Gange and Michael Ledger-Lomas. Cambridge: Cambridge University Press, 2013, pp. 39–70, p. 46.

coherence within complex structures" and "truth as personal relevance,"[48] Person concludes that "traditional history can be twice as true as modern history."[49]

One might observe critically, however, that this statement only reiterates what literary theory has claimed for centuries by substituting the term "(traditional) history" for "literature." The celebratory tone misses the point that coherence and personal relevance are recognized qualities of literature; referentiality, by contrast, is not, as Oatley points out as well: "But fiction is not empirical truth. It is simulation that runs on minds of readers just as computer simulations run on computers."[50]

What, then, is gained and what is lost by the weakening of generic boundaries? A recent volume edited by Paulina Kewes has looked at *The Uses of History in Early Modern England* (2006). In her introductory statement, Kewes maintains that "Renaissance poetry, drama, and prose historiography, which were often written by the same people, routinely shared aims and preoccupations."[51] As a consequence, she suggests that scholars should look at "the uses of history in all its shapes and forms"[52] and proposes to investigate "'literary' and 'factual' writings side by side, avoiding traditional chronological and disciplinary divisions and the artificial separation of secular from ecclesiastical history."[53] Kewes' ambitious project to attain a holistic view of "the deployment of history for political, religious, moral, aesthetic, or commercial purposes"[54] is clearly to be praised. The premise that literature and historiography were "often" written by the same people is, however, open to doubt, at least as far as canonized authors with popular audiences are concerned. The most important objection to arise is that the equation of historiography and literature negates the special rhetorical mode of fictional literature, its function as a historiosophic or metahistorical discourse. Early modern English drama, to stay with a pertinent example, routinely introduces metatheatrical witticisms that challenge the statement at the surface level. In Shakespeare's *Henry VIII* (c. 1612), the archbishop Cranmer looks at an

---

48 Raymond Person, Jr. "Biblical Historiography as Traditional History." *The Oxford Handbook of Biblical Narrative*, edited by Danna Fewell. Oxford: Oxford University Press, 2016, pp. 73–83, p. 78.
49 Ibid.
50 Keith Oatley. "Why Fiction May be Twice as True as Fact: Fiction as Cognitive and Emotional Simulation." *Review of General Psychology* 3 (1999), pp. 101–117.
51 Paulina Kewes. "History and its Uses." *The Uses of History in Early Modern England*, edited by Paulina Kewes. San Marino: Huntington Library, 2006, pp. 1–30, p. 7.
52 Ibid., p. 11.
53 Ibid., p. 30.
54 Ibid., p. 11.

infant, Elizabeth, and tells the king how his daughter will grow up to be a marvelously felicitous and long-lived monarch. Henry replies:

> This oracle of comfort has so pleased me,
> That when I am in heaven I shall desire
> To see what this child does, and praise my Maker.[55]

The play here produces two effects: on the one hand, it functions as a eulogy for the deceased Queen Elizabeth, prompting the audience to ponder the loss. On the other hand, the play discloses its function as an ideological tool, as an "oracle of comfort." Much like the humanists, who did not tire of explaining the ancients' reasons for fusing myth and history (to glorify their origins), the play polemically asks whether such ideological motives are not inherent in any historicizing text. If so, its polysemy gives literature the upper hand, or so the banter of the epilogue, only a few lines after the supposed tribute to Elizabeth, implies. Rather than unite the audience as a homogeneous group of mourners, the play promises to stimulate debate and uncover different agendas:

> 'Tis ten to one this play can never please
> All that are here: some come to take their ease,
> And sleep an act or two; but those, we fear,
> We have frighted with our trumpets; so, 'tis clear,
> They'll say 'tis naught: others, to hear the city
> Abused extremely, and to cry 'That's witty!'[56]

English Renaissance drama playfully resists Sidney's notion that literature must be monadically doctrinal to legitimize its existence. History is not reduced to the role of an example, rolled, perhaps, into pleasurable scenes to be palatable for the masses, but otherwise similar to prose historiography. Instead, many plays question what the average groundling will, in the end, take away from the performances. Shakespeare's *The Taming of the Shrew* (c. 1590) pokes fun at the drunkard Christopher Sly, who is apparently a regular playgoer, but misquotes Thomas Kyd's *Spanish Tragedy* and cannot exactly remember the names of historical monarchs: "The Slys are no rogues. Look in the chronicles. We came in with Richard Conqueror."[57] Far from a didactically useful piece, to Sly, a chronicle is nothing but a historicizing record of his family's worth and station. Similarly, Ben Jonson's satirical comedy *The Devil Is an Ass* (1616) features a dialogue between

---

55 Shakespeare, Henry *VIII*, 5.5.65–67.
56 Ibid., Epi.1–6.
57 Shakespeare, *Taming*, 1.1.3–4.

the wealthy gentleman Fitzdottrel and the confidence trickster Meercraft. As Fitzdottrel proves unable to transfer the lessons of history – to beware of flatterers and backstabbers – to his own situation, the dialogue calls into question the reformative power of historical drama:

> Fitzdottrel. But Thomas of Woodstock,
> I'm sure, was Duke, and he was made away
> at Calais, as Duke Humphery was at Bury;
> And Richard the Third, you know what end he came too.
>
> Meercraft. By m'faith, you are cunning i'the Chronicle, Sir.
>
> Fitzdottrel. No, I confess I ha't from the playbooks,
> And think they are more authentic.[58]

The play simultaneously travesties and affirms the value of historical drama by representing a character that does not profit from it and by re-framing the audience's perception with a metatheatrical gag. This strategy is comparable to the intertwined discussion of history and literature in Miguel de Cervantes' *Don Quixote* (1605–1615). Although the novel ridicules its protagonist for failing to differentiate between fiction and reality, one should not neglect the fact that the text poses as a work of historiography, i.e. an edition and translation of Arab sources. In the course of the narrative, Quixote emerges as a naive reader of both literature and historiography; he refuses to acknowledge that the libidinous space that is opened up by fictional literature remains confined to the text and the reader's mind, but he also buys into the historians' hubristic self-image: "History is a sacred kind of writing, because truth is essential to it; and where truth is, there God Himself is, so far as truth is concerned."[59] Quixote, however, applies a double standard; earlier in the same debate, he considers himself unlucky that the historians have recorded his defeats as well:

> "They might, indeed, as well have omitted them," said Don Quixote, "since there is no necessity of recording those actions, which do not change nor alter the truth of the story, and especially if they redound to the discredit of the hero. In good faith, Aeneas was not altogether so pious as Virgil paints him, nor Ulysses so prudent as Homer describes him."[60]

What Quixote outlines here is not the "sacred" historiography he propagates soon after; after all, the humanist historians are adamant that nothing be left out or

---

58 Ben Jonson. *The Devil is an Ass. The Devil is an Ass and Other Plays*, edited by Margaret Kidnie. Oxford: Oxford University Press, 2000, 2.4.8–14.
59 Miguel de Cervantes. *Don Quixote de la Mancha*, edited and translated by Edward C. Riley. Oxford: Oxford University Press, 2008, p. 489, II, 3.
60 Ibid., p. 486, II, 3.

added: "The first office of an Historiographer, is to write no lye. The second, that he shall conceal no truth for favour, displeasure or fear."[61] What Quixote describes is rather a literary truth, the one grounded in the Aristotelian concept of verisimilitude that calls for a hero with certain qualities. To complicate matters further, the novel *Don Quixote* does record its protagonist's foibles, which would make it – according to the definitions given there – more historiographical than fictional. As so often, literature uses its code elasticity and freedom from empirical referentiality to transcribe, test, and travesty the central tenets of other discourses.

Skipping a few centuries, one can still encounter this playfully rhetorical mode in recent fiction, where it emerges once more as the defining quality of the literary discourse. Despite the theoretical celebration of the shared semiotic field of literature and historiography, postmodernist novels have, by and large, resisted the impulse to declare themselves, in the tradition of Sidney, the more dignified form; instead, they continue to open up spaces for the discussion of historical meaning. It is only on the surface, for example, that Julian Barnes' novel *A History of the World in 10½ Chapters* (1989) backs certain postmodernist values:

> History isn't what happened. History is just what historians tell us. There was a pattern, a plan, a movement, expansion, the march of democracy; it is a tapestry, a flow of events, a complex narrative, connected, explicable. [...] And we, the readers of history, the sufferers from history, we scan the pattern for hopeful conclusions, for the way ahead.[62]

This statement, which echoes White's reflections about the moral quest of historiography, seems to be underscored by the novel's approach, which, if one believes the title, champions incompleteness ("½") and a relativistic openness to other narratives ("*a* history"). Looking at the first chapter, however, the reader will soon become aware of the pitfalls of revisionist history: the story of Noah's ark is told by a woodworm that constantly insists on his impartiality and his reliability as a narrator. As suspicious gaps in the chain of events make clear, however, his eye-witness report is hardly more trustworthy than the Biblical account. The "half-chapter," by contrast, turns out to belie its unfinished state and perpetual *différance*. It unfolds a quasi-authorial digression whose "insistence on love and on 'objective' truth as regulative ideas which enable us to take a stand and

---

[61] Polydore Vergil. *De Rerum Omnibus*, chapter X. Translation quoted after *The Works of the Famous Antiquary, Polidore Virgil Containing the Original of all Arts, Sciences, Mysteries, Orders, Rites, and Ceremonies, Both Ecclesiastical and Civil*, translated by John [*recte* Thomas] Langley. London: Simon Miller, 1663, p. 37. *Early English Books Online*. https://quod.lib.umich.edu/e/eebo/A65093.0001.001. Accessed 18 April 2018.
[62] Julian Barnes. *A History of the World in 10½ Chapters*. London: Jonathan Cape, 1989.

thus make moral decisions" has been described as the novel's main ideological thrust – one that, quite literally, "interrupts and disrupts the postmodern 'logic' of the ten stories."[63]

A similar impetus is discernible in post-millennial fiction. Arthur Phillips' *The Tragedy of Arthur* (2011) purports to be the first modern edition of Shakespeare's (allegedly) lost Arthurian play. However, its introduction by the editor/narrator Arthur Phillips (who, due to complex legal reasons, is said to have the sole rights to the play) turns out to be a lengthy memoir, during which the narrator muses on his complicated relationship with his absent father, Arthur Phillips senior, who has spent most of his life in jail for forgery. The narrator suspects that the Arthurian drama is another of his father's frauds. The text of "Shakespeare's" play is thus almost reduced to a coda,[64] whereas the paratext, i.e. the "introduction," is turned into the main event. In this way, the novel implicitly acknowledges the commercial pressures on the literary market and the ascendancy of prose texts since the eighteenth century. However, the sidelining of "Shakespeare" also represents the narrator's struggle to resolve the oedipal relationship with his father and, by extension, the relationship between himself as a writer and his models.[65] Whether this is a successful enterprise, is left open. The narrator wonders whether he is right to recognize himself and his family in the various characters of the Arthurian play; the novel thus seems to argue that drama – based on identification rather than illusion – still has relevance alongside the reality effect of latter-day narratives. With regard to his autobiography, though, the narrator cannot help but note the inadequacy of restructuring his life according to literary models: "What sort of story is this, then? Not quite a tragedy, not for anyone else, anyhow. Not quite a comedy, not for me, anyhow."[66] The triple sense of the novel's title, which alludes to "Shakespeare's" play and the narrator's and his father's lives as "tragedies," reminds the reader how literary patterns continue to shape our perception of contingent developments. The novel tenders an alternative. Completing a ritual of atonement inspired by *Love's Labour's Lost*, Phillips

---

63 Christina Kotte. *Ethical Dimensions in British Historiographic Metafiction: Julian Barnes, Graham Swift, Penelope Lively*. Trier: WVT, 2001, p. 105.
64 It is worth reading nonetheless, as Philips has achieved an impressive imitation of Shakespeare's style.
65 Sujata Iyengar has pointed out that one of the interpretative riddles that the novel presents is the question "whether Arthur Phillips is prevented by his own Oedipal fantasies from acknowledging the genuineness of the play." See "Shakespeare and the Post-Millennial Cancer Novel." *Shakespeare and Millennial Fiction*, edited by Andrew James Hartley. Cambridge: Cambridge University Press, 2018, pp. 159–176, p. 172.
66 Arthur Phillips. *The Tragedy of Arthur*. 2011. London: Duckworth Overlook, 2012, p. 255.

is barred from seeing his family for a year. Harsh though this may seem, the narrator connects his conscious performance of an old dramatic plot to his epiphanic self-awareness: "All my empathy has gone into trying to understand fictional characters, fantasies of my own making."[67] By defamiliarizing tragedy, the novel adjusts its readers' perspective, simultaneosuly celebrating this particular potential of literature and warning against mistaking narratives for 'life.'

Analyzing the pseudo-historiographical novels of the eighteenth-century, which often claim to rest upon found documents such as Crusoe's notebook, Everett Zimmermann has argued that this parody of the historian's method ultimately affirms the validity of representations:

> Through these often skeptical explorations and evocations of historicist procedures, eighteenth-century fiction makes history vulnerable. [...] Yet [...] the eighteenth-century novel is not pyrrhonist any more than eighteenth-century historiography is. Its demonstration of the capacities of fictional construction is also an imputation of potency to historical narration. History is challenged to differentiate the traces it accepts as foundational from those teased into meaning by novelistic narration, yet both historical and novelistic narrative retain their potential for meaningfulness.[68]

This seems to be a recurrent trend in literature, which remains bound up with historiography – not as something identical nor as something entirely separate – in many ways. Literature, we posit in what follows, is not merely a way of making history palatable. The education of the recipients is indubitably relevant for many texts, at least as a strategy of legitimation, but as the existence of "unteachable" characters like Sly and Fitzdottrel shows, literature tends to mock and subvert the demands of literary and historical theory. The provision of popular pleasures certainly forms another motive for the deployment of history (ultimately, a commercial one); the battle scenes of history plays provide a tantalizing spectacle, as attested by the fact that London's Globe theater burnt down in 1613 when a theatrical cannon was improperly handled during a performance of *Henry VIII*. However, history is also the touchstone against which literature measures the limits of linguistic representation: "Can this cockpit hold/the vasty fields of France? Or may we cram/Within this wooden O the very casques/That did affright the air at Agincourt?"[69]

---

67 Ibid., p. 230.
68 Everett Zimmermann. *The Boundaries of Fiction: History and the Eighteenth-Century British Novel*. Ithaca: Cornell University Press, 1996, p. 55.
69 Shakespeare, *Henry V*, Pro.13–15.

In order to investigate the manifold ways in which literary texts engage with history, and to explore the functions that history takes on in literature, from ideological hegemony to parodic criticism, the research group "Early Modern European Drama and the Cultural Net (DramaNet)" dedicated a conference to the pan-European tradition of history and drama, bringing together experts on medieval and modern literature and culture. Due to its paradigmatic status as the first mass medium,[70] the focus was set on early modern drama, but glances at romances and the realist novel in terms of genre, and at classical times and the nineteenth century in terms of periodization, provide many links and ensure broad applicability. The case studies offer thorough interpretations of drama as a rhetorical mode that is as open to royal self-fashioning and soteriology as it is to travestying and subverting the means and ends of historical interpretation. In addition, the comparative analysis of metapoetic and historiosophic aspects sheds light on drama as a transnational phenomenon, demonstrating the importance of the cultural net that links the multifaceted textual examples from France, Russia, England, Italy, the Netherlands, and the Germanophone lands.

The collection opens with an essay by Joachim Küpper that discusses the relation between history and literature, starting from Aristotle's *Poetics* ("Literature and Historiography in Aristotle and in Modern Times"). Küpper introduces *eikós* (the verisimilar, probable, or likely) as one of the most prominent concepts of the *Poetics*, whose ninth chapter makes a broad distinction between texts that deal with the universal, i.e. philosophical texts, and texts that deal with the particular, i.e. literature and historiography. The difference within the latter category is that literary texts ought to take recourse to *eikós*, whereas historiographical texts may, according to the Stagirite, dispense with it. Küpper elucidates the important function of that stricture: by conceding to literature a slightly higher degree of universality than to historiography, Aristotle defends it against charges of futility; the recipients' impression that there is an "isomorphic relation between the causal laws governing the text's actions and the 'laws' of human reality" gives fiction a greater philosophical quality. The essay proceeds to compare the ancient philosopher's position with modern answers to the question why one should prefer the verisimilar over the real, i.e. why one should read a novel rather than a history book. Küpper argues that aesthetic pleasure cannot be a generally satisfactory answer and contends that the realist novel does not, in fact, offer any answer at all. Rather, novels of this type gloss over the fact that they represent made-up characters and events by insisting on the truth of what is told. The lasting success of realism, the essay concludes, is founded on this *effet de réel*, a technique most

---

70 Cf. Joachim Küpper. *The Cultural Net: Early Modern Drama as a Paradigm*. Berlin: de Gruyter, 2018.

suited to the post-heroic society in which identification must be supplanted by illusion.

Küpper's contribution is supplemented, but also problematized in Blair Hoxby's brief statement ("History, Myth, and Early Modern Drama"). Hoxby suggests that the distinction between history and myth is less consequential than the distinction between "material that is treated as if it were myth – distilled into a fable – and material that is treated as if it were history: composed of a series of events and happenstances, of [...] recalcitrant particulars." Observing that dramatists who distill history into myth have been superseded by playwrights who, like Shakespeare, highlight the contingency of history in their works, Hoxby argues that this pervasive change in taste took root during the historical turn of eighteenth-century Western philosophy. In evidence of this development, which he connects to the naturalization of Adam Müller's conceptualization of history as tragedy, Hoxby cites philosophers like Johann Herder and literary critics like Maurice Morgann, both of whom championed the historical quality of Shakespearean drama. *Pace* Aristotle, such a 'drama of contingency' must, as Hoxby implies, not necessarily be regarded as an endeavor in futility because it facilitates, as Georg Wilhelm Friedrich Hegel and others have emphasized, the negotiation of moral freedom, which is, almost by definition, anthropocentric – and hence offers, one might gloss, a narcissistic pleasure.

The collection continues with two essays on history and literature in the Middle Ages. Gaia Gubbini introduces the Arthurian legend as a "tangled mix of reality and imagination," arguing that even though the evidence for the historical existence of Arthur is thin, the Arthurian myth is best understood as a nexus in which history and fiction intersect ("King Arthur in Medieval French Literature: History and Fiction, the Sense of the Tragic and the Role of Dreams in *La Mort le Roi Artu*"). King Henry II, to name but one example, used the 'discovery' of Arthur's grave at Glastonbury, identified with the mythical Avalon, to promote his political ends. Building on these observations, the second part of the essay draws attention to the anonymous thirteenth-century romance *La Mort le Roi Artu*. Gubbini argues that if the "thèse de l'architecte" is correct, that is, if the texts in the *Lancelot-Graal* cycle were written independently but constructed according to an overarching plan (much like a medieval cathedral), *La Mort le Roi Artu* may have been consciously conceived as the last part. This claim is borne out by an analysis of the text's emphasis on death and corruption, both in its title and through the reintroduction of the traitorous character of Mordret, Arthur's illegitimate son. Further illuminating the link between history and fiction, the essay demonstrates the potency of the idea of the tragic across genres. Employing ancient and medieval theories of dreams, Gubbini shows that Arthur's dream of the Wheel of Fortune must be understood as a prophecy, not as a lie or false vision; she submits, therefore, that the tragic, defined as the inevitability of destiny, is the predominant trait of *Le Roi Artu*.

Gubbini's paper is complemented by Susanne Friede's transmedial approach to the Arthurian material ("When History Does Not Fit into Drama: Some Thoughts on the Absence of King Arthur in Early Modern Plays"). Friede points out that the Arthurian tradition was hugely popular in the romances of the Middle Ages (and has become so again in latter-day movies); in early modern times, however, Arthur featured peripherally at best, e.g. in some German carnival plays. Using this conspicuous absence as the vanishing point of her analysis, Friede compares the fictional worlds of the mystery plays, where heroes display their impeccable ethos and serve as typological examples for biblical protagonists and Christian virtues, with the Arthurian cosmos, which, replete with adultery and incest, hardly fits the requirements. One example for the heroic role model espoused by the mystery plays is *Les Épitaphes d'Hector et d'Achille* (1454), which represents Alexander the Great as an ideal prince. As the essay notes, the text takes its liberties with history so that Alexander dies an "appropriate" death: he is murdered by his servants, an occurrence that shows his generous nature whilst also teaching that social stratification is justified – noblemen should not trust their retainers. By contrast, the moral ambivalence of Arthur and the Knights of the Round Table does not lend itself to the propagation of the heroic model. The complex Arthurian world, Friede concludes, requires a narrative voice in order to establish the links between the protagonists' subjective guilt, objective guilt, and the metaphysical framework represented by the Wheel of Fortune. In drama, the legend of the king who is a hero and a victim, the ideal and its corruption, cannot actualize its full meaning.

The third section of the present volume is dedicated to the early modern age. Julia V. Ivanova illuminates the genealogy of *Mandragola* by investigating discursive elements and rhetorical strategies that Niccolò Machiavelli's text has in common with the Renaissance novel and the dialogue of the Quattrocento ("Machiavelli's Soteriology and the Humanist Quattrocento Dialogue"). Ivanova points out that the humanists' dialogues tend to stage quarrels about some given definite concept, e.g. the virtues of law and medicine, so as to hide their rhetorical propensities: feigning several interlocutors, the authors could deny responsibility and enjoy greater discursive liberty. Highlighting how the dialogues turned anthropology and ethics into negotiable, experimental domains, Ivanova cites contemporary stories about wicked clerics who try to seduce young women through selective wording, metonymy, and false logic. If the dialogues and narratives create this rich context for the refutation of the New Testament's evangelical message, *Mandragola*, Ivanova contends, must be interpreted as one such play that inverts or carnivalizes the gospel. Analyzing how the play inherited not just the plots, but also the logic of the dialogues and the anti-clerical stories, the essay shows that the familiar interpretation of *Mandragola* as a political allegory, with Lucretia as Florence, is complemented by the new approach.

The analysis of the redefinition or rhetorical shift of values, i.e. *paradiastole*, is taken up in Pavel V. Sokolov's essay on civic values in the early-modern Netherlands ("Lucretia without Poniard: Pieter Corneliszoon Hooft's *Geeraerdt van Velsen* between Livy and Tacitus"). Connecting the female protagonist of Pieter C. Hooft's play, Machtelt van Velsen, to the "archetypal" rape victim Lucretia, Sokolov observes that rape accounts have traditionally been used to negotiate turning points in the development of a state. In Cicero and Ovid, the woman who takes her life after setting her family on a course of revenge features is a pivotal figure of Roman liberty; in Livy, Lucretia is an emblem of the republican virtues of *gloria*, *modestia*, and *castitas*. This changes, as Sokolov observes, with Tacitus, who is more pessimistic and posits Livia Drusilla, who yields to Augustus, as an "Anti-Lucretia" whose cowardice leads to tyranny. In all of these cases, however, rape is the *experimentum crucis* that puts ethical terms like liberty, prudence, and virtue to the test. Acknowledging Hooft as a writer who was esteemed for his lucid demonstration of the best principles of government, Sokolov embarks on a political interpretation of *Geeraerdt van Velsen* (1613). Remarking that the medieval history of the Netherlands had been fit into a macro-historical framework – the fall of Rome and its promised rebirth –, Sokolov reads Hooft's early modern tragedy as a palimpsest that takes recourse to Tacitist historiography and post-Machiavellian political rhetoric in order to stage heroic behavior for a monarchical age, that is, as useless and potentially harmful. In addition, Sokolov shows how Hooft adapted history to his needs: the suicide of the historical Mechtelt is omitted; instead, the character is shown to hide her sorrow and to suffer for the future glory of the state. He concludes that Hooft uses the marginalized female voice to stage the triumph of prudence and Stoic providentialism over the heroic ethos.

The investigation of monarchical ideology in early modern literature is continued in the next paper, in which Ekaterina Boltunova focusses on the relationship between history and drama, specifically on the functionalization of nonfictional and fictional spaces, in the political system of absolutism ("The Historical Writing of Catherine II: Dynasty and Self-Fashioning in *The Chesme Palace* [*Chesmenskii Dvorets*]"). She introduces Chesme Palace as a site with a 'double' topography: Chesme is a *maison de plaisance* that was designed by Yury Felten and completed in 1777, but it is also the name and setting of a text that Catherine II wrote in the mid-1780s, i.e. at a time when the real palace contained 59 portraits of contemporary European monarchs as well as bas-reliefs of former Russian rulers. In the text, these representations come to life and discuss their historical roles. Whereas modern interpretations tend to read Catherine's written work as a glorification of Russian culture (and as a stylistic exercise, i.e. a dialogue of the dead), contemporaries tended to focus on the political allusions and the expression of political views. It is with this strand of interpretation in mind that Boltunova reads *Chesme Palace* as a reassessment of Russian monarchs and as Catherine's attempt to tip the scales in her own favor at the expense of Peter I, the first emperor of Russia. The text has satirical elements, showing dysfunctional rulers besotted with love, but it gives more positive examples as well, e.g. judicious rulers whose designs only ran awry due to ill health. Catherine's purpose, then, is to legitimize her position by highlighting her European kinship and by assessing her own person and position vis-à-vis her predecessors. Underlining the "masculine" features of successful female rulers, the dialogue presents Catherine II as an ideal sovereign whose profile emerges from the portrayal of others.

Boltunova's essay is complemented by Kirsten Dickhaut's characterization of the situation in absolutist France ("History – Drama – Mythology"). Adapting theories that view drama as a model for the court and as an instrument of power and self-fashioning, Dickhaut regards Louis XIV as a king who actively sought to naturalize the relationship between history, drama, and mythology. As a first case in point, Dickhaut investigates the Sun King's use of the Apollo myth, taking the *Ballet de Cassandre* (1651), in which Louis played the sun on stage, as her main example. The ideological entwining of the theater, mythology, and political and historical reality is further borne out by the observation that Louis supported the Copernican revolution, i.e. the dissemination of the heliocentric world picture. As a second case in point, Dickhaut revisits the Perseus myth, which served to ascribe heroic values to the monarch. Corneille's *Andromède*, for example, forges a link between Perseus and the virtues of justice, prudence, and temperance – the attributes of a worthy hero and, by extension, the king. Under the absolute monarchy in France, the essay maintains, "drama becomes the place to show history in an allegorical-mythical way on stage."

The fourth section comprises articles on eighteenth- and nineteenth-century texts. Elena N. Penskaya characterizes farce as an "adjustable commentary" that accompanies grand genres and enters into dialogue with other texts ("Fielding's Farces: Travestying the Historiosophical Discourse"). Farce is shown to thrive on exaggerated situations, physical humor, and nonsense; it is an ambivalent form that revolts against order and propriety but may also restore the social order it attacks. Over time, it developed into a sophisticated, internally consistent "travesty model of a specific [...] canon." Mapping out the genealogy of that "travesty model," Penskaya cites Francis Beaumont's *The Knight of the Burning Pestle* (c. 1607) as a play that presents the 'heroic' deeds of a grocer's apprentice. Exploring the castigation of literary 'sinners' in this and other plays, e.g. audiences that consider themselves co-actors and co-authors during a dramatic performance, Penskaya brings the metaliterary aspects of farce to the fore. She goes on to argue that the heyday of farce, the 1720s and 1730s, was the time when tragic clichés exercised particular power. Against this background, she presents Henry Fielding as an author who gave much thought to history and theatrical aesthetics and developed a "travesty-based model of life theatricalization," in which farcical elements would question the relationship of historical and dramatic characters. As a result, this "burlesque historiosophic commentary" ought to be able to dispel the impression that extraliterary *realia* and literary representations coincide; the use of theatrical metaphors and symbols in the historical discourse is subverted. By way of example, the essay analyzes Fielding's *Tom Thumb*, which was reworked as *The Tragedy of Tragedies* in the early 1730s. Penskaya conducts a philological comparison of the four versions of the *Tragedy of Tragedies*, which are geared towards different modes of reception. She finds that for Fielding, as for Aristotle, history presents itself as a contingent series of events. Far from imprinting moral patterns on historical events, Fielding's plays deploy farcical characters like Lockehobbes to undercut the interpretative patterns of historiography: "These instances, just like those, teach us/They teach us I don't really know what."

Turning from Fielding's metaliterary criticism of clichés and textual recycling to a Russian playwright who was concerned about what he perceived to be the all-too narrow archive of contemporary literature, the following paper introduces Alexander Ostrovsky (1823–1886) as a polyglot who sought to broaden the repertoire. Olga Kuptsova takes particular issue with the idea that Ostrovsky primarily wrote "slice-of-life" plays that capture, in the words of Jules Patouillet, "les mœurs russes" ("Ostrovsky's Experience of the Creation of the European Theatrical Canon and Russian Stage Practice: Personal Preferences and General Trends"). As evidence for her position, Kuptsova cites the contents of Ostrovsky's vast library, which contained works of the Western stages as well as tomes of literary criticism. Emphasizing the importance of understanding Ostrovsky in the pan-European context, she notes that the playwright translated from five different languages, and did so, from the 1860s onwards, with a view to repertoire. In order to substantiate this biographical evidence with a reading of Ostrovsky's plays, Kuptsova ties the "Hamlet mania" that gripped Ostrovsky's generation to the *The Forest* (1871), a play about two actors who behave theatrically in real life. She then observes the importance of Shakespeare for Russian drama, noting how competing traditions of translation (the "free" adaptations of Germany and the "bound" translations of France) became influential in Russia at about the same time. Having offered dramas of France and the Spanish Golden Age as further examples, the essay concludes that Ostrovsky did "localize" his work – his plays often represent the lifestyle and sociolect of the merchant class in a specific part of Moscow –, but that he went out of his way to fertilize his plays with plot elements that he found elsewhere, merging what is a local social reality in contact with globally disseminated literary artefacts to achieve verisimilitude in his plays.

Natalia Sarana's essay adds some remarks on Ostrovsky in the context of a subgenre that she calls *Bildungsdrama*, or 'drama of formation' ("The *Bildungsdrama* and Alexander Ostrovsky's Plays"). Sarana contests the critical opinion that *Bildung* – a protagonist's eventual achievement of maturity through his or her interaction with society – is a concept that, due to its processual character, belongs to the novel, not to drama. Having enlisted biographical criticism to show that Ostrovsky was interested in the psychological and educational possibilities of plays, she employs drama theory to demonstrate that plays can accommodate the protagonists' shifts in perspectives and evoke empathy and understanding for the protagonists' changing circumstances (and their reaction thereto). Applying this notion of *Bildungsdrama* to Ostrovsky's works, Sarana finds that the idea of *Bildung* is often tied to a female character's experience of marriage, which either features as the final step of the process or as a challenge that is resisted by the woman. This is the case, for example, in *Belugin's Marriage* (1877), a play that has an evident connection to the nexus of novels that Elaine Hoffmann Baruch has called the "feminine Bildungsroman" – and hence to the tradition in Britain, France, Russia, and beyond (*Emma, Jane Eyre, Madame Bovary, Anna Karenina*). *The Storm* (1859) and *Without a Dowry* (1879) are analyzed as further examples of this patriarchal ideal of *Bildung* that sees life trajectories end in happiness or ruin, depending on the protagonist's attitude towards marriage. The discussion then turns to *Guilty Innocents* (1883). In a play that is presented as Ostrovsky's most elaborate examination of the theme, the pregnant protagonist is abandoned by her lover; her baby is soon left for dead. The dramatic action condenses no less than seventeen years: the woman becomes a successful actress and eventually learns that her son is still alive. Their reunion serves as an emblem of patience rewarded, but, Sarana argues, also as a structural reduplication of the pattern of *Bildung* when the son's own journey towards maturity is retold by one of his fellows.

The final section of the volume engages with texts that are on their way into a new canon of world literature. Gautam Chakrabarti approaches nineteenth-century India as an interstitial space in which an Anglophile Bengal playwright tried to bridge notions of the Orient and the Occident, the past and the future ("'Sail[ing] on the Pathless Deep:' Michael Madhusudan Datta's Dramatic Entanglements"). This agument is borne out by a careful analysis of biographical facts and documents, e.g. Michael M. Datta's letters to friends, which show the playwright's awareness and conscious cultivation of his "Western ideas and *modes of thinking.*" In his interpretation of Datta's literary works, Chakrabarti focuses on the dramatist's interweaving of the "historical" and the "mythological," particularly in his play *Sermista* (1859), which draws upon an episode from a Sanskrit epic and was immediately translated into English by the playwright himself. Postulating that cultural historiography is a "prism" through which the consolidation of the literary canon in colonial and, by extension, post-colonial India can be fruitfully analyzed, the essay argues that "Datta's plays [...] serve as discursive models for the entangled process through which history and drama permeate each other." Chakrabarti's central metaphor of "entanglements" – which captures, among other things, Datta's life between India and Europe, Datta's plays between ancient texts and the modern vernacular, and the relation between literature and history in colonial India – is further corroborated by a comparative reading of *Sermista* and Schiller's *Mary Stuart*. Employing Johann W. von Goethe's notion of world literature and recent critical adaptations of that concept, Chakrabarti highlights the structural similarities of the two plays, each of which features two female protagonists in respective positions of power and subalternity.

The dissemination of texts through the (virtual) cultural net is also central to Toni Bernhart and Janina Janke's understanding of folk literature and their report on how they staged a newly discovered German folk play that is, in turn, derived from a novella in Giovanni Boccaccio's *Decameron* ("The Crystallization of Early Modern European Drama in the Folk-Theater Tradition in Tyrol: The Marienberg *Griseldis* from 1713, Staged in 2016"). The essay initially familiarizes its readers with the German-speaking South as a space with a vibrant tradition of popular theater. Acknowledging that the reduplication of existing genres as folk poetry, folk plays, etc. serves no critical purpose, the authors problematize the notion of folk literature and suggest a typological approach: a plausible concept of folk literature ought to be tied to the use of a marginal language, a place of production that is distant from politico-cultural centers, and a heterogeneous audience. Ideologically, folk literature resisted the industrial age and was sometimes intended to define a communal cultural identity against the otherness of, for example, French 'civilization' (to use Herder's dichotomy). Bernhart and Janke tender the Griselda myth, based on the last novella in the *Decameron*, as an example of a narrative complex whose spread throughout global literatures is well-documented, but whose traces in the German folk-play tradition have not been sufficiently studied. During their archival research, the authors discovered an anonymous Griselda play from 1713 in the Benedictine abbey of Marienberg in South Tyrol. Describing the tension between the present and the original cultural contexts of the play as particularly intriguing and productive, the authors go on to report about their own staging of the Marienberg *Griseldis* in the newly-constructed subterranean library building of the abbey. The authors discuss their decisions during the production, not least their invitation to eight local amateur troupes, which ultimately led to the proliferation of the character of Griselda – she was played by five actresses of three generations in every performance. Bernhart and Janke's scholarly and creative approach to the constellation of history and literature is an important reminder that literature, as part of the cultural net, has two ties to the historical process: in its creation and its reception.

The volume concludes by presenting DS Mayfield's deliberations on literature and rhetorical ventriloquism ("Rhetorical Ventriloquism in Application"). The essay addresses the functions of putting personified voices into writing (or on stage) by assigning, for example, invented speeches to dramatic characters that are based on historical figures, by imagining, within a given text, the recipients' response to it ("you will say that…") or by insisting on the 'famous last words' of this or that person. Introducing the topic with an analysis of autobiographical writing, specifically Augustine's *Confessions*, Mayfield proceeds to give a historical overview of the use of "rhetorical ventriloquism" in historiography, philosophy, and literature. His heuristic approach highlights the enormous variety of applications across different times and genres and supports a careful and thorough differentiation between the phenomenological variants of the textual strategy, e.g. the differences in application and function of rhetorical concepts such as *prosopopoeia*, *sermocinatio*, and *ethopoeia*. Mayfield shows how "ventriloquism" is an indispensable part of dramatic writing, where it lends a particular "immediacy and intensity" to the dialogic exchanges between characters; it is, in the most general terms, a technique of citation which fabricates or subverts authority in both fictional and allegedly referential texts – and thus a phenomenon that adds another angle to the question initially discussed here: whether it is possible to keep the entwined strands of literature and history apart.

Joachim Küpper
Literature and Historiography in Aristotle and in Modern Times

It is a well-known fact that the Aristotelian *Poetics* belongs to that part of the Stagirite's works commonly qualified as "esoteric," that is, the texts written down for the internal use of the academy at which the philosopher taught. This fact is reflected within the tract itself by a structuring that appears erratic in many regards, when considered from the standpoint of an exoteric reader. There are lengthy passages concerning points that are not that difficult to grasp – I am thinking of the chapters which discuss questions of *lexis*. There are, on the other hand, extremely concise, even elliptical paragraphs concerning questions with regard to which it would have been highly desirable to get some more information – I am thinking in particular of the argumentation by which the central effect of a well-conceived tragedy is introduced: *hêdonê*, provoked by a previous catharsis of *phóbos* and *éleos*, a mechanism which is not at all as evident as it seems to have been to the person who wrote down the tract.[1] And there are even flagrant contradictions, the most famous being the one between the qualification of *Oedipus the King* as the best and most beautiful of all tragedies (*kallistê tragôedia*; 1453a 23) to be found in chapter 13, and the attribution of this predicate to *Iphigeneia in Tauris* (1454a 8 sq.) in chapter 14, a piece with a happy ending, that is, a device Aristotle judges in chapter 13 (1453a 30–35), with reference to, amongst other texts, the *Odyssey*, in a rather condescending way to be complying with the illusions about the world and its mechanisms cultivated by the less intelligent readers and spectators. The situation briefly characterized is complicated by the fact that a standard philological procedure, that is, the search for parallel arguments in other works by the author, does not produce many results in this case; the *Poetics* is a relatively isolated text within the entire oeuvre.

The remarks I will formulate in the following are thus to be considered with an explicit caveat: any interpretation of the *Poetics* and its most important concepts will remain by necessity thetical or even hypothetical.

---

[1] Many specialists believe that the actual text as transmitted was fixed in writing by a pupil (or several pupils) rather than by Aristotle himself (who may then have revised it, without, however, investing too much effort in the process); although the Stagirite's position towards literature is much more welcoming than that of his teacher Plato, literary artefacts ranked rather low within his hierarchy of human-made objects.

There is one concept, namely the *eikós* (which might be best translated as something that is verisimilar, likely, or probable), which seems to hold a particularly outstanding position within the entire edifice of thought underlying the text. It occurs in the text at a higher frequency than any other of the terms that hold a privileged position, such as *mimêsis, kátharsis, sýnthesis ton pragmáton, phóbos, éleos, hêdonê*, etc. This eminent role is underpinned by the fact that it is introduced in a passage of peculiarly high importance to the argument in its entirety. In chapter 9, Aristotle establishes two comprehensive categories of texts referring to reality: on the one hand, there are texts that dedicate themselves to representing the "universal" (*kathólou*), on the other, there are those representing the "particular" (*kat'hékaston*; 1451b 7). The first category is comprised of philosophical texts, the second one includes literary texts (especially tragedies and epics) and also those texts that render what has really happened, that is, historiographical texts. The conceptual subdivision of this latter category – texts presenting particular items – is established by recourse to the concept of *eikós*: literary texts have to respect this criterion by necessity; exceptions are of low quality and not even worth the effort of considering on a theoretical level. Historiographical texts, by contrast, may well dispense with this criterion of verisimilitude, since their veracity is guaranteed by the fact that the events represented did, indeed, occur: "until something happens we remain uncertain of its possibility, but what has happened obviously is possible, since, if impossible, it would not have happened" – this is the core argument concerning the entire problem, as can be read in chapter 9 of the text (1451b 17–20).[2] From a present-day perspective informed by questioning the possibility of representing reality by means of texts, and the stressing of all of textual "reproduction" of the real as being a construction rather than a representation, one could, of course, characterize Aristotle's argument as somewhat naive; the respective theses are, however, rather recent, and it remains to be seen whether a future, post-postmodernist period will continue to accept Hayden White's reasoning unreservedly, or will rather reject it for being somewhat exaggerated.

The *eikós*, the verisimilar, is, then, according to Aristotle the indispensable characteristic of texts presenting particular persons and particular events without being able to pretend that what is narrated represents real items; it is the characteristic of literary texts, or, to put it precisely, of literary texts that deserve consideration at all. As it cannot be excluded that certain parts of reality (in the sense of events that did factually occur) follow a path of evolution that

---

[2] All quotations are taken from Aristotle. *Poetics*, edited and translated by James Hutton. New York: Norton, 1982.

one could qualify as verisimilar, Aristotle allows that poets may have recourse to historical plots when they are thinking of conceiving a tragedy or an epic text (1451b 30 sqq.). This license conceded to poets and writers, which subverts, in a certain way, a separation clearly established previously (literature on the one hand, historiography on the other),[3] underpins the unique role that the concept of verisimilitude holds within Aristotle's conceptualization of what a literary text is. And the central importance of this concept is corroborated by a famous sentence in chapter 24, by which Aristotle advises choosing an impossible element (*adýnaton*) that is verisimilar (or may be presented as such) rather than a possible element which is not credible (*apíthanon*; 1460a 26 sqq.); he repeats the advice in chapter 25 (1460b 5 sqq.). The exact signification of the underlying thought is not rendered in the text in a precise way – Aristotle does not give any examples of events that are "impossible but at the same time verisimilar." I should like to link this conceptual syndrome to the close relation of the verisimilar and the *dóxa* as established in that same chapter (cf. 1461b 10). And one might add that the acceptance of the traditional mythical stories as true, or at least as possible, is considered by the philosopher to be an important element of *dóxa*, that is, of generally held views (cf. 1460 b 30 sqq.); as for items that are at the same time impossible and verisimilar, one could thus think of elements taken from the mythical tradition, as, e.g., the existence of sphinxes (in archaic times).

Although Aristotle does not discuss extensively the reasons why he attributes such a visible role to the concept of the verisimilar, one major point can be extrapolated, in my opinion, from the chapter I have been talking about: a fictional story, that is, a story which cannot refer to a reality that would justify what is told, presented, diffused, has to evince a profile that distances it from outright futility. As Aristotle rejects any explicit abstraction with respect to literary texts, such as, for instance, explicit allegorical personifications or extended reflexive or argumentative passages, and advises sticking to a strictly mimetic mode, the only device that can liberate the fictional text from the suspicion of non-pertinence is, consequently, that of bringing it closer to a rendering of the factual by implementing structures the recipients – readers or viewers – are prepared to accept as something that could possibly have occurred, or that may occur in the future, that is, as something that resembles the real or factual, something that is, as we say in all Western vernaculars, "verisimilar" ("vraisemblable," "verosimile," "verosímil," "wahrscheinlich").

---

[3] It should be stressed that there is a dissimilarity concerning the license to transgress this separation; Aristotle does not say that historians are free to make use of fictional elements or structures of emplotment.

The verisimilitude that characterizes well-wrought fictional stories not only frees them from the suspicion of non-pertinence, it also confers upon them an intellectual dignity that elevates them to a level higher than that of texts that render the factual; they are *philosophóteron* (1451b 5), "more philosophical," than historiographical texts because, although, like the latter, they present particular events, they give expression to something more "universal" (*kathólou*) than factographical texts.

There are endless discussions amongst the specialists as to what textual level is referred to by the "universal" claimed by Aristotle in the above-mentioned context. But the more comprehensive interpretations – claiming that Aristotle has something like a "global view" in mind – as well as the more cautious readings – claiming that the "universal" is meant to be no more than the adequate rendering of characters and their deeds[4] –, all these interpretations of the *kathólou* which is, according to Aristotle, a necessary constituent of literary texts, may be subsumed under the category of the verisimilar. The *kathólou* which we as recipients are ready to ascribe to a text that we know does not by necessity represent factual events emanates from a sort of isomorphic relation between the causal laws governing the text's actions and the "laws" of human reality, of "life," as we, recipients, conceive them on a level that precedes critical, that is, epistemologically relevant reflection. It is particularly this link to a more abstract level of what we call "real" or "true" that brings literary texts closer to philosophical texts. But I should like to stress that the Stagirite neither says that literary texts would be equivalent to philosophical texts in this respect, nor that they would be at an equal distance to historiographical texts on the one hand, to philosophical texts on the other. Aristotle just says that, put in perspective, they are closer to philosophical texts than historiographical texts are. It would thus be hazardous to reclaim Aristotle in order to substantiate the thesis, widespread in postmodernist literary theory, that literary texts have a cognitive dignity equal to philosophical texts.

This, in a nutshell, is what Aristotle says concerning the *eikós* in the famous ninth chapter of his tract. It is indeed remarkable that, even though he stresses the importance of this characteristic in almost every other chapter, he does not go into the details of why he deems it so important. That said, Aristotle's position seems to me far superior to those given by certain theoreticians of modern narrative, namely the advocates of literary realism, for the simple reason that Aristotle's text allows readers to construct an acceptable answer to a question that remains

---

4 – a position, as I might say in parenthesis, that I find not very convincing, because within the frame of a text of fiction, the characteristics of the personages are not something that could exist prior to the text proper, they are an abstraction of their actions.

unresolved within the poetic tracts emerging in the age of realism: why should one represent the verisimilar, and why not the real, when it comes to presenting a historical scenario? Why should one read *Le Père Goriot* (1835) rather than a historiographical text on Restauration France; why should one read *L'Éducation sentimentale* (1869) instead of a text such as, for instance, *The eighteenth Brumaire of Louis Napoléon* (1852)? The current answer: "because this is more pleasurable an enterprise" may well be pertinent to the novel by Balzac, but certainly not to the text by Flaubert, which is difficult to read; the attribute of "lisibilité" (as it has been called within the structuralists' polemics against the Balzacian model),[5] however, calls into question truthfulness, a feature ostentatiously claimed by the text ("Ah, sachez-le! Ce drame n'est ni une fiction ni un roman, All is true!")[6]: is the text a trustworthy rendering of reality, or, rather, a construction of reality conceived with respect to the common readers' somewhat trivial wishes concerning reality? Flaubert's text, to which one could reasonably attribute an authentic verisimilitude,[7] is not only difficult to read. The fact that there is, in the text, an aporia at the point where one would like to be given an answer to the question, "Why narrate something verisimilar if it is possible to present something that really happened?" provokes speculative functionalizations that indulge in characterizing the text in a way that cannot be called anything other than highly anachronistic: as an exposure of its devices, as autoreferential, etc.

I have allowed myself this first short digression in order to create a background from which the comprehensive Aristotelian argument proper will detach itself in a clear-cut way: the verisimilar, in Aristotle, is the central component of a specific theorizing of the *function* of tragedies and epics. This functionalization has, however, been rendered obsolete by the historical process.

In order not to neglect the second part of my paper, namely, the question of what has become of this syndrome of verisimilitude and literature in more recent times, I will only briefly characterize the further steps of Aristotle's comprehensive theory concerning the function of literary texts: an ingredient no less difficult to understand than the ones discussed previously is the rules he advises for the construction of well-conceived central personages, or, heroes. At times he seems

---

5 See Roland Barthes. *S/Z*. Paris: Seuil, 1970.
6 – these are the words advanced by the text's narrator in the second chapter of *Le Père Goriot*. The quotation continues: "[...] il est si véritable que chacun peut en reconnaître les éléments chez soi [...]" (Honoré de Balzac. *Le Père Goriot. La Comédie humaine*, edited by Marcel Bouteron, vol. 2. Paris: Gallimard, 1963, pp. 847–1085, p. 848).
7 – with the exception, perhaps, of Frédéric's inheritance, which is, this should not be forgotten, the basis of his unproblematic, although somewhat uneventful – and in that sense: verisimilar – existence of over two decades as narrated in the penultimate chapter.

to have in mind characters far more outstanding than regular humans (*epieikês*); at times he says that heroes need not be better than common human beings.[8] In any case, he claims that the hero should be *hómoion* – equal, comparable – to the spectators.

It seems that we find a first solution to the difficult question of why there was, 2,500 years ago, a theorizing of literary texts which is at first sight so very close to positions we are familiar with from nineteenth-century poetology, in those passages where Aristotle begins to discuss the effects of a well-wrought tragedy: it is to arouse *phóbos* and *éleos*. But it is not the arousal that is the final goal, it is rather the purification, or, as I would rather say, the evacuation of these affects, that constitutes the final point, as well as the pleasure that accompanies this *kátharsis*.

What is the logic behind this rather odd theorizing? – it is a literary text's primary function to first stimulate and then evacuate certain specific emotions. I would suggest taking a look at the question for whom the playwrights of that age conceived their pieces. The recipients were not a general public in the modern sense, they were constituted by the (male) adult full citizens, that is, those allowed but also obliged to carry arms – which means at the same time that they were obliged to fight for the polity, should this become necessary.

In order to complete the panorama of the elements on which Aristotle's theory builds one has to add that the Stagirite polemically engages his teacher Plato with respect to the nature of the affects. While Plato holds that affects can be disciplined and even totally controlled by reason, Aristotle considers such a view to be one of the many illusions concerning humans that would only come to the mind of a theorizer. Aristotle was the son of a physician, and in many respects his anthropology is much more materialistic, physical, than Plato's. Affects are, according to the Stagirite, bodily reactions to external stimuli which occur without the intervention of volition. According to a conceptualization that has been handed down to us by Galenic humoral pathology, the concrete intensity of the affective reaction is contingent upon the configuration of the various bodily fluids in a certain specific person. To put it very concisely: to artificially arouse and then cathartically purge certain specific affects might help reduce the quantity of bodily fluids prone to arousal. To put it in more concrete terms: periodically submitting the warrior class of Athens to artificially feeling fear and pity may have helped to immunize them against feeling fear and pity when fighting on a real, factual battle-field. Verisimilitude with respect to the action, and *homoiôsis* with regard to the hero of a tragedy are thus to be conceived as the structural enabling of identification, which is an indispensable prerequisite of emotionalization.

---

[8] Meaning of course: humans from the ruling class, I shall come back to this point.

When we now risk an audacious jump right into the eighteenth century, it should not astonish us that very many details regarding the theorizing of drama and epics have changed. But it is interesting to observe that many arguments were continued while being given an, at times, completely different meaning.[9] When Balzac frequently calls his novels "*drame*,"[10] he is referring to a generic label introduced by Denis Diderot in his reflections concerning the problem of how a tragedy adapted to modern times might best be conceived. In the *Entretiens sur 'Le Fils naturel'* (1757) and in the *Discours sur la poésie dramatique* (1758), Diderot continues the Aristotelian argument that it is the primary goal of drama to emotionalize the spectators. His concept of "emotions" is, however, much broader than the Aristotelian reduction to *phóbos* and *éleos*. It also comprises less intense affects like sympathy and empathy. Diderot's most important argument for creating a substitute for the (according to him) obsolete genre of tragedy is linked to the recipients he has in mind: why should late eighteenth-century middle-class Parisians be emotionalized when confronted with situations pertaining specifically to the lifeworld of princes and kings, with regard to which they had become more and more critical, if not hostile, in the process of political enlightenment? Some decades later, it was François-René de Chateaubriand who gave the most impressive characterization of this shift in literary demand linked to a shift in the audience, the latter being contingent on a dramatic political shift, namely the abolition of the feudal system: "Avant la Révolution, on n'interrogeait les manuscrits que relativement aux prêtres, aux nobles et aux rois. Nous ne nous enquérons que de ce qui regarde les peuples et les transformations sociales."[11]

Diderot, for his part, invested some energy in theorizing what the preconditions are for an arousal of emotion linked to situations borrowed from the lifeworld, no longer of kings, but of bourgeois people. Is it possible to feel deeply shocked by the vicissitudes ascribed to a humble "père de famille" (this is the title of one of Diderot's *drames*, created in 1758), rather than to a king whose horrible, but unconscious past mistakes lead the entire polis into destabilization and a foreseeable disaster? Diderot's answer, once again, has recourse to basic arguments already found in the *Poetics*, while, once again, changing the relative

---

9 See Hans Robert Jauss. "Diderots Paradox über das Schauspiel (*Entretiens sur 'Le Fils naturel'*)." *Germanisch-Romanische Monatsschrift* 42 (1961), pp. 380–413; see also my *Ästhetik der Wirklichkeitsdarstellung und Evolution des Romans von der französischen Spätaufklärung bis zu Robbe-Grillet*. Stuttgart: Steiner, 1987, chs. I–IV.
10 See the reference in n. 6.
11 François-René de Chateaubriand. "Preface." *Études historiques. Œuvres complètes*, vol. 9. Paris: Garnier, 1861, pp. 5–99, p. 29. Chateaubriand's observation is all the more remarkable as he was, as to his political opinions, a fierce reactionary.

weight of the argument in question. As already explained, Aristotle indeed emphasizes that there is a prerequisite for empathy, namely the possibility on the recipients' part of considering themselves as *hómoion*[12] – that is: equal or similar – to the tragic hero. It seems that in Aristotle this clause is mainly meant to refer to the psychic and intellectual profile of the hero, and not primarily to his social status. That said, the "democratic" Athens of the fifth century BCE was structured in a way that differs dramatically from Europe in the eighteenth and nineteenth centuries CE. The audience of the classical Greek tragedy performances was patrician. The distance between their lifeworld and the situations represented on stage was factual, but it was not unbridgeable, at least not in terms of imaginary identification. Things were drastically different in Europe in the age of absolutism. Bourgeois (*tiers état*) people's lifeworld experience was so far removed from the life at court that emotional identification may have been a difficult thing. And the closer we get to the actual revolution of 1789, the more there may have been a conscious unwillingness on the *tiers état*'s part to identify with the stage analogues of people whom they considered to be oppressors and decadent profligates. Consequently, Diderot proposes that the genre of *drame*, that is, modern-style tragedy, should present "dramatic" scenes of bourgeois life.

Still, there is the question of how to reach a level of identification that is sufficient to provoke empathy, emotion. Is everyday misery (looming bankruptcy, the pregnancy of an unmarried daughter,[13] etc.) apt to provoke emotions in the audience? Diderot's answer to the question is inspired by the novels by Samuel Richardson.[14] Without disclosing to his readers the rationale of so doing, Richardson distinguishes, according to Diderot, his écriture, as regards the setting in which the action of novels like *Pamela* (1740) and *Clarissa* (1748) takes place, by a peculiar feature, namely a "multitude de petites choses [auxquelles] tient l'illusion; il y a bien de la difficulté à les imaginer."[15] The effect of all these – at first sight contingent, that is, meaningless – details is, according to Diderot, the impression, on the recipients' part, that the entire action is not something invented, something fictional, but something real.[16] It is no longer the immensity of catastrophe that provides the basis for the recipients' emotional arousal; it is the "reality effect,"

---

12 Aristotle, *Poetics*, 1453a 4–6 (see also 1454a 24).
13 I am referring not only to Diderot's, but also to Mercier's contributions to the new genre.
14 On his *Éloge de Richardson* (1762), see my *Ästhetik der Wirklichkeitsdarstellung*, pp. 13–55.
15 Denis Diderot. *Éloge de Richardson. Œuvres esthétiques*, edited by P. Vernière. Paris: Garnier, 1959, p. 29–48, pp. 35.
16 Let me add in parenthesis that Roland Barthes built his theory of literary realism as developed in his famous essay "L'Effet de réel" (first printed in *Communications* 11 [1968], pp. 84–89) on this argument first advanced by Diderot.

the conviction that "all [this] is true,"[17] that provides the emotional engagement that is a prerequisite for the readers' positive response to a given text.

To summarize: it seems that literary realism's most conspicuous device, namely substituting the novel for tragedy, owes its "origins" to a shift in the recipients of literary products, a shift that occurred in the eighteenth century, especially in its pre-revolutionary second half. The quantitatively dominant part of the demand side of the emerging modern book-market was constituted by the bourgeois class, whose members attained literacy during that century. The demand of these new recipients could no longer be satisfied by the "old" genre of classical and classicist tragedy, which seemed all too different from eighteenth-century bourgeois lifeworld experience to be able to provoke emotions. The "new" genre of *drame*, proposed by Diderot as an adequate substitute, is, according to the theoretician, a combination of tragedy and comedy.[18] From comedy it takes the setting of everyday bourgeois life; from tragedy it adopts the element of disaster hitting the principal personages. The question of identification on the recipients' part – provided for within the reception process of classical tragedies by the narcissistically fueled imaginary "bridging" of the gap between kings and patrician audience – is resolved by "lowering" the impression of fictionality and by increasing the level of alleged "reality." This should be done, according to Diderot, by way of creating reality-effects based on an accumulation of descriptive details without an obvious function in the narrative as a whole.

If one accepts this position, it is evident that drama as a genre characterized by a relatively reduced quantity of descriptive passages can no longer be the adequate generic frame for this "new" variant of tragedy. But it was not Diderot himself[19] who put into practice the ideas first devised by him. The "new" technique of how to create identification under the conditions of a post-heroic society, to be found in a somewhat embryonic stage in Richardson, was systematically implemented only from the time of Balzac, who extracted the specific descriptive techniques from a pragmatic genre that already existed, the Mercier-style *Tableau de Paris* which, while based on the classical genre of "praise of one's (native) city," is distinguished from its model by focusing on the "interesting," "curious" features of present-day city-life, thus catering to the needs of a "new" readership which, on account of its social position, was no longer interested in questions of origin and provenance but was, rather, looking to be presented with its own everyday world as a scene or

---

17 – to quote, once again, from Balzac's *Le Père Goriot* (see n. 6).
18 See Denis Diderot. *Entretiens sur 'Le Fils naturel.' Œuvres esthétiques,* edited by Paul Vernière. Paris: Garnier, 1959, pp. 77–175. On the description of *drame*, see specifically pp. 137–140.
19 – who, as said, tried to conceive some pieces according to his theorizing of the shift in recipients, but was not very successful as a dramatist.

a stage.[20] As a result of all these processes of extraction-from-the-archive, recombination, and refunctionalization, there is, finally, the "new" genre of the realistic novel with its accent on literary topography.

In conclusion, I should like to summarize my argument while relating it to the general topic of this volume: Aristotle does not propagate, but permits the integration of history into drama, though with the qualification that only such episodes of what did factually occur may be selected that comply with or allow for modeling according to the standards of verisimilitude. Early modern European drama, heavily influenced by Neo-Aristotelian poetology, made use of Aristotle's position in order to create historical dramas, mainly tragedies, while relegating to the background the strict rules concerning the presence of history in drama as established by Aristotle. The best examples of the latter attitude may be Shakespeare's histories that present history in the same way as it is already conceived by Aristotle, that is, as a contingent chain of events, which implies that the pieces build upon a material that, according to the Stagirite, is not suitable for constructing well-wrought plays. The "more general" meaning they thus convey is, accordingly, the one contained in the structuring of the plot: factual history is the realm of inscrutable contingency, "signifying nothing," to quote *Macbeth*, a nihilistic attitude Aristotle would have most probably rejected, if only for ethical reasons.

This model of early modern historical tragedy loses ground with the inception of the bourgeois age. For the reasons explained previously, identification as the basic device for engaging the recipients gets replaced by illusion. The latter effect is created mainly by integrating a huge amount of descriptive detail into the stories, which means at the same time that drama as the "leading" genre gets replaced by the novel.

Description, however, links a narrative to a certain specific time and place, which means that history becomes, once again, a central topic in "modern-style" tragedies, that is, in realistic novels. The question already hinted at in Aristotle's text remains open, however. The modeling of history is either submitted to the structuring principle of the fiction created by the narrator (or author), which means, as can be seen most prominently in Balzac, that it becomes distorted. Or, as may be seen in Flaubert, history is preserved in its essential inscrutability, which, as such, undermines the pertinence of the fictional narrative: why *invent* something futile, if reality as such *is* futile all the way? With hindsight, the skeptical attitude towards a fusion of history and fiction, as displayed by Aristotle, seems to be a very sound position.

---

20 – a mentality that later became the basis of the middle-class style of tourism.

Blair Hoxby
History, Myth, and Early Modern Drama

History and myth have been rubbing shoulders ever since the first Renaissance humanists revived classical, regular tragedy: scarcely had Gian Giorgio Trissino composed his *Sofonisba* (1515) before his friend, Giovanni di Bernardo Rucellai, wrote *Oreste* and *Rosmunda*. Trissino's historical tragedy dramatizes a minor episode in the Punic Wars recorded by Livy and Appian. Rucellai's plays reanimate Euripides' mythic *Iphigenia in Tauris* and *Hecuba*. Trissino's decision to dramatize an episode of Roman history is striking because we know of only three plays from the fifth century BCE that dealt with verifiable history (as opposed to legendary material): Phrynicus' *Capture of Miletus* and *Phoenician Women*, and Aeschylus' *Persians*.[1] Only the last has been preserved for posterity. To be sure, the third-century BCE Latin poet Naevius did introduce a species of tragedy based on Roman history that was known as the *fabula praetexta* – thus founding a tradition to which Ennius, Pacuvius, and Accius contributed. The existence of this genre was attested by Cicero, Horace, Tacitus, Diomedes, Evanthius, and Donatus,[2] not to mention their Renaissance commentators, so it might have emboldened some humanists to write tragedies based on history, whether Rome's or their own. But it would be hard to imagine that authors from Miguel de Cervantes to William Shakespeare to Joost van den Vondel would *not* have dramatized national histories but for the classical imprimatur of the *fabula praetexta*: the impulse to dramatize history needed no impetus from the ancients.

The more important distinction on the early modern stage, I would argue, is not between myth and history but between material that is treated as if it were myth – distilled into a fable – and material that is treated as if it were history: composed of a series of events and happenstances, of individualized, even idiosyncratic, manners and dispositions, of recalcitrant particulars. The *locus classicus* of this distinction is Aristotle's *Poetics*, where the Stagirite asserts that "the poet's task is to speak not of events which have occurred, but of the kinds of events which *could* occur, and are possible by the standards of probability or necessity." That makes poetry "both more philosophical and more serious than history, since poetry speaks more of universals, history of particulars." "A 'universal' comprises the *kind* of speech or action which belongs by probability

---

[1] Alan H. Sommerstein. "Tragedy and Myth." *A Companion to Tragedy*, edited by Rebecca Bushnell. London: Wiley-Blackwell, 2009, pp. 164–180, p. 164.
[2] Gesine Manuwald. *Fabulae praetextae: Spuren einer literarischen Gattung der Römer*. Munich: Beck, 2001, ch. A.

or necessity to a certain *kind* of [person]," while "a 'particular', by contrast is (for example) what Alcibiades did or experienced."³ From the sixteenth through the eighteenth centuries, this distinction was often invoked to censure early modern plays – such as those of Lope de Vega or Shakespeare – that were "neither right comedies, nor right tragedies" but "representations of history."⁴ For as Thomas Rymer explains in *The Tragedies of the Last Age Consider'd and Examined by the Practice of the Ancients* (1678), the ancients had demonstrated "that *History*, grosly taken, was neither proper to *instruct*, nor apt to *please*; and therefore would not trust History for their examples, but refin'd upon the History; and thence contriv'd something more *philosophical* and more *accurate* than *History*."⁵ Exemplary plays by Rymer's standard might have included Jean Racine's *Britannicus* (1670) and *Bérénice* (1671). In the preface to the former, Racine declared his preference for a "simple action burdened with little matter," one that proceeded "step by step to its end."⁶ In his preface to the latter, Racine claimed to take his subject from a single sentence in Suetonius: "Titus, who loved Berenice passionately, and who even, as was believed, had promised to marry her, sent her away from Rome, against his will and against hers, in the first days of his reign." Suetonius's under-elaboration of the incident, he claimed, permitted him as a poet "to write a tragedy of that simplicity of action which was so much to the Ancients' taste."⁷

Shakespeare's histories and tragedies could scarcely be described as simple in Racine's sense, and that proved a major sticking point for many of his readers in the late seventeenth and early eighteenth centuries, when critics often took their starting point from Aristotle. Lisideius' judgment of Shakespeare's history plays in *An Essay of Dramatick Poesie* (1668) may stand in for many others: they are, he complains, "rather so many Chronicles of Kings, or the business many times of thirty or forty years, crampt into a representation two hours and an half, which is not to imitate or paint Nature, but rather to draw her in miniature, to take her in little; to look upon her through the wrong end of a Perspective, and receive her Images not only much less, but infinitely more imperfect then

---

3 Aristotle. *Poetics*, translated and with a commentary by Stephen Halliwell. Chapel Hill: The University of North Carolina Press, 1987, pp. 40–41, 1451 a36–b15.
4 John Florio. *Florios Second Frutes*. London: Printed for Thomas Woodcock, 1591, p. 123.
5 Thomas Rymer. *Tragedies of the Last Age*. London: Richard Tonson, 1678, pp. 15–16.
6 Jean Racine. *Œuvres complètes I: Théâtre-Poésie*, edited by Georges Forestier. Paris: Gallimard, 1989, p. 374.
7 Racine, *Œuvres complètes I*, pp. 450–451. See Alain Niderst. "Analyse de la preface de *Bérénice*." *Ouverture et Dialogue: Mélanges offerts à Wolfgang Leiner à l'occasion de son soixantième anniversaire*, edited by Ulrich Doring, Antiopy Lyroudias, and Rainer Zaiser. Tubingen: Gunter Narr, 1988, pp. 319–24. See also Forestier in Racine, *Œuvres complètes* I, p. 1468.

the life." Equating truth with verisimilitude and *distinguishing* it from the particulars of history, Lisideius declares such plays ridiculous "because the Spirit of man cannot be satisfied but with truth, or at least verisimility."[8] Nicholas Rowe, Shakespeare's first editor of note, was equally struck by Shakespeare's refusal to confine himself to a single action, remarking that in all the plays taken "from the *English* or *Roman* History," one finds "the Character as exact in the Poet as the Historian": "so far from proposing to himself any one Action for a Subject," Shakespeare often entitles his plays "lives."[9]

Johann Gottfried Herder and Maurice Morgann's seminal essays on Shakespeare in 1777 mark an important shift in the priorities of dramatic critics, a shift that coincides with a more general "historical turn" in Western philosophy,[10] for they champion the historical quality of Shakespearean drama. Shakespeare "took history as he found it," announces Herder: the "changes of time and place, over which the poet rules, proclaim most loudly: 'This is not a poet but a creator! Here is the history of the world!'"[11] In the case of Shakespearean dramatis personae, said Morgann, "it may be fit to consider them rather as Historic than Dramatic beings."[12] In Adam Müller, we find the complementary impulse to describe history *as* tragedy (rather than tragedy as history). Citing Friedrich Schlegel's observation that England had "dealt in advance and single-handedly with all the revolutions that Europe as a whole [had] been forced to undergo," Müller claimed that British history was itself "a drama in which Europe might find its own history reflected in coherent and idealized form." He then added that

---

8 John Dryden. *The Works of John Dryden*, vol. 17, edited by Edward N. Hooker and Hugh T. Swedenberg, Jr. Berkeley: University of California Press, 1956–89, p. 36.
9 William Shakespeare. *The Works of Mr. William Shakespear*, vol. 1, edited by Nicholas Rowe. London: Jacob Tonson, 1714, p. xxviii.
10 For the larger context of this historical turn, see Isaiah Berlin. *The Proper Study of Mankind: An Anthology of Essays*. New York: Farrar, Straus and Giroux, 1998, pp. 326–435; Herbert Butterfield. *Man on His Past: The Study of the History of Historical Scholarship*. Cambridge: Cambridge University Press, 1955; Friedrich Meinecke. *Historicism: The Rise of a New Historical Outlook*, translated by James E. Anderson. London: Routledge & Kegan Paul, 1972; Hans Peter Reill. *The German Enlightenment and the Rise of Historicism*. Berkeley: University of California Press, 1975; Robert Leventhal. *The Disciplines of Interpretation: Lessing, Herder, Schlegel and Hermeneutics in Germany, 1750–1800*. Berlin: de Gruyter, 1994; Theodore Ziolkowski. *Clio the Romantic Muse: Historicizing the Faculties in Germany*. Ithaca: Cornell University Press, 2004; Frederick A. Beiser. *The German Historicist Tradition*. Oxford: Oxford University Press, 2011.
11 Herder quoted in Jonathan Bate, editor. *The Romantics on Shakespeare*. London: Penguin, 1992, pp. 168, 170–171.
12 Maurice Morgann. "An Essay on the Dramatic Character of Sir John Falstaff." *Eighteenth Century Essays on Shakespeare*, edited by David Nichol Smith, 2nd edition. Oxford: Clarendon Press, 1963, pp. 278–364, p. 231, n. 1.

study of "the dramatic character of the British constitution," which united a monological element in the shape of king, clergy, and aristocracy with the dialogical element in the shape of the House of Commons "to form a single beautiful and dramatic whole" was "a fine preparatory exercise for the dramatic poet" because it would teach him not to become engrossed in monologic contemplation of a single hero but to let his attention be seized continually by new ones.[13] Georg W. F. Hegel's contribution to this discussion would prove the most perdurable: Beholding in history a panorama of sin and suffering, he perceived in the very inadequacy of things as they were a groundwork for the individual exercise of moral freedom. To be sure, those who attempted to impose their private desires and personal conceptions of the good on society might fare no better than the typical tragic hero; but the conflicts of history produced the very gain that Hegel found in tragedy, for Spirit emerged exalted and glorified.[14] This was the theory that Andrew C. Bradley developed with such brilliance in *Shakespearean Tragedy* (1904), thus naturalizing the relationship between history and tragedy for the twentieth century.

This newly discovered kinship between history and tragedy secured Shakespeare's place in the canon as the poet who "wrote the text of modern life"[15] while marginalizing many other dramatists who sought to distill history into myth. By writing as a "historian," Shakespeare created a drama that could satisfy a new set of criteria for truth-claims by reproducing the particulars and the occlusions of history, one that could immerse audiences in the theatrical experience of enduring *being* through time.

---

[13] Müller quoted in Bate, *The Romantics on Shakespeare*, p. 85.
[14] Hayden White. *Metahistory: The Historical Imagination in Nineteenth-Century Europe*. Baltimore: Johns Hopkins University Press, 1975, pp. 88–131.
[15] Ralph Waldo Emerson. *Representative Men*, edited by Pamela Schirmeister. 1850. New York: Marsilio Publishers, 1995, p. 142. See also Peter Holbrook. *Shakespeare's Individualism*. Cambridge: Cambridge University Press, 2010.

Gaia Gubbini
King Arthur in Medieval French Literature: History and Fiction, the Sense of the Tragic, and the Role of Dreams in *La Mort le Roi Artu*

Camelot, Avalon: it is enough to briefly mention such places to evoke a myth that has haunted European literature – and, more broadly, culture – for centuries. These are some of the places where the stories of King Arthur and the Round Table are located: places probably unreal, but places whose names form part of the European cultural imagination. In this sense, a very interesting representation is to be found in the French book *La légende arthurienne*, where a map – significantly entitled "carte de l'imaginaire arthurien" – shows both real places and imaginary ones, the latter existing only in literary sources.[1] This tangled mix of reality and imagination is, in my view, the key element of the French medieval texts about King Arthur and the so-called "Breton cycle."[2] My contribution will focus first more broadly on this literary tradition, and on its relationship with history and fiction. Thereafter, I will develop an analysis of these themes in the thirteenth-century French prose masterpiece *La Mort le Roi Artu*, focusing in particular on its sense of the tragic and on the role played by dreams in the text.

As suggested at the beginning, it is not overstated to define the character of King Arthur as a 'myth' of European culture. The trajectory of the theme of Arthur and the Round Table is a typically literary one. Still, its evolution is deeply embedded in historical developments and it has been repeatedly used for political legitimation. It also combines a key set of mythical and historical elements that remain a constant presence in European medieval culture. The charm this figure and the literary texts pertaining to the "Breton cycle" exercise on readers has a long history. In fact, the medieval public was already deeply aware of the seductive power of this kind of literature. For example, the French poet Jean Bodel distinguished three major literary materials – the texts of ancient Rome, the Carolingian ones from France, and the Breton cycle – and argued that the texts pertaining to the last are "vains et plaisantes," unreal and charming.[3] And Dante Alighieri, in his *De Vulgari Eloquentia*, defined these texts as "Arthuri regis

---

[1] Danielle Régnier-Bohler, editor. *La légende arthurienne: Le Graal et la Table Ronde*. Paris: Éditions Robert Laffont, 1989, pp. 1888–1889.

[2] On this literary tradition, see Richard Trachsler. *Clôtures du Cycle Arthurien: Étude et Textes*. Geneva: Droz, 1996.

[3] Régnier-Bohler, *La légende arthurienne*, p. II.

Open Access. © 2019 Gaia Gubbini, published by De Gruyter. This work is licensed under the Creative Commons Attribution-NonCommercial-NoDerivatives 4.0 License.
https://doi.org/10.1515/9783110604276-004

ambages pulcerrimae" ("the wonderful adventures of King Arthur").[4] One of the reasons for the irresistible charm of these texts is to be found in their peculiar relationship with imagination, space, and time. In fact, the fantastic imagery plays a crucial role in the narrative of Arthurian romances, where the presence of the supernatural is a key driver of the plot and deeply affects the characters' destiny. The relationship of these texts with time is also peculiar.[5] The romances of the Breton cycle mostly have a cyclical view of time, which, following the Celtic tradition, is governed by the alternation of seasons, and is hybridized with the main Christian celebrations.[6] These texts therefore give an impression of 'timelessness.' Mikhail Bakhtin, in his study "Forms of Time and of the Chronotope in the Novel" (1938), has already highlighted the "subjective play with time" of chivalric romances that distort temporal coordinates in the double direction of "a poetical and an emotional expansion and reduction."[7] The same combination of imaginary and historical elements shapes the main character of the Breton cycle, King Arthur. In fact, whether the 'myth' of Arthur has a historical foundation or whether, on the contrary, it is a fictional one, is an issue that has caused rivers of ink to flow. Historians, archeologists, and literary historians have carefully analyzed the weak traces of the possible real existence of the king.

The name *Arturus*, referring to a military leader who successfully supported the Celtic Britons against the Saxons in the sixth century, appears very late, in ninth-century texts such as, for example, the *Historia Brittonum* written by Nennius. The fact that the name Arthur does not appear earlier, i.e. in sixth-century chronicles – that is to say in texts that are contemporary to the historical struggle between Britons and Saxons –, combined with the fact that he is not even mentioned by the careful eighth-century *Historia ecclesiastica gentis Anglorum* written by the Venerable Bede, has led modern historians to doubt the historical existence of Arthur.[8]

---

4 Dante Alighieri. *De vulgari eloquentia*, edited by Steven Botterill. Cambridge: Cambridge University Press, 1996, I.10.2.
5 See Gaia Gubbini. "Le chronotope du sommeil-rêve dans les lais et dans les romans arthuriens français en vers." *Forme del tempo e del cronotopo nelle letterature romanze e orientali (X convegno Società italiana di Filologia Romanza, VIII Colloquio internazionale Medioevo romanzo e orientale, Roma, 25–29 settembre 2012)*, edited by Gaetano Lalomia, Antonio Pioletti, Arianna Punzi, and Francesca Rizzo Nervo. Soveria Mannelli: Rubbettino, 2014, pp. 479–489.
6 For this cyclical conception of time and for all the considerations that follow on the historical discussion of the existence of King Arthur, see Philippe Walter. *Arthur: L'ours et le roi*. Paris: Imago, 2002, pp. 8–30.
7 Mikhail Bakhtin. *Estetica e romanzo*, translated by Clara Strada Janovic. Turin: Einaudi, 1979, pp. 301–302. The English translation is mine.
8 Walter, *Arthur*, p. 18.

However, as Philippe Walter has persuasively observed,[9] the importance of the figure of King Arthur is not to be found in his (highly dubious) historicity, but in the symbolic role he has played in European culture, especially from the twelfth century onward.[10] At that time, the history of Arthur also had a political function: in this perspective, it is crucial to recall the alleged 'discovery' of Arthur's grave, promoted by Henry II, the first Plantagenet King of England, in Glastonbury Abbey, mistakenly identified with the Isle of Avalon – the island of apples, Arthur's last place of rest, according to literary texts. Such an operation was instrumental in consolidating the legitimacy of the Plantagenet kingdom, suggesting continuity between Arthur and Henry II and building on the appeal that the Arthurian tradition held for contemporaries.[11] In fact, artistic and literary evidence attest to the European spread of the Arthurian legend; we may cite as an example the famous twelfth-century image on the mosaic pavement of the cathedral of Otranto, in the deep south of Italy, showing King Arthur riding a supernatural buck.

Among the textual sources, the Latin chronicle *Historia regum Britanniae*, written around 1135 by Geoffrey of Monmouth, is of particular importance. This text, together with its Anglo-Norman translation and re-elaboration entitled *Roman de Brut* (written by Wace in about 1155, i.e. 20 years later),[12] plays a crucial role in the development of major Arthurian characters.[13] Here, the wife of King Arthur, Guenièvre, is already part of an adulterous triangle that connects herself, her husband Arthur, and Mordret, who is the nephew and incestuous son of Arthur and his half-sister Morgan le Fay. Such an incestuous triangle is at the root of many medieval texts of Celtic origin – one is formed, for example, by Tristan, his uncle King Mark, and his uncle's wife Iseult the Blonde. This ancestral setting of love, power, and family relationships was entirely reframed by Chrétien de Troyes – a crucial author for the development and history of the Arthurian novel.[14] In his famous twelfth-century verse romance *Lancelot ou le chevalier de la Charrette*, Chrétien in fact stages a character, Lancelot, destined for great popularity in the evolution of European literature. Lancelot, the most valiant knight of the Round Table, is in Chrétien's romance the lover of Guenièvre, replacing in

---

9 Ibid., p. 27.
10 On Arthur (and Charlemagne) as "roi imaginaire," see Dominique Boutet. *Charlemagne et Arthur ou le roi imaginaire*. Paris: Champion, 1992.
11 On the Plantagenet empire, see Martin Aurell. *L'empire des Plantagenêts*. Paris: Tempus, 2003.
12 On Wace, see Gioia Paradisi. *Le passioni della storia: Scrittura e memoria nell'opera di Wace*. Rome: Bagatto Libri, 2002.
13 Régnier-Bohler, *La légende arthurienne*, p. III.
14 For a full picture of Chrétien de Troyes and his masterpieces, see Chrétien de Troyes. *Œuvres complètes*, edited by Daniel Poirion et al. Paris: Gallimard, 1994.

the adulterous triangle the treacherous and incestuous character of Mordret and therefore reorganizing the narrative into a courtly – and more socially acceptable – framework. In the wake of Chrétien, this remains at the heart of the plot in the anonymous prose cycle called *Lancelot-Graal*: the narration of the exploits of King Arthur, Lancelot, and the Knights of the Round Table, and the adultery between Lancelot and Guenièvre, finally leading to the end of the Round Table. However, in the very last part of the so-called *Lancelot-Graal* cycle – that is to say in the thirteenth-century romance entitled *La Mort le Roi Artu* –, one may encounter not only the triangle formed by Arthur-Guenièvre-Lancelot, but once again the disquieting presence of Mordret. The text *La Mort le Roi Artu* – a somber, haunted text about the end of King Arthur and the Round Table – in fact presents itself as the perfect 'conclusion' of the Breton cycle. As Jean Frappier has importantly suggested, *La Mort le Roi Artu* is in fact conceived by the anonymous author as the 'epilogue' of the endless Arthurian tradition.[15] Moreover, the three last masterpieces of the vast cycle called *Lancelot-Graal* – that is to say, the texts *Lancelot-propre*, *Queste del Saint Graal*, and *La Mort le Roi Artu* – have been recognized as the result of a coherent process of creation – especially thanks to the "thèse de l'architecte" developed by Jean Frappier. Frappier supposes that different authors contributed to the *Lancelot-Graal* cycle, but identifies, in analogy to what happened in the construction of the cathedrals during the Middle Ages, the presence of a "plan d'ensemble dans son unité," conceived by "celui qui mérite d'être appelé le premier maître de l'œuvre ou, d'un seul mot, l'Architecte."[16] The third and last part of such a 'triptych' and the final text of the entire cycle, *La Mort le Roi Artu*, stages the end of the Arthurian world with a tragic perception of the changes caused by time and, most of all, by the destructive power of the adulterous passion between Lancelot and Guenièvre. I will therefore now concentrate my attention on this text, and in particular on its sense of the tragic and on the role played by dreams in this masterpiece, adding some considerations on the concept of the tragic and on dream theories during the Middle Ages.

A brief summary of the key episodes of the plot of *La Mort le Roi Artu* will be useful for the remarks that follow.[17] One of the brothers of Gauvain – King Arthur's favorite nephew – becomes aware of the relationship between Lancelot and Guenièvre: the two lovers, who, for a long time, have restrained their mutual passion, now experience it openly. Venomous rumors about this adulterous relationship circulate at

---

15 Jean Frappier. *Étude sur* La mort le roi Artu, *roman du XIIIe siècle, dernière partie du "Lancelot" en prose*. Geneva: Droz, 1961, spec. p. 9. The entire following section of my essay will rely on the excellent analysis of the text provided by Frappier.
16 Ibid., p. 144.
17 For a detailed summary, see ibid., pp. 9–20.

court. A young and beautiful woman named "la demoiselle d'Escalot" (the Lady of Shalott) nurtures a passion for Lancelot, which he cannot requite as he is already deeply in love with the queen. However, at the start of her passion for the knight, the young woman does not know of his love affair with Guenièvre, and, following a *topos* widespread in Arthurian and Breton literature, the "don contraignant" – that is to say, according to the definition given by Philippe Ménard, the "don en blanc qui lie le donateur"[18] –, she asks him to wear a sleeve of her dress at the tourney of Winchester as a courtly homage. Lancelot reluctantly accepts, nevertheless fearing Guenièvre's jealousy. Guenièvre, who does not know the real reason that has led Lancelot to wear the young woman's sleeve, indeed becomes terribly jealous and decides not to speak to him any more. Afterwards, accusations against Guenièvre develop at the court; she is finally condemned to be burned alive. In the meantime, the corpse of the "demoiselle d'Escalot," who died from the sorrow of not being loved by Lancelot, is magically transported by a ship without crew to Arthur's court, together with a letter explaining the reason for her death. Guenièvre and Lancelot's misunderstanding is therefore resolved, and Guenièvre's jealous rage disappears. The faithful Lancelot decides to rescue the queen from the fire; he saves her and they resume their adulterous relationship. The two lovers are discovered and leave Arthur's court together. A cruel war ensues, which sees Arthur and his nephew Gauvain fight against Lancelot. The latter is winning but generously returns the queen to the king. Arthur and Gauvain are still not satisfied and decide to continue the war. Lancelot has left the country and Arthur follows him, entrusting his kingdom and his wife Guenièvre to Mordret, his incestuous son. Mordret wants the kingdom and desires Guenièvre; he organizes a coup, spreading the word that Arthur has died. To escape Mordret, Guenièvre hides in the Tower of London. Arthur is fighting both Lancelot and the Romans; he learns of Mordret's betrayal and dreams of the Wheel of Fortune predicting his fall. He does not change course, however, nor does he ask for Lancelot's help. When he faces Mordred in the final battle, this results in the death of both and, in the end, of the Round Table.

As we can see already from this brief synopsis of the plot, the dominant note of the text *La Mort le Roi Artu* is the sense of the tragic, as Frappier has observed.[19]

---

18 See Philippe Ménard. "Le don en blanc qui lie le donateur: Réflexions sur un motif de conte." *An Arthurian Tapestry: Essays in Honor of Lewis Thorpe*, edited by Kenneth Varty. Glasgow: Glasgow University Press, 1981, pp. 37–53. – On the same theme, see also Jean Frappier. *Amour Courtois et Table Ronde*. Geneva: Droz, 1973. A more recent study is Corinne Cooper-Deniau. "Culture cléricale et motif du 'don contraignant': Contre-enquête sur la théorie de l'origine celtique de ce motif dans la littérature française du XIIe siècle et dans les romans arthuriens." *Le Moyen Âge* 111 (2005), pp. 9–39.
19 Frappier, *Étude*, speaks of the "grandeur tragique de son sujet" (p. 25); in this regard, see also p. 253.

Let us now review in detail some of the key themes that reflect this sense of the tragic in the text – that is to say, what from a modern perspective could be captured by the term "tragic."

A crucial theme for the development of the sense of the tragic in the text is the concept of inevitability that affects the destiny of characters, first of all, the inevitability of the *force d'amors* – the power of love. Near the beginning, the romance offers a bitter update on Lancelot's emotional troubles: having engaged in the Quest of the Holy Grail, he has renounced his passion for the queen for a long time. But even after such a chaste period, when he meets Guenièvre again he falls once more – and all of a sudden – into the old sin:

> Mes comment que Lancelos se fust tenuz chastement [...] quant il fu en la queste del Seint Graal et eüst del tout renoiee la reïne Guenievre [...], si tost comme il fu venuz a cort, il ne demora pas un mois aprés que il fu autresi espris et alumez come il avoit onques esté plus nul jor, si qu'i rencheï el pechié de la reïne autresi comme il avoit fet autrefoiz. Et se il avoit devant meintenu celui pechié si sagement et si couvertement que nus ne s'en estoit aperceüz, si le meintint aprés si folement que Agravains [...] tant s'en prist garde que il le sot veraiement, que Lancelos amoit la reïne de fole amour et la reïne lui autresi.[20]

The inevitability of the adulterous relationship of Lancelot and Guenièvre – a risk many times avoided, but, in the end, openly taken by the two lovers – is a *fil rouge* that crosses the whole *Lancelot-Graal* cycle. However, this complex mixture of guilt and, at the same time, lack of resistance and shame which characterizes Lancelot and the queen is part of the psychological investigation present in particular in *La Mort le Roi Artu*. This *amour fou* between Lancelot and Guenièvre is at the root of many tragic episodes in the plot of the masterpiece: from the death of the valorous knights of King Arthur, to the sad story of the "demoiselle d'Escalot," and finally to the end of the Round Table, all of which occur under the tragic 'sign' of inevitability.

The "demoiselle d'Escalot," for example, is aware, despite her youth, that she could not avoid pursuing her passion for Lancelot (and thus escape her destiny of death), as she clearly states to her brother:

---

[20] Jean Frappier, editor. *La Mort le Roi Artu: Roman du XIIIᵉ siècle*. Genève: Droz, 1996, §4, p. 3. – "When he was engaged in the Quest of the Holy Grail, Lancelot had lived in a state of perfect chastity [...]. He had then renounced the queen Guenièvre [...] but, once he returned to the court, within a month he was more than ever enflamed by his love for her. He thus fell again – as he did before – into the sin of loving the queen. But while in the past he committed his sin in such a cautious and hidden way that no one had realized it, after his return he madly allowed his sentiments to emerge openly, to the point that Agravain [...] followed the affair so well that he became certain that Lancelot loved the queen in a foolish love and that she felt the same for Lancelot."

> Lors vint la damoisele a son frere et li descouvri meintenant trestout son pensé; et si li dist qu'ele amoit Lancelot de si grant amor que ele en estoit a la mort venue, se il ne fesoit tant qu'ele eüst toute sa volenté. [...] "car il m'est ensi destiné que je muire por lui; si en morrai que vos le verroiz apertement."²¹

Such an insistence on the inevitability of passion is a textual representation of the theme of lovesickness – a *topos* par excellence of medieval literature²² – and constitutes the perfect textual *pendant* of the "fole amour" already depicted with the couple Lancelot-Gueniève.²³ In fact, the young woman lets herself slowly die in bed, without offering resistance to her malady: "Lors se parti la damoisele devant lui et s'en vint a son lit et se cocha a tel ëur que onques puis s'en leva, se morte non, si com l'estoire le devisera apertement."²⁴ The beauty of the "demoiselle d'Escalot" appears remarkable even after her death, but highly disquieting as her corpse suddenly appears at Arthur's court, transported by a ship without crew – this magic translation being another *leitmotif* of Breton literature.²⁵ Such a macabre apparition starts the series of episodes related to death that are present in the romance and that culminate in the final battle between father and son, gloriously staged by the anonymous author on Salisbury Plain. In fact, closely linked to the theme of death that permeates the entire text is the cosmic dimension which the death of King Arthur and the end of the Round Table acquire in *La Mort le Roi Artu.* The text clearly states that the sun-ray that shines through the wound of the traitor Mordret is a sign of God's wrath: "et l'estoire dit que aprés l'estordre del glaive passa par mi la plaie

---

21 Ibid., pp. 42–43. – "Then the young woman went to her brother and revealed to him all her thoughts. And she told him that she loved Lancelot so deeply that she would die if he did not agree to her having him at her will. [...] 'because it is my destiny, to die for him; I will die, and you will clearly see it.'"
22 Among the rich bibliography on the theme, see Massimo Ciavolella. *La "malattia d'amore" dall'Antichità al Medioevo.* Rome: Bulzoni, 1976; Mary-Frances Wack. *Lovesickness in the Middle Ages: The* Viaticum *and Its Commentaries.* Philadelphia: University of Pennsylvania Press, 1990; Joachim Küpper. *Petrarca: Das Schweigen der Veritas und die Worte des Dichters.* Berlin: de Gruyter, 2002, esp. pp. 115–161. For updated and extensive bibliographical references on the subject, see also Gaia Gubbini. "Patologia amorosa: Due fenomeni nella lirica d'oïl." *Ragionar d'amore: Il lessico delle emozioni nella lirica medievale*, edited by Alessio Decaria and Lino Leonardi. Florence: Edizioni del Galluzzo per la Fondazione Ezio Franceschini, 2015, pp. 83–97.
23 "Lancelos amoit la reïne de *fole amour* et la reïne lui autresi" (Frappier, *La Mort*, p. 3).
24 Ibid., p. 68. – "Then she went away from him, she went to bed and lay down and from that time she would never get up but only dead, as the story will openly narrate."
25 For this *topos*, see Laurence Harf-Lancner. *Les Fées au Moyen Age. Morgane et Mélusine: La naissance des fées.* Paris: Champion, 1984.

uns rais de soleill si apertement que Girflet le vit, dont cil del païs distrent que ce avoit esté sygnes de corrouz de Nostre Seigneur."[26]

The fatality and the inevitability that affect the destiny of characters are also elements crucial for Arthur. Two passages in particular seem to me to convey this inevitability: the dream of the Wheel of Fortune and the inscription on a rock on Salisbury Plain announcing that at that same site the final and tragic battle will take place. I will not comment on this second plot element, i.e. the inscription, which is introduced after the dream and, more importantly, after the idea of inevitability has already been strongly conveyed by the text. I will focus, rather, on the dream of the Wheel of Fortune. Arthur in fact has two dreams shortly before the battle of Salisbury. In the first one, Gauvain (who has recently been buried) appears to the king to dissuade him from engaging in the battle against Mordret – or, at least, to convince him to have Lancelot back by his side in order to defeat Mordret. In the dream, Arthur does not listen to Gauvain's advice. The night after this first dream, Arthur experiences another vision. A wondrous woman who embodies Fortune makes the king sit on her wheel and ultimately lets him fall to the ground; this dream is a prediction of his fall:

> Quant il fu endormiz, il li fu avis que une dame venoit devant lui, la plus bele qu'il eüst onques mes veüe el monde, qui le levoit de terre et l'enportoit en la plus haute montaigne qu'il onques veïst; illuec l'asseoit seur une roe. En cele roe avoit sieges dont li un montoient et li autre avaloient; li rois regardoit en quel leu de la roe il estoit assis et voit que ses sieges estoit li plus hauz. La dame li demandoit: "Artus, ou ies tu? – Dame, fet-il, ge sui en une haute roe, mes ge ne sei quele ele est. – C'est, fet ele, la roe de la Fortune". Lors li demandoit: "Artus, que voiz tu? – Dame, il me semble que ge voie tout le monde. – Voire, fet ele, tu le voiz, n'il n'i a granment chose dont tu n'aies esté sires jusques ci, et de toute la circuitude que tu voiz as tu esté li plus puissanz rois qui i fust. Mes tel sont li orgueil terrien qu'il n'i a nul si haut assiz qu'il ne le coviegne cheoir de la poesté del monde". Et lors le prenoit et le trebuschoit a terre si felenessement que au cheoir estoit avis au roi Artu qu'il estoit touz debrisiez et qu'il perdoit tout le pooir del cors et des membres.[27]

---

26 Frappier, *La Mort*, §190, p. 245. – "The story says that, when King Arthur extracts his sword, a ray of sun goes through the wound with so much intensity that Girflet could see it; also the local people said that it was a sign of the wrath of God."
27 Ibid., §176, pp. 226–227. – "Once asleep, he had a vision: a lady got close to him, more beautiful than all the ladies he had seen before in this world; she raised him from the ground and took him to the top of the highest mountain he had ever seen. There she made him sit on a wheel provided with seats, which moved up and down as the wheel turned. Arthur, seeing where he was, saw that his seat was the highest of all. The lady asked him: 'Arthur, where are you?' 'My Lady, I am at the top of a high wheel, but I do not know which wheel is this one.' 'This is the wheel of fortune,' she said. And then she asked: 'Arthur, what do you see?' 'My Lady, it appears to me that I see the whole universe.' 'In truth,' she said, 'you do see it, and of all the kingdoms that you can

We will come back soon to the sense of prophecy that Arthur's dream has in the text, framing the theme in the medieval cultural context regarding dreams. For the moment, it is crucial to highlight how the prophetic nature of Arthur's dream has to be understood as a part of the 'inevitability' which marks the character of the king in particular in *La Mort le Roi Artu*, and which contributes to generating the sense of the tragic we have analyzed so far. But what is the sense of the tragic for the Middle Ages? As analyzed by Henry Ansgar Kelly in his book on the conceptions of tragedy through the centuries – from Aristotle to the Middle Ages – the concept was already ductile in Antiquity, and even more so in Late Antiquity and during the medieval era.²⁸ One well-known aspect, which is, however, crucial in the present context, is the fact that the concept of the tragic could apply to different literary genres, and not only to drama, and was mostly linked to the sublime in terms of the subject, style, and characters. What is perhaps even more important for our analysis of the tragic dimension of Arthur in *La Mort le Roi Artu* – and in particular of his dream of the Wheel of Fortune – is the strong role that the twelfth- and thirteenth-century concept of the tragic attributes to Fortune.²⁹ For example, the long version of William of Conches' twelfth-century commentary on Boethius' *Consolatio Philosophiae* clearly highlights the close relationship between tragedy, the theme of Fortune, and the falls of "kings and highly placed men": "*Quid tragediarum*, etc. [...] In hoc carmine potuisti perpendere reges et provectos deprimi per Fortunam indiscrete percucientem, id est improvise, quia nescitur dies vel hora miseriarum."³⁰

Boethius found in tragedies, as William of Conches states in his *Commentary*, perfect examples of the mutability of Fortune, in fact: "Tragedia

---

see you have been the Lord; until now you have been the most powerful king that ever existed. But such is the pride of men that there is no one in the world, however highly placed he might be, that he should not fall down and lose his power over the world.' Then she took him and made him fall on the ground in such a treacherous way that, in his fall, the king felt like he had broken all his bones and had lost control of his body and limbs."

28 See Henry Ansgar Kelly. *Ideas and Forms of Tragedy from Aristotle to the Middle Ages*. Cambridge: Cambridge University Press, 1993, pp. xiii-xvi. On the specific theme of *La Mort le Roi Artu* as a tragedy, see Karen Pratt, who discusses the possible analogies between the medieval masterpiece and classical and late antique theories of tragedy: "Aristotle, Augustine or Boethius? *La mort le roi Artu* as Tragedy." *Nottingham French Studies* 30 (1991), pp. 81–109.

29 On the relationship between Arthur and Fortune as a tragic theme, see Karl Joseph Höltgen. "König Arthur und Fortuna." *Anglia* 75 (1957), pp. 35–54.

30 William of Conches, *Glose super Librum Boecii de Consolacione*, II.2, British Library MS Royal 15 B 3, fol. 39v., quoted in Kelly, *Ideas and Forms of Tragedy*, p. 71. For the English translation, see ibid.: "In this sort of poem [that is, tragedy], you could have taken to heart examples of kings and highly placed men brought down by Fortune's striking without discernment – that is without expectation, because one knows neither the day nor the hour of one's miseries."

est scriptum de magnis iniquitatibus a prosperitate incipiens, in aduersitate desinens. Et est contraria comediae quae ab aliqua aduersitate incipiens in prosperitate finitur."[31]

Like many authors in the twelfth century, John of Salisbury "considers the main feature of the tragedy to be the mournful ending,"[32] and Geoffrey of Vinsauf summarizes this tradition, putting at the center of the concept of tragedy the misfortune of an eminent character.[33] We will see how this element (the eminence of the character at the center of the fall) is also crucial for the medieval theory of dreams, in Macrobius as well as in the later tradition. The theme of the Wheel of Fortune is a frequent *topos* in medieval literature and, more broadly, culture, as scholars have highlighted.[34] One beautiful example is to be found in the famous text of the *Carmina Burana, O fortuna*:

> O *Fortuna*,
> velut luna
> *statu variabilis*,
> semper crescis
> aut decrescis
> [...]
> Sors immanis
> et inanis,
> *rota tu volubilis*,
> status malus,
> vana salus
> semper dissolubilis
> [...]
> nunc per ludum
> dorsum nudum
> fero tui sceleris.[35]

---

[31] I quote this passage from the recent edition of the works of William de Conches by Édouard Jeauneau. See *Guillelmi de Conchis Opera Omnia*. Turnhout: Brepols, 1999, p. 105.
[32] Kelly, *Ideas*, p. 80.
[33] Ibid., p. 99.
[34] On the subject in classical literature, see David M. Robinson. "The Wheel of Fortune." *Classical Philology* 41 (1946), pp. 207–216. For the relevance of the Wheel of Fortune in medieval literature, history of art and culture, see Edmond Faral. *Recherches sur les sources latines des contes et romans courtois du moyen âge*. Paris: Champion, 1913; Frappier, *Étude*, pp. 258–288; Yasmina Foehr-Janssens and Emmanuelle Métry, editors. *La Fortune: thèmes, répresentations, discours*. Geneva: Droz, 2003.
[35] *O Fortuna, CB* 17, quoted in Alfons Hilka and Otto Schumann, editors. *Carmina Burana*. Heidelberg: Winter, 1930–1970.

The theme is also widespread in illuminations in medieval manuscripts, and it is represented in manuscripts within the Arthurian tradition,[36] very often presenting the detail of the bare back of man in his downfall, an element we have also encountered in the text of the *Carmina Burana*. As a perfect example, we can cite the illumination showing King Arthur on Fortune's wheel present in the manuscript London, British Library, Ms. Additional 10294, f. 89.[37] Man helplessly facing his destiny is a medieval topos that reaches a particularly tragic degree in *La Mort le Roi Artu*, where we find concentrated all the relevant elements of the sublime: an eminent character, the Wheel of Fortune, the inevitability of destiny. Moreover, they are staged in a dramatic, narrative *crescendo* that culminates in the final battle where, as the texts says, "Einsi ocist li peres le fill, et li fils navra le pere a mort" ("the father killed his son and the son gave his father a mortal wound"). In this way the Round Table comes to its end, and Arthur's death leaves his kingdom "orphaned," as the prophecy inscribed on the rock on Salisbury Plain clearly announces: "En ceste plaingne doit estre la bataille mortel par quoi li roiaumes de Logres remeindra orfelins."[38]

As anticipated above, the tragic mood of Arthur's dream is not only conveyed by the presence of the tragic topos *par excellence* for the Middle Ages (the Wheel of Fortune), but also by the prophetic nature of the dream, which implies that all the predictions present in the vision will come true, regardless of the choices made by the king. However, in order to fully understand the meaning of such a prophetic dream in the plot of *La Mort le Roi Artu*, we have to contextualize it among the medieval theories about dreams. The distinction between dreams and visions is made, for example, by Augustine, especially in his *De genesi ad litteram*. In the twelfth book of this text, Augustine explains the formation of images and of visions and establishes a 'hierarchy' between different types of vision: the spiritual vision is superior to that of the body; in turn, the intellectual vision is superior to the spiritual one.[39] According to this logic, "at its most powerful, imagination was thought to channel divine influence in the form of proph-

---

[36] On the illuminations representing the dreams in *Lancelot-Graal* manuscripts, see Mireille Demaules and Christiane Marchello-Nizia. "Träume in der Dichtung: Die Ikonographie des *Lancelot-Graal* (13.–15. Jh.)." *Träume im Mittelalter: Ikonologische Studien*, edited by Agostino Paravicini Bagliani and Giorgio Stabile. Stuttgart: Belser, 1989, pp. 209–226.
[37] The illumination can be seen here: http://www.bl.uk/catalogues/illuminatedmanuscripts/ILLUMIN.ASP?Size=mid&IllID=858. Accessed 25 July 2018.
[38] Frappier, *La Mort*, p. 228. – "In this plain will take place the deadly battle after which the realm of Logres will become orphaned."
[39] *De genesi ad litteram*, XII.24.51.

ecy."⁴⁰ However, medieval knowledge of dreams, as has been argued by Jacques Le Goff,⁴¹ largely draws on the typology of dreams in Macrobius' fifth-century *Commentary on the Dream of Scipio* and that in Calcidius' fourth-century Latin commentary on Plato's *Timaeus*. In the twelfth century, these ideas were developed by William of Conches and the School of Chartres⁴² – an important point of reference for the Troubadours and, more broadly, for the vernacular literary production of medieval France.⁴³ Calcidius distinguished between the prophetic dream, the truthful dream, and the dream-lie. In his *Commentary on the Dream of Scipio*, Macrobius proposes a schema of five categories. I quote from Le Goff's seminal article:

> Les rêves prémonitoires se répartissent en trois catégories: l'*oneiros* (*somnium*) ou rêve énigmatique, l'*horama* (*visio*) ou vision claire, le *chrematismos* (*oraculum*) ou rêve envoyé par la divinité et souvent énigmatique. Les rêves non prémonitoires se divisent en deux types: l'*enupnion* (*insomnium*), rêve, symbolique ou non, qui n'a de référence que dans le passé ou le quotidien, et le *phantasma* (*visum*), pure illusion.⁴⁴

In the case of Arthur's dream⁴⁵ of the Wheel of Fortune, it seems to me that we are at the crossroads between *oraculum* and *visio*: the dream is apparently enigmatic,

---

40 Quoted in Michelle Karnes. *Imagination, Meditation, and Cognition in the Middle Ages*. Chicago: University of Chicago Press, 2011, p. 6.
41 Jacques Le Goff. "Le christianisme et les rêves (IIᵉ–VIIᵉ siècle)." *I sogni nel Medioevo: Seminario Internazionale (Roma, 2–4 ottobre 1983)*, edited by Tullio Gregory. Rome: Edizioni dell'Ateneo, 1985, pp. 171–218.
42 See the following studies: Alyson M. Peden. "Macrobius and Mediaeval Dream Literature." *Medium Aevum* 54 (1985), pp. 59–73; Thomas Ricklin. *Der Traum der Philosophie im 12. Jahrhundert: Traumtheorien zwischen Constantinus Africanus und Aristoteles*. Leiden: Brill, 1998; Michel Lemoine. *Intorno a Chartres: Naturalismo platonico nella tradizione cristiana del XII secolo*. Milan: Jaca Book, 1998; Michel Lemoine and Clotilde Picard-Parra, editors. *L'École de Chartres: Bernard de Chartres – Guillaume de Conches – Thierry de Chartres– Clarembaud d'Arras. Théologie et cosmologie au XIIᵉ siècle*. Paris: Les Belles Lettres, 2004. – More broadly on the role of dreams in the Middle Ages, see *I sogni nel Medioevo*, edited by Tullio Gregory, passim; Steven F. Kruger. *Dreaming in the Middle Ages*. Cambridge: Cambridge University Press, 1992; Jean-Claude Schmitt. *Le Corps, les rites, les rêves, le temps: Essais d'anthropologie médiévale*. Paris: Gallimard, 2001.
43 In this regard, cf. Gaia Gubbini. "Soupir, esprit: Bernard de Ventadour, *Can lo boschatges es floritz*." *Romanistisches Jahrbuch* 65/66 (2015), pp. 86–102.
44 Le Goff, "Le christianisme et les rêves," p. 178.
45 On the dreams in *La Mort le Roi Artu*, see Jehanne Joly. "Rêves prémonitoires et fin du monde arthurien." *Fin des temps et temps de la fin dans l'univers medieval*. Aix-en-Provence: Centre universitaire d'études et de recherches médiévales d'Aix, 1993, pp. 259–284. – For a broader analysis of the dreams in the *Lancelot-Graal* cycle, see Klaus Speckenbach. "Form, Funktion und Bedeutung der Träume im Lancelot-Gral-Zyklus." *I sogni nel Medioevo*, pp. 317–55.

but clear enough to let Arthur realize, as soon as he awakes, that it constitutes a prophecy of the catastrophes to come ("Einsi vit li rois Artus les mescheances qui li estoient a venir").[46] Therefore, in *La Mort le Roi Artu*, the prophetic dream plays an important role in foreshadowing the narrative plot. Such a view of the dream as a prophecy that has to be trusted seems the antipode of the medieval literary *topos* of the dream-lie. In fact, in early French texts, dream-lies are especially present in courtly production, particularly in romances, where we find a frequent use of the rhyming pair *songe/mençonge*, as has been highlighted in the secondary literature.[47] Arthur's interpretation of the dream as a prophecy is furthermore confirmed by the priest who hears his confession in the morning after the vision. The fact that the king has correctly understood the meaning of the dream and that he has received a prophecy rather than a dream-lie probably has to do with his eminent status. As Le Goff has highlighted, Macrobius inherited from Antiquity (and then developed, and delivered to the Middle Ages) the concept of a "hierarchy of dreamers": according to such a hierarchy, "seuls peuvent être considérés comme rêves prémonitoires d'une authenticité irréfutable des rêves de personnages revêtus d'une autorité suprême."[48] This is actually the case of Arthur, whom the same Fortune clearly designates in the text as "li plus puissanz rois qui i fust."[49]

This theme – the dream-prophecy, or the vision that is reserved for an eminent character – seems significant for the understanding of the development

---

[46] Frappier, *La Mort*, §177, p. 227. – "In this way King Arthur saw the misfortunes that were ready to come."
[47] Within a rich bibliography, see at least Herman Braet. "*Visio Amoris*: Genèse et signification d'un thème de la poésie Provençale." *Mélanges d'Histoire littéraire, de Linguistique et de Philologie romanes offerts à Charles Rostaing*. Liège: Association des romanistes de l'Université de Liège, 1974, pp. 89–99; Christiane Marchello-Nizia. "La rhétorique des songes et le songe comme rhétorique dans la littérature française médiévale." *I sogni nel Medioevo*, pp. 244–259; Francesco Zambon. "L'amante onirica di Guglielmo IX," *Romanistische Zeitschrift für Literaturgeschichte* 15 (1991), pp. 247–261; Alain Corbellari and Jean-Yves Tilliette, editors. *Le Rêve medieval*. Geneva: Droz, 2007; Yasmina Foehr-Janssens. "Songes creux et insomnies dans les récits médiévaux (fabliaux, dits, exempla)." *Le Rêve médiéval*, edited by Alain Corbellari and Jean-Yves Tilliette. Geneva: Droz, 2007, pp. 111–136; Christine Ferlampin-Acher, Elisabeth Gaucher, and Denis Hüe, editors. *Sommeil, songes et insomnies: Actes du colloque de Rennes (28–29 septembre 2006). Perspectives médiévales* 32, supplement (2008); Mireille Demaules. *La Corne et l'Ivoire: Étude sur le récit de rêve dans la littérature romanesque des XIIe et XIIIe siècles*. Paris: Champion, 2010.
[48] Le Goff, "Le christianisme et les rêves," p. 183.
[49] Frappier, *La Mort*, p. 227.

of European medieval literature: from the revelations received by the saints[50] and by Charlemagne, to the prophecy about the end of the Round Table given to Arthur, to the vision of the *status animarum post mortem* of Dante's *Divine Comedy*.[51]

---

[50] See Alain Corbellari. "Pour une étude générique et synthétique du récit de rêve dans la littérature française médiévale." *Le Rêve médiéval*, pp. 53–71.
[51] In this regard, see Mirko Tavoni. "Dante 'Imagining' His Journey through the Afterlife." *Dante Studies* 133 (2015), pp. 70–97.

Susanne Friede
When History Does Not Fit into Drama: Some Thoughts on the Absence of King Arthur in Early Modern Plays

King Arthur – and perhaps his realm as a whole – is one of the most important, if not *the* most important character, or topic, in medieval narrative literature. Today, his literary prominence is as relevant as ever. Next to many modern literary (re)interpretations set in King Arthur's reign (for example, the works of T. H. White and Marion Zimmer Bradley), there are more and more cinematic adaptations that show the life and the death of Arthur (for example, *King Arthur*, 2004, directed by Antoine Fuqua; *King Arthur: Legend of the Sword*, 2017, directed by Guy Ritchie). Given the medieval literary prominence of the figure of King Arthur, the following question arises: why is there no historical play about Arthur in the early modern period? It is, to be sure, difficult, if not impossible, to consult the entire output of the early modern stage. However, there is certainly no prominent play that includes the (pseudo)historical King Arthur.

This absence of a historical early modern Arthurian play must not be taken for granted, as the enormous dissemination of Thomas Malory's *Morte d'Arthur* (first published in 1485) proves. There are, in fact, also some German carnival plays (*Fastnachtsspiele*) that are randomly based on the quasi-mythological background of the Arthurian world. At least three *Fastnachtsspiele* from different cultural backgrounds refer to Arthurian material. Two of them, *Das vasnachtspil mit der kroon* and *Der Luneten Mantel* (whose manuscripts date from 1455 to 1458) are from Nuremberg. However, these two plays, which refer solely to the 'frame' of the Arthurian world and its heroes, do not introduce King Arthur as a character. They only use Arthurian 'narrative elements' to stage a 'test of chastity,' or conjugal fidelity. A third, more complex example, *Ain hupsches Vasnacht Spill von Künig Artus*, comes from Swabia (the manuscripts dating from 1486–1520).[1]

---

[1] I warmly thank Thomas Habel for his gracious hints and explanations. – The plays can be found in Adalbert von Keller's anthology *Fastnachtsspiele aus dem fünfzehnten Jahrhundert*. 4 vols. Stuttgart: Bibliothek des Litterarischen Vereins, 1853–1858. [Reprint: Darmstadt: Wissenschaftliche Buchgesellschaft, 1965–1966]. *Das vasnachtspil mit der kron* appears as no. 80, *Der Luneten Mantel* is no. 81, and *Ain hupsches Vasnacht Spill von Künig Artus* is no. 127. Cf. also Kurt Ruh, editor. *Die deutsche Literatur des Mittelalters: Verfasserlexikon*, vol. 5. Berlin: de Gruyter, 1985. All three plays are mentioned there: *Das vasnachtspil mit der kron* (p. 384),

Still, why is there no historical play about King Arthur in the early modern period? One explanation of remarkable importance is that the history of Arthur cannot provide a heroic model. First, it is necessary to underline the fact that the Middle Ages and the early modern period knew considerably more religious (i.e. biblical or salvific) plays than secular historical plays. While the notion of 'secular theater' does not refer to a homogeneous group of texts, the distinction between religious and profane theater is rather sharp.[2] For example, a manuscript from Wolfenbüttel edited by Alan E. Knight[3] gives a clear idea of this difference and underscores preferences of Renaissance playwrights with regard to content. It contains a collection of *mystères* performed during the processions at Lille. From these 74 *mystères*, almost all, i. e. 69, are religious plays, and only 5 are historical *mystères* treating episodes from Roman history. 'Historical' playwrights could select their topics from biblical history, saints' lives, or, *à la limite*, secular history, as is the case in the *mystères* of Lille. However, they *had* to include a moral, or at least stage a hero with outstanding values and comportment,[4] who would ideally serve as a typological example for biblical protagonists and Christian virtues. A play about King Arthur could not have belonged to Roman history, and it would have been difficult to represent Arthur's life as a praiseworthy example of biblical, or as a part of salvific history.[5]

In her article in this volume, Gaia Gubbini discusses different factors that caused the decline of King Arthur and his reign as told in *La Mort le Roi Artu*, the last part of the Prose Lancelot-Grail Cycle, a complex cycle generated in growing stages between 1210 and 1235/40. In *La Mort le Roi Artu*, the narrator provides a lot of overt explanations to rationalize the decline of the Arthurian empire. Explicit comments on Lancelot's, Guinevere's, and indirectly also on Arthur's behavior stress both their subjective guilt (also through the Christian term *pechié*) and their objective guilt (without any sense of misbehavior on the part of the heroes). The latter, the objective guilt, is, for example, evoked by the incestuous relationship

---

Der Luneten Mantel (p. 1221) and *Ain hupsches Vasnacht Spill von Künig Artus*, i.e. *König Artus' Horn* (pp. 70–72).
2 Cf. Alan E. Knight. *Aspects of Genre in Late Medieval French Drama*. Manchester: Manchester University Press, 1983, esp. pp. 17–40, as well as Charles Mazouer. *Le théâtre français du Moyen Âge*. Paris: Sedes, 1998, chapters I and IV.
3 Alan E. Knight, editor. *Les mystères de la procession de Lille*. 2 vols. Geneva: Droz, 2001/2003.
4 See the excellent article by Konrad Schoell. "Le théâtre historique au XVe siècle." Divers toyes mengled: *Essays on Medieval and Renaissance Culture in Honour of André Lascombes*, edited by Michel Bitot. Tours: Université François Rabelais, 1996, pp. 189–196.
5 In a purely technical sense, it would have been difficult to give (as is regularly done in the *mystères* of Lyon) a moral of the play in the epilogue or to mention its precise historical sources in an *argumentum* at the beginning.

between Arthur and Morgane that is insinuated in the text. It is true that the very first vernacular text mentioning King Arthur, Wace's chronicle (*Roman de*) *Brut*, depicts him as a strong and combative, successful, and very courageous hero (which is why the Plantagenets could refer to this 'historical' figure for the legitimization of their claim to power). However, in other texts of the twelfth century that belong to different genres, he is described as a rather weak and passive king whose significance is not as great as that of the other knights of the Round Table. This is, for instance, true of the lai *Lanval* and Chrétien's courtly romances, including *Lancelot, ou le Chevalier de la charrette* and *Perceval, ou le Conte del Graal*. In the Prose Lancelot-Grail Cycle, and notably in *La Mort le Roi Artu*, King Arthur's position weakens even further, and finally he is lethally wounded by his own nephew. In this way, medieval French texts about King Arthur provide an impressive example of how reworking existing figures can be provocative in literature.

In fact, from the beginning of the thirteenth century at the latest, the history of Arthur was no longer able to provide a heroic model, as had been the case, albeit for a very short period, in the middle of the twelfth century (Wace's *Roman de Brut*). It therefore does not necessarily matter whether a potential early modern play about King Arthur would have been conceptualized and perceived as a literary or as a historiographical drama.

To point out further probable reasons for the absence of a historical play about King Arthur in the early modern period, it will be helpful to look at the – in some regards contrary – example of Alexander the Great. In his study of theological and humanistic erudition in the early French theater, Tobias Leuker analyzes the *mystère* called *Les Épitaphes d'Hector et d'Achille* by George Chastelain, which was staged in Nevers in 1454.[6] He examines and outlines the novel perspective that this play aims to offer on ancient history. The main character, Alexander the Great, reads and judges the epitaphs of the two great heroes of the Trojan War, Hector and Achilles. To redeem Hector, whose epitaph declares that he has been perfidiously killed by Achilles, Alexander calls Achilles up from the depths of the netherworld and arranges a 'confession conversation' between Achilles and Hector.

Apart from the single flaw that he is not a Christian, Alexander (like Hector) functions as a nearly perfect example of ideal behavior as prescribed by the idea of nobility in most ancient and medieval romances, which partly appear in the shape of a 'mirror of princes.' That is why Alexander and Hector are both held in the *limbus* (the *siège des Preux*) in Chastelain's play.[7]

---

[6] Tobias Leuker. *Vom Adamsspiel bis Jodelle: Theologische und humanistische Gelehrsamkeit im frühen französischen Theater*. Köln: Böhlau, 2016, pp. 109–130.
[7] Cf. ibid., p. 130.

Although Alexander was always perceived as a historical figure in medieval literature (which was not always and not necessarily the case for Arthur),[8] both heroes experience a literarily stylized tragic ending. While Arthur is lethally wounded by his nephew Mordred, Alexander is poisoned by two of his servants, whom he has overly trusted. Chastelain's play further examines Hector's death and its influence on the hero's posthumous fate. In this way, it shows how important it is for a literary character based on a mythological or historical hero to experience an 'appropriate' death.

Given this context, Alexander, as opposed to Arthur, represents the ideal kind of hero that fits into a historical (and necessarily moral) early modern play. Even the moral of his death and destiny emphasized in medieval romances: not to trust the non-noble, could indirectly refer to his remarkable noble qualities. On the contrary, Arthur's death, caused by a treacherous relative, only underlines the deep corruption of his whole kin.

Finally, the question regarding the absence of King Arthur from early modern plays is also a matter of genre. During the thirteenth century at the latest, the *matière de Bretagne* established a considerable tie to the romance genre, which is especially evident in the Prose Lancelot-Grail Cycle. To show the possible, the credible, and to develop fully its own narrative power (to be φιλοσοφώτερον in a figurative sense), the Arthurian material clearly required a narrator's voice rather than a *mise en scène*. However, only the long narrative genre allows the establishment of a link between the topic of subjective and objective guilt of the heroes and the mythological level of explanation culminating in the motif of the Wheel of Fortune. The aspects underlying the complex portrait of King Arthur and his world required explanations and comments that could only be provided by a narrator. These aspects included the highly contradictory display of King Arthur as a hero and as a victim, of his realm as an ideal and at the same time disrupted world, as well as of the manifold forms of guilt of the king, the queen, and the Knights of the Round Table. This is perhaps one of the most important reasons why it was difficult to put the Arthurian heroes and Arthur himself on stage (or in a play) without a narrator's commenting voice. Until today, long narrative genres (including film, which is 'more narrative' than the stage play) seem to have been the only means to explain the Arthurian 'universe.'

---

8 See, for example, the following three studies: Martin Gosmann. *La légende d'Alexandre le Grand dans la littérature française du 12e siècle: Une réécriture permanente*. Amsterdam: Rodopi, 1997; Catherine Gaullier-Bougassas. *Les* Romans d'Alexandre: *Aux frontières de l'épique et du romanesque*. Paris: Champion, 1998; Susanne Friede. *Die Wahrnehmung des Wunderbaren: Der Roman* d'Alexandre *im Kontext der französischen Literatur des 12. Jahrhunderts*. Tübingen: Niemeyer, 2003.

Julia V. Ivanova
Machiavelli's Soteriology and the Humanist Quattrocento Dialogue

In order to reconstruct the genealogy of Niccolò Machiavelli's *Mandragola*, we will consider this work against the background of the Quattrocento dialogue and Renaissance novel, singling out common discursive elements and rhetorical strategies. In the first half of the fifteenth century, the authors of humanist experimental dialogues sought to prevent their readers from making the attempt at reading any univocal sense or unambiguous authorial intention into their texts. They made no straightforward claims, however, noting only *en passant* in the expositions to their dialogues that their sole aim was that of rhetorical exercise. This subterfuge made it possible to disguise the main topic of the dialogue – the rhetorical art – under the cloak of a quarrel around a definite concept or an entire theory (be it the poetry of *tre corone fiorentine*, or the virtues of laws and medicine, nobility, the true and false good, etc.).[1]

The claim to combine objective reasoning with rhetorical exercise grants the participants of the dialogue an unprecedented discursive liberty – a liberty shared not only by the interlocutors, but by the author, too. Together with his characters, the author thus disclaims all responsibility for the utterances they make as the dialogue unfolds. The rules of the game are defined in the exposition: once the author has defined his work as (at least partly) a fiction, he acts beyond the reach of any appeals to objective reality and is subjected only to aesthetic judgment. The literary aspect, wearing the mask of objective reality, foments infinite exchange and inversion of opinions, life attitudes, and social roles (the early humanist writers often have their characters defend positions that contradict those to which they adhere in real life).

This strategy has the characters articulate scandalous and occasionally nonsensical things. One of the characters in Lorenzo Valla's *De vero falsoque bono*

---

[1] For an analysis of the most famous fifteenth-century humanist dialogues, see David Marsh. *The Quattrocento Dialogue: Classical Tradition and Humanist Innovation.* Cambridge: Harvard University Press, 1980.

Note: The research at the basis of this paper was conducted as part of the Basic Research Programme at the National Research University Higher School of Economics (HSE) and supported within the framework of a subsidy granted to the HSE by the Government of the Russian Federation for the implementation of the Global Competitiveness Programme.

ә Open Access. © 2019 Julia V. Ivanova, published by De Gruyter. This work is licensed under the Creative Commons Attribution-NonCommercial-NoDerivatives 4.0 License.
https://doi.org/10.1515/9783110604276-006

thus states that the true good consists, among other things, in cuckolding others (especially if the husbands are negligent in performing their conjugal duty) – the only condition is not to upset the betrayed husbands by revealing to them who they are.[2] The void nominal difference being removed, the thing itself (*res*) proves to be entirely identical: in both cases, be it a *connubium* or a *conjugium*, the woman either has sexual contact with a man (*cum uiro coniungitur*), or conceives a child with him, becoming a mother (*mater per maritum efficitur*). Both acts, as stated by Valla's character, who displays the "Epicurean" attitude, can be performed by a lover (*adulter*) with even greater success, given that he is a male (*mas*) no less, and perhaps even more so than the husband. We see here how the struggle against empty terms stumbles at a self-contradiction: having removed the difference between *connubium* and *conjugium* as a barely nominal difference, the "Epicurean" than equates the husband and the lover on the basis of their common denomination (*mas*). We may hypothesise that these semantic experiments are to be considered against the background of Valla's full-scale destruction of Aristotelian-Porphyrian taxonomical principles in his *Repastinatio dialecticae et philosophiae* (1439).[3]

Thanks to a whole system of mediations, we can see that each statement of the dialogue turns out to be, on the one hand, securely protected from literalism in interpretation, and, on the other, almost completely isolated from the particular historical situation in which it emerges. This system of mediations has been a constitutive trait of the dialogue genre since Plato (many of whose dialogues are staged as a retelling of quasi-real conversations, myths, speeches, etc.).[4]

What happens, then, to the meanings that emerge and develop as the dialogue unfolds? If the meaning of a concept is at stake (as a rule, Quattrocento

---

2 "Omnino nihil interest utrum cum marito coeat mulier, an cum amatore. Semoue nanque differentiam peruersi nominis connubij, unam eademque rem effecisti adulterij et conjugij. Etenim quid aliud est siue coniugium, siue connubium, siue matrimonium, nisi quod foemina uel cum uiro coniungitur, uel mater per maritum efficitur? Quæ duo etiam alius non maritus praestare foeminis potest. Maritus quod quid aliud quam marem significat? An non et adulter mas? Vide ne forte sit ipso interdum marito marior" (Lorenzo Valla. *De voluptate ac vero bono libri III*. Basel: Anreas Cartander, 1519, pp. 29–30).
3 On Valla's logical and semantic reform, see Salvatore Camporeale. "Lorenzo Valla. *Repastinatio, liber primus*: retorica e linguaggio." *Lorenzo Valla e l'Umanesimo Italiano*, edited by Ottavio Besomi and Mariangela Regoliosi. Padua: Editrice Antenore, 1986, pp. 217–239; Peter Mack. *A History of Renaissance Rhetoric, 1380–1620*. Oxford: Oxford University Press, 2011, pp. 22–73; Lodi Nauta. *In Defense of Common Sense: Lorenzo Valla's Humanist Critique of Scholastic Philosophy*. Cambridge: Harvard University Press, 2009, pp. 13–128.
4 See the section "*L'ontologie comme chef-d'œuvre sophistique*" in Barbara Cassin. *L'Effet sophistique*. Paris: Éditions Gallimard, 1995, pp. 23–65.

authors chose the verification of a concept as the subject matter for their dialogues), the dialogue is transformed into a sophistic game with a so-called meaning without denotation, that is, with a meaning which is not investigated, but arbitrarily assigned to the concept in question. Usually, the assignment of a given signification relies on the fact that some of the meanings the term has in ordinary language effectively enable the sophist to associate with it the required sense. But meaning does not exist in a void: the assignment of a meaning inevitably entails "the creation of a world," in which the concept endowed with the required meaning is inscribed. Given that the humanists usually discussed anthropological and ethical notions, the worlds emerging in their dialogues are usually ethical, i.e. systems which enable a person to realise one of the possible ways of conduct. But ethics, by its very nature, may be the ethics of only one world – the real one; the freedom in producing different ethical worlds may only be that of dissociating from your own personality or of forging literary fictions. The fact that, at the dawn of the Renaissance, anthropology and ethics are transformed into a kind of an experimental field therefore merits special interest.

In the light of these preliminary remarks, let us now turn to *Mandragola*. In one of his articles, Ruf I. Khlodovsky traces the genealogy of the plot of Machiavelli's play, outlining its affinity to the third novel of the third day of Giovanni Boccaccio's *Decameron*.[5] In fifteenth-century Latin humanist literature, we also find a story in which a cleric, using a simple confusion of terms, seduces a pious woman who ignores the fact that it is illicit to understand the desire to serve God metonymically (by giving oneself to one of His servants). This plot may be found, for instance, in Poggio Bracciolini. In his dialogue *Against Hypocrites*, one of the characters, Carlo Marsuppini, and Poggio himself retell a number of similar stories: a hermit from Pisa claimed that in being with a prostitute, he only seeks to exhaust his despicable body; another, being surprised during the act of coitus and harshly reprimanded, pretended that he had only wanted to bridle the mischievous flesh. Some hermits from Bologna, convincing a woman that the worthiest thing in the eyes of God is obedience, ordered her to go to bed and conceive a child, while one of the hermits consented to play the role of the husband – not for the pleasure of doing it, but for the sake of obedience and in order to give birth to a new being.[6]

---

[5] Ruf I. Khlodovsky. "Lorenzo Medici mezhdu Giovanni Boccaccio i Niccolò Machiavelli: Transformatsiya odnogo novellisticheskogo syuzheta" [Lorenzo Medici between Giovanni Boccaccio and Niccolò Machiavelli: The Transformation of a Novelistic Plot]. *Pyatnadtsatyiy vek v evropeyskom literaturnom razvitii*. Moscow: Nasledie, 2001, pp. 52–111.

[6] Francesco Poggio Bracciolini. *Contro l'ipocrisia (i frati ipocriti)*, edited by Giulio Vallese. Naples: Tullio Pironti, 1946, pp. 89–90.

It seems unnecessary to quote all the examples, given that there are a dozen of them in Poggio's dialogue. What matters is the logic the wicked clerics use in order to bolster their arguments. The depraved spirituals exploit the lack of an immediate logical transition from the corporeal to the spiritual. As a matter of fact, according to the Christian doctrine, this transition takes place in the historical world; it is exemplified by the Incarnation, in which matter is expiated, as the "lascivious body" is transformed into a "temple of the Holy Spirit." The body becomes immortal; it has been promised Resurrection. In the historical perspective, it cannot be dissociated from the spirit inhabiting it. Therefore the Law, given after the Incarnation, forbids and censors evil not only in deeds, but in thoughts as well. The spiritual sense cannot exist alone: it is given in the Revelation that operates in the history of mankind. But there is a gap in this logic, one which many heretics and enemies of Christianity have used: they ascribe to the Christians the most incredible acts of depravity, allegedly practiced under the cloak of spiritual love (cf., for example, the *Octavius* by Minucius Felix). The domain of the historical is self-contradictory: it is easy to skip the historical, passing from the body to the spirit. Being detached from history, the body loses its own right. By putting aside the aspect of the temporal embodiment of sense, one may introduce a kind of a selective semiotics, arbitrarily assigning meanings chosen at random to whatever bodily phenomenon one pleases. This is especially easy to do by paradiastolically misinterpreting the words of ordinary speech with neighboring significations, e.g., by identifying simple bodily love with the spiritual, or by drawing a parallel between the exhaustion of the body by erotic exercises to the ascetic *mortificatio carnis*.

Another dialogue in which we may find a story of a depraved cleric is Gioviano Pontano's *Charon*. A shade in Hell tells the infernal boatman a story about having dedicated her virginity to God, an act that was mediated by one of His servants. As a young girl, she attended church praying for a successful marriage, but the priest ordered her to remain unmarried and to dedicate herself to God. It turns out that this dedication is to be understood in very concrete, material terms: her virginity is dedicated to the church with which this priest is affiliated, and he also has the exclusive right to accept the offerings. The act of 'dedication' is described in detail: the priest proclaims the various limbs of the girl to be the property of the church. However, the ending of the novel is a sad one: the maiden falls pregnant and dies in labor.[7]

---

[7] Giovanni Gioviano Pontano. *Opera omnia soluta oratione composita*, vol. 1. Venice: Aldus et Socerus, 1518, p. 64.

Both Poggio and Pontano used dialogues to exploit the topic of seduction of a woman by a cleric, though Poggio preferred the narrative form – that of the anecdote – for these erotic stories from the lives of the clergy, while Pontano was more inclined to the dramatic form. His novel consists almost entirely of the lines spoken by the priest and his innocent victim.

In general, if we were to sum up Pontano's role in the development of the Quattrocento dialogue, we should say that we owe to him the lending of the theatrical to the dialogue, its transformation into a series of comic scenes. Still, this sequence of scenes remains incomplete. The main omission is the absence of the intrigue which would unify the separate sketches. The binding element in Pontano's voluminous works is not intrigue but, as in classical dialogue, the unity of the topic. But the reasoning, a typical trait of the dialogue, progressively gives way in *Charon* to the demonstration: in front of a few stable characters, there files a procession of secondary figures, permitted only to utter short speeches – at best, to tell the audience a brief story.

In this way, the system of mediations that provides the author and the characters of the dialogue with the possibility of distancing themselves from the points of view expressed comes to a critical moment of its existence. From the very beginning, the utterances proffered in the fictitious conversation tend to merge with objective reality. The different meanings emerging in the conditions of the theatricalization of the dialogue undergo a process of emancipation, breaking free from the control of the author as well as of the characters who articulate them. Though the authors of the early Quattrocento dialogues insisted on the non-identity, even dissociation, between the images of their characters and their utterances within the framework of a fictitious conversation, here we see that the characters and their judgments merge. The characters, embodying particular ideas, enjoy the right to an independent way of conduct, displaying the idea that each of them transports. Acting in a definite way on stage, the characters relentlessly forge the illusion of the autonomy of their life. This autonomy is confined to the limits of the stage – a fictive space, fancying its own reality.

These are, according to our interpretation, the components of the historical-cultural situation in which such an enigmatic play as Machiavelli's *Mandragola* appears. The space in which its action unfolds is the last in this series of the objectification of ideas, whose spokesmen dared not assume responsibility for them. Its plot has been tested many times, by the novel on the one hand and the dialogue on the other; the dialogue made it possible to instill the logic of heretics and sophists into the play, the logic of arbitrariness, violently transgressing any actual reality and spinning its own illusory world from its transient phantoms. As Khlodovsky has convincingly demonstrated, *Mandragola*'s characters originate from the novel – a genre containing an irremediable contradiction.

From its very beginnings, this genre considered itself a fragmentary reflection of a particular event – and obviously a secular one. But at the same time, the memory of this genre also included elements drawn from spiritual literature – *exempla* of the church sermon and hagiographic episodes that necessarily presuppose miracles. An element of spontaneity, of unpredictability, is included in the very name of this genre. In this sense, its paradigm is the Gospel, a book containing ground-breaking good news; the Gospel and the central point of its poetics – the paradox, refuting and rejecting the narrow old logic and revealing to man the endlessness of his new, unprecedented possibilities: a paradox opening the way for human boldness.

Now we can, at least, put forward one of the, in my opinion, very probable interpretations of *Mandragola*'s plot. There is a striking affinity between the plot of *Mandragola* and the evangelical story of the Annunciation.[8] In both cases, the miraculous birth of a child is expected. Before the news of this child spreads, the characters languish in despair: Messer Nicia is lamenting the childlessness of Lucrezia, his wife, while Callimaco, haunted by love's passion, suffers the torments of Hell. Let us note that the characters, describing their situation and state of mind, speak suspiciously often of death. Of course, the story of a deceptive conception presented as a supernatural event had been exploited long before Machiavelli: it may be found as far back as the early Christian era, not only in apocrypha and various polemical writings hostile to Christianity, but indirectly in the New Testament as well: Saint Joseph "was minded to put her [his pregnant wife] away privily" (Matthew 1:19). The motif of procreation turns out to be connected with that of an alleged relocation of Messer Nicia and Lucrezia from their home to another place (which, however, does not take place – I.2; an allusion to the trip to Bethlehem for the Census).

Machiavelli goes further, linking the childless Lucrezia to John the Baptist's mother Elizabeth, who, according to the Gospel of Luke, was barren and yet miraculously enabled to conceive a child by her old husband. In the third act of *Mandragola*, Ligurio, who wants to put to the test the measure of Fra' Timoteo's

---

8 The fact that Machiavelli names his main character Lucrezia points to another theological allusion in *Mandragola*. At the beginning of *De Civitate Dei*, Saint Augustine scrutinizes in detail the problem of how Christian women, molested by wicked men, could preserve their chastity and holiness (I, chs. 18–19). Dealing with this question, Augustine also considers in the context of theological ethics the suicide of Lucretia, a Roman matron molested by the Roman king's son Sextus Tarquinius. There is no doubt that Machiavelli had read *De Civitate Dei*. On *Mandragola* as a rewriting of the circulating 'Lucretia stories,' see Melissa M. Matthes. *The Rape of Lucretia and the Founding of Republics: Readings in Livy, Machiavelli, and Rousseau*. Pennsylvania: The Pennsylvania State University Press, 2000, pp. 51–98.

dishonesty, informs him of a fictitious pregnancy of a non-existent maiden, whom Fra' Timoteo would have to talk into taking the medicine that enables her to get rid of the unwanted child. This imaginary maiden is in the fifth month of pregnancy when Lucrezia is told of the future conception.

Besides the affinity of the plots, we may cite a long series of quotations that confirm the exalted condition of Machiavelli's Lucrezia and create, so to say, a *theotokic* context for the reception of her person. Besides the fact that word of Lucrezia's beauty and grace even reaches Paris – this may be considered simply as a commonplace of courtly literature –, there are a number of sayings testifying that neither Lucrezia nor the other characters perceive her eventual pregnancy as a result of natural causes. Messer Nicia, for instance, narrates at length that Lucrezia considers endless prayer the best means against infertility – devoting all of her time to it while paying no attention to the circumstances that might physically hinder conception: "she spends four hours on her knees with her Our Fathers before she'll go off to bed; and she's a tough one with the cold."[9] Callimaco speaks of "the most honest" nature of Lucrezia, "totally alien to love affairs." Nicia characterises Lucrezia as the "the sweetest person in the world and the most obliging."[10] At the same time, Ligurio, also pointing to Lucrezia's virtuous nature, affirms that she is "fit to rule a kingdom."[11] Lucrezia's own statements are also of some interest. When her mother proposes that she take the mandrake potion and give herself to a man, she says: "even if I was the last woman left in the world and if the human race was to rise again from me, I don't believe that I would be allowed to do something like this."[12] Apropos, the motif of Lucrezia's pregnancy emerges at least twice. Fra Timoteo seeks to persuade Lucrezia by using the following example: "The Bible says that the daughters of Lot, thinking that they were the last women left in the world, lay with their father. And because their intention was good, they did not sin."[13] When

---

[9] "[...] ma la sta quattro ore ginocchioni a infilzar paternostri, innanzi che la se ne vadi a letto, ad è una bestia a patire freddo" (I.6). – From here on, the Italian original is quoted from Niccolò Machiavelli. *Opere scelte*, edited by Gian Franco Berardi, 2nd edition. Rome: Editori Riuniti, 1973. The English translation is quoted from Niccolò Machiavelli. *Mandragola*, translated by Nerida Newbigin, 2009. http://www.personal.usyd.edu.au/~nnew4107/Texts/Sixteenth-century_Florence_files/Mandragola_Translation.pdf. Accessed 23 July 2018.
[10] "Ell'era la più dolce persona del mondo e la più facile" (III.2).
[11] "[...] bella donna, savia, costumata ed atta a governare un regno" (I.3).
[12] "[...] ché io non crederei, se io fussi sola rimasa al mondo, e da me avessi a resurgere l'umana natura, che mi fussi simile partito concesso" (III.10).
[13] "Dice la Bibbia che le figliuole di Lotto, credendosi essere rimase sole nel mondo, usorono con el padre; e, perché la loro intenzione fu buona, non peccarono" (III.11).

Fra Timoteo tells Lucrezia what she has to do, she replies: "[...] of all the things discussed, this seems to me the strangest."[14] The characters who change their clothes for the feigned hunt for a lover for Lucrezia use as a password the words "saint cuckold" – an obvious allusion to Saint Joseph. And finally, again, Lucrezia's words, transmitted by Callimaco, that she pronounced after the adulterous night: "I will judge that it is the result of a heavenly disposition that so desires, and I am not capable of refusing what heaven wants me to accept. Therefore I take you as lord, master, guide. I want you as my father, my defender, and as my dearest good"[15] (cf. the Holy Virgin's canticle: "My soul doth magnify the Lord, and my spirit hath rejoiced in God my Saviour"). After the night with Lucrezia, Callimaco says: "As a result, I find myself the happiest, most contented man ever in the world; and if death and time do not bring this happiness to an end, I'll be more blessed than the blest, more sainted than the saints."[16] Another Biblical context that the author implicitly refers to is the Book of Tobit. The evil demon Asmodeus falls in love with Sarah, Raguel's only child, and kills every man she attempts to marry. In the play, this context is introduced by mentioning of the name of the Archangel Raphael (according to the Holy Writ, it was he who delivered the maiden from the demon). Fra' Timoteo, blessing Lucrezia's union with Callimaco, says that he will recite the Archangel Raphael's prayer (this prayer forms part of the order of a Catholic wedding mass). The Middle Ages knew the demon Asmodeus as King Solomon's rival, who had once managed to assume the king's form and take power over his harem for a short period of time. Significantly, Asmodeus was unmasked thanks to the testimonies of Solomon's wives, outraged and surprised by the fact that their husband, who had previously been a jealous enthusiast of the Law, had suddenly given up on the rules of conduct with women and began indulging in debauchery and excess. In this context, it is worth recalling the words of the song Callimaco was singing shortly before his date with Lucrezia: "Since you won't let me come to your bed,/may the devil come instead!"[17] It is worth noticing that the coitus of a chaste and virtuous woman with a demon (with Asmodeus, as a rule), and the resultant conception of a child, was a wide-spread topic by Machiavelli's time.

---

14 "[...] ma questa mi pare la più strana cosa che mai si udissi" (III.11).
15 "[...] io voglio iudicare che è venga da una celeste disposizione che abbi voluto così, e non sono sufficiente a recusare quello che 'l cielo vuole che io accetti. Però io ti prendo per signore, padrone, guida; tu mio padre, tu mio defensore, e tu voglio che sia ogni mio bene [...]" (V.4).
16 "Tanto che io mi trovo el più felice e contento uomo che fussi mai nel mondo; e se questa felicità non mi mancassi o per morte o per tempo, io sarei più beato ch'e beati, più santo che e' santi" (ibid.).
17 "Venir vi possa el diavolo al letto. / Da poi che io non ci posso venire io!" (IV.9).

The intertwining of the stories taken from the Book of Tobit and the Gospel, and the transformation of the ideas they contain through the means of the novel and the dialogue, enabled the author to create a rich context for the total refutation of the New Testament's evangelic message. It is not by chance that *Mandragola* is filled with words and expressions connected with salvific good news. The recognition – a customary device for any comedy – is preceded by agonizing suspense and takes place when the characters are already on the verge of desperation, at the crossroads between life and death. Machiavelli's main characters – Callimaco, Messer Nicia, and Lucrezia – from time to time threaten to die – until, that is, the coitus between Lucrezia and Callimaco occurs. On the verge of and immediately after this event, they acknowledge that they have experienced a second birth. When Ligurio informs Messer Nicia that Fra' Timoteo has agreed to induce Lucrezia into committing adultery, he exclaims:

Nicia: You've given me new life. Will it be a boy?

Ligurio: A boy.[18]

Lucrezia's husband assures her that after having committed the act she seems completely renewed: "because this morning it is just as if you were reborn."[19] He notices in her the signs of audacity, when she had formerly always been meek: "You're very bold this morning. Yesterday evening she seemed half dead."[20]

We must mention yet another event binding these two contexts – the *theotokic* and the "Lucrezian": the celebration of the wedding of Lucrezia Borgia and Alfonso I d'Este in Ferrara at the beginning of 1502, marked by a theatrical performance based on the story of the Annunciation. Kristin Phillips-Court quotes a fragment from the description of this event made by Isabella d'Este in 1503 and observes that, according to this description of the performance, the scenography of the Ferrara Annunciation turns out to be quite similar to the composition of Piero della Francesca's 1455 Annunciation panel.[21] Phillips-Court's research is not dedicated to the biography of Alexander VI's legendary daughter, however, but to the fifteenth-century *sacre rappresentazioni*, and the main character in her work is Feo Belcari with his famous *Rappresentazione quando la Nostra Donna*

---

18 "*Nicia*: Tu mi ricrei tutto quanto. Fia egli maschio? - *Ligurio*: Maschio" (III.8).
19 "[...] perché gli è proprio, stamane, come se tu rinascessi" (V.5).
20 "Tu se' stamani molto ardita! Ella pareva iersera mezza morta" (ibid.).
21 Kristin Phillips-Court. "Framing the Miracle in Feo Belcari's 'Rappresentazione quando la Nostra Donna Vergine Maria fu annunziata dall'Angelo Gabriello'." *Annali d'Italianistica* 25 (2007), pp. 233–261, p. 233.

Vergine Maria fu annunziata dall'Angelo Gabriello. In the Middle Ages, the feast of the Annunciation played a particular role in the life of Florence and other cities of Tuscany: the New Year began on this day, and it was only in November 1749 that this was moved to 1 January by decree of Duke Francis II of Lorraine. In the Quattrocento, the celebrations of the Annunciation in Florence were particularly magnificent and ingenious. As Phillips-Court writes in her article:

> In addition to feast day celebrations organised by convents and confraternities, the plays richly flourished under Lorenzo de' Medici during the last decades of the fifteenth century. Nuptial and diplomatic celebrations alike included elaborate productions of the sacred representations in churches, performed mainly by confraternities and religious companies, but sometimes also by professional actors, courtiers and poets.[22]

Perhaps it was these numerous Florentine sacred representations of the Annunciation, often used by the politicians who organized them to impose appropriate political views on their audience, that instilled in Machiavelli the idea of carnivalizing the Gospel story.[23] It is also probable that Machiavelli, who demonstrated a lively interest in the history of the Borgia family, was aware of the fact that the representation of the Annunciation had formed part of the luxuriant feasts on the occasion of Lucrezia's wedding. In the first years of the sixteenth century, Lucrezia's reputation was already somewhat ambiguous: on the one hand, it had been tainted by participation in her father's and brother's intrigues – it remaining unclear how far this was intentional or not; and on the other, the most famous politicians and writers of her time, who had maintained friendly relations with her (the very pious Aldo Manuzio featuring among them), characterized her as a highly intelligent, pious, and modest woman.[24] Her husband, Alfonso d'Este, officially delegated the administration of the duchy to her during his absence from Ferrara. (Perhaps this fact explains the characteristic of Machiavelli's Lucre-

---

[22] Ibid., p. 237.
[23] Still, we must mention here the interpretation of *Mandragola* as a parody on another Christian plot, a *missa parodia* inverting the order of the Catholic Mass and deriding the transubstantiation – cf. Paolo Dall'Olio. *Alcune note sull'interpretazione della Mandragola di Niccolò Machiavelli.* http://www.bibliomanie.it/interpretazione_mandragola_machiavelli_paolo_dallolio.htm. Accessed 23 July 2018.
[24] Agostino Paravicini Bagliani quotes some extracts from the reports addressed to Alfonso d'Este by one of the Ferrara ambassadors: "Lucrezia è donna molto prudente, discreta e di buona indole [...] è ad un tempo modesta, bella e onesta"; "Nulla di sinistro si debba o si possa sospettare di lei." Cf. Agostino Paravicini Bagliani. "Lucrezia Borgia preghiere e veleni." *La Repubblica*, 10 August 2007. http://ricerca.repubblica.it/repubblica/archivio/repubblica/2007/08/10/lucrezia-borgia-preghiere-veleni.html. Accessed 23 July 2018.

zia as "atta a governare un regno"?) A special line of research exists that investigates the connection between two Lucrezias – Borgia's daughter and Machiavelli's character. The ambiguous reputation of the name "Lucrezia" ("from Lucretia Romana[25] to Lucrezia Borgia and famous Lucrezias – Cinquecento courtesans") in sixteenth-century Italian culture has been examined by Giusi Baldissone.[26] In fact, the affinity between the two Lucrezias, separated by two millennia, is quite striking, at least if we proceed from the image of Lucrezia elaborated in the secondary literature of recent decades – as a reasonable, virtuous, pious, and refined being forced to serve the vile intentions of the men who had power over her.[27] Viewed in this way, Lucrezia Borgia is transformed into a symbol of the Machiavellian period and of the Machiavellian understanding of political wisdom, appropriate to his time – perhaps, no less than Lucrezia in *Mandragola*, in her interpretation by Luigi Russo: "una vera eroina della moralità 'Machiavelliana.'"[28]

In this way, these repetitive acts of parodying Scripture – i.e. the progressive plunge into the abyss of sin – take the form of the good news of the revival of life. Trampling and inverting the Gospel and the Law becomes a means of gaining this renewed existence. It seems very important that the spectator of the play

---

25 An allusion to Livy's account of Collatinus' virtuous wife may be found in *Mandragola*, I.1. Like Tarquinius, Callimaco learns about the woman he will come to desire during a friendly conversation at a party. As in Livy, *Mandragola* mentions a competition regarding the superiority of women. (The Romans compare their own wives, while Callimaco and his friends compare French and Italian women [Tit. Liv., *Ab urbe cond.*, I.57].) Just as in *Ab urbe condita*, the hero-lover in *Mandragola* is far away from his beloved when the desire to possess her awakens in his soul, and this desire prompts him to undertake a trip. Finally, Collatinus' wife attracts Sextus Tarquinius by her virtue no less than by her beauty ("Ibi Sex. Tarquinium mala libido Lucretiae per vim stuprandae capit; cum forma tum spectata castitas incitat" – I.57.10); Callimaco likewise says: "First of all, what's most against me is her character: she is completely virtuous and quite against anything that has to do with love" ("in prima mi fa guerra la natura di lei, che è onestissima ed al tutto aliena dalle cose d'amore" – *Mandragola*, I.1). Both Lucretias – Livy's and Machiavelli's – are not fond of entertainments or paying visits to friends; both make their servants work hard and live a virtuous life.

26 Baldissone points out the contrasting contexts in which this name functioned: Perugino depicts a Roman matron with jewelry which had once belonged to Lucrezia Borgia; the Cinquecento courtesans willingly used this name as a pseudonym. Aretino, for example, names one of the characters of his obscene work "Lucrezia." Cf. Giusi Baldissone. "Un nome contaminato: Lucrezia nella Mandragola." *Il nome nel testo: Rivista internazionale di onomastica letteraria X (2008). Atti del Convegno internazionale di Onomastica & Letteratura. Università degli studi di Pisa, 31 maggio – 1 giugno 2007*, pp. 27–38. http://riviste.edizioniets.com/innt/index.php/innt/article/view/278. Accessed 23 July 2018.

27 Cf., e.g., the works by Agostino Paravicini Bagliani and Bruno Capaci.

28 Luigi Russo. *Machiavelli*. Rome: Laterza, 1974.

remains unaware whether the coitus of Lucrezia and Callimaco has resulted in conception, or whether this conception turns out to be a fiction – as is the case with the other pregnancy mentioned in the play. In fact, we see here a continuation of the logic of the wicked clerics from Boccaccio's *Decameron* on the one hand, and on the other that of the Quattrocento humanists, who systematically evaded responsibility for their own utterances and sought to create a variety of semantic worlds, revolving around the most incredible versions of ethical relativism and inconceivable without the possibility of declaring them non-existent, of dispelling them at any moment as a nightmare. Machiavelli's play, inheriting the plots of the novel and of the dialogue, could not help but inherit the logic born and elaborated within these genres.

Let us note that our interpretation of *Mandragola* as an inversion of the Gospel in no way contradicts the conception according to which this comedy constitutes a political allegory in which Lucretia symbolically represents Florence and the Florentine people. Rather, these two notions fit each other perfectly. It is not by chance that, in the prologue, the author expresses a wish regarding his Florentine audience: "I would wish that you,/just as she was, might be deceived too ("[...] ed io vorrei/Che voi fussi ingannate come lei"), while other characters assume the roles of the politicians in whose hands the destiny of the city lies.[29]

In conclusion, we should stress that we have so far discussed exclusively the inversion of the Gospel in *Mandragola*, and not its parodying. These two concepts are entirely different. If we were to deal with the parodying of the Gospel – which would be a very fruitful topic to examine – it would require investigating the carnivalesque aspect of Machiavelli's play, and in this light the very concept of death acquires a radically new sense: it is clear that, in the world of the Carnival, death occupies a completely different place than in the phantasmatic worlds generated in sophistic games.

---

29 Cf. Carnes Lord. "On Machiavelli's Mandragola." *The Journal of Politics* 41 (1979), pp. 806–827. Lucrezia, in the author's opinion, represents the Florentine people, who become the playthings of the city's rulers: Messer Nicia is Piero Soderini (even Roberto Ridolfi, while not accepting the allegoric interpretation of the play, recognizes his affinity to Machiavelli); Fra Timoteo, stingy and greedy, is Pope Julius II; Sostrata, Lucrezia's mother, participating in the plot against Lucretia's chastity, is Francesco Soderini, Piero's brother, a rich and ambitious cleric who became a cardinal in 1503 under Julius II and was the Florentine ambassador at the Papal Curia in 1504. In Machiavelli himself, Lord sees a similarity with Ligurio, who, as is typical for a smart servant, is the moving principle of the whole intrigue. Callimaco, who at the end of the play happily takes possession of Lucretia, is the future prince, young and audacious, who is able to save Florence. In his article, the author also cites the works of his opponents, who refuse to see any topical political content in *Mandragola* at all.

Pavel V. Sokolov
Lucretia without Poniard: Pieter Corneliszoon Hooft's *Geeraerdt van Velsen* between Livy and Tacitus

In this paper we set ourselves the goal of examining the figure of the female protagonist of Pieter Corneliszoon Hooft's historical tragedy *Geeraerdt van Velsen* (1613), Machtelt van Velsen, in its connection with the classical "archetypical rape victim"[1] Lucretia, transformed by Livy into an *exemplum* of republican *virtus*, feminine *gloria*, conjugal *modestia*, and *castitas*. The intertextual analysis of Dutch early modern dramatic female characters has already proven fruitful, for instance, in the case of Joost van den Vondel's historical drama *Gysbreght van Aemstel*, as studied by Marco Prandoni.[2] But, obviously, in the case of *Geeraerdt van Velsen*, the historical accounts are by no means less relevant as intertexts than the literary sources. According to Geeraardt Brandt, Hooft's first biographer, his play was highly appreciated by all its erudite spectators ("alle geleerden, die daar van oordeelen konden") especially due to its author's capacity to epitomize and clearly represent the best principles of rule and civil wisdom, as carried out by the ancient and modern political and historical writers ("geen kleen deel der burgerlyke wysheit, en beste regeerregels der oude en nieuwe Schryveren, in zoo weining blaaden beknoptelyk begreep, en klaarlyk ontvoude").[3] Bringing on stage rival political theories, Hooft bears in mind not only the medieval history of the Netherlands, but also the 'grand narrative' of Roman history: the motif of the fall of Rome, lamented by the Chorus of Amsterdam Maidens, and its rebirth, prophesied by the god of the river Vecht, constitutes the 'macro-historical' frame,

---

[1] Daniela Hammer-Tugendhat. *The Visible and the Invisible: On Seventeenth-Century Dutch Painting*. Berlin, Munich, and Boston: de Gruyter, 2015, p. 58.
[2] Marco Prandoni. "Intertextuality – Gysbreght van Aemstel (1637)." *Joost van den Vondel (1587–1679): Dutch Playwright in the Golden Age*, edited by Jan Bloemendal and Willem Korsten. Leiden: Brill, 2012, pp. 271–284.
[3] Geeraardt Brandt. *Het leven van Pieter Corn: Hooft en de lykreeden*, edited by Pieter Leendertz, Jr. The Hague: Nijhoff, 1932, pp. 12–13.

Note: The research that is at the basis of this paper was conducted within the framework of the Basic Research Program at the National Research University Higher School of Economics (HSE) and supported within the framework of a subsidy granted to the HSE by the Government of the Russian Federation for the implementation of the Global Competitiveness Program.

 Open Access. © 2019 Pavel V. Sokolov, published by De Gruyter. This work is licensed under the Creative Commons Attribution-NonCommercial-NoDerivatives 4.0 License.
https://doi.org/10.1515/9783110604276-007

in which the particular episode of Van Velsen's disastrous hubris and Floris V's inglorious murder is only a small part.

As a number of classical scholars have justly observed, in Roman historiography, especially in Livy and Tacitus, the turning points of the development of the state were tightly connected with rape accounts: let us recall the stories of Rhea Silvia, the Sabine Women, and Lucretia herself. Christina Kraus has even coined a special term for this recurrent theme of ancient historical writing – a 'Lucretia story.'[4] Along with the Livian female hero, Tacitus, moving away from the glorious retrospective *ab urbe condita* to the pessimistic one *ab excessu divi Augusti*, creates the image of an 'anti-Lucretia' – Livia Drusilla, a woman whom Augustus has "stolen away" (*abducta*, a term also connoting rape) from her husband, the great pontiff Tiberius Nero, breaking the legal marriage while she is pregnant.[5] Instead of committing suicide in the footsteps of Lucretia, she yields to Augustus' decision without any attempt at resistance (Tacitus wonders whether it was done willingly or not) and becomes "terrible to the State as a mother, terrible to the house of the Caesars as a stepmother."[6] Quite naturally, the prudential cowardice of the elder Tiberius degenerates into the tyrannical laxity of his son, Emperor Tiberius, and the *principatus* becomes a shameful link between trampled freedom and full-fledged tyranny. The shared premise of the two major Roman historians, borrowed by their early modern commentators, was summed up by Jan Gruter (de Gruytere, 1560–1627), the long-standing director of the Bibliotheca Palatina in Heidelberg, in his notes on Livy's expression *spectata castitas*: he writes that "a certain trait of tyranny consists in seeking to offend, as much as possible, the virtues as such" ("nota vera tyrannidis: inquinare velle ipsas, se posset modo, virtutes").[7] Commenting

---

4 Christina S. Kraus. "INITIUM TURBANDI OMNIA A FEMINA ORTUM EST: Fabia Minor and the Election of 367 B.C." *Phoenix* 24 (1991), pp. 314–325.
5 Let us quote the passage from Tacitus (which has been analyzed thoroughly by Thomas E. Strunk. "Rape and Revolution: Tacitus on Livia and Augustus." *Latomus* 73 [2014], pp. 126–148): "abducta Neroni uxor et consulti per ludibrium pontifices an concepto necdum edito partu rite nuberet; †que tedii et† Vedii Pollionis luxus; postremo Liuia grauis in rem publicam mater, grauis domui Caesarum nouerca" (Tacitus. *Annales ab excessu divi Augusti*, edited by Charles Dennis Fisher. Oxford: Clarendon Press, 1906, I.10.5. http://www.perseus.tufts.edu/hopper/text?doc=Perseus:text:1999.02.0077. Accessed 25 July 2018). – The analogy with the 'Lucretia story' is reinforced by the use of the formula "cupidine formae" that echoes literally the Livian narrative. See Christina S. Kraus. "The Tiberian Hexad." *The Cambridge Companion to Tacitus*, edited by Anthony J. Woodman. Cambridge: Cambridge University Press, 2009, pp. 100–115, p. 114.
6 Tacitus, *Ann.*, I.10.5.
7 Jan Gruter. "Notae politicae ad T. Livii Historiarum librum I." *Titi Livii Patavini historicorum romanorum principis Libri omnes superstites*. Frankfurt: Guolphgangi Hofmanni, 1627, p. 28.

on Livy's statement that Tarquinius was attracted not only by Lucretia's beauty but by her virtue as well, Gruter backs up his statement by referring to Tacitus' interpretation of the rapes of free-born adolescents by Tiberius: "neque formam tantum & decora corpora; sed in his modestam pueritiam, in aliis imagines majorum."[8] Gruter's observation explains the centrality of the 'rape accounts' for political theory: the rape of a noble matron functions as an *experimentum crucis*, which is a kind of a 'Machiavellian moment' for any political community. The way in which a given *civitas* reacts to this crucial event determines both its political form (republic or tyranny) and also the meaning of pivotal ethical terms (liberty, virtue, prudence, etc.).

Since the early Renaissance, the 'Lucretia story' has had a fascinating impact on European intellectual and artistic imagery: the interest in it has been considerably fomented by the discovery, around 1500, of an ancient statue interpreted as Lucretia. The 'Lucretia fever,' ranging from numerous representations of this *exemplum* of Roman *pudicitia* and *fides* on Italian *forzieri* and *cassetoni* to the most prominent works of art and literature, puts at stake the pivotal values associated with this figure. Containing the seeds of ambivalence from the very beginning (the 'erotic component' introduced by Ovid and reinforced by Augustine), this archetype of feminine virtue underwent infinite semantic shifts in various narrative, pictorial, and performative contexts in the course of the sixteenth century. As a part of the Livian rhetorical narrative on the origins of Roman grandeur, it was affected by the tectonic change in fashion in early modern political thought pointed out by Giuseppe Toffanin[9] and a number of scholars following in his footsteps: while in the fifteenth century an interest in Livy prevailed, the following century witnessed a fascination with Tacitus – the number of editions of Tacitus' works in Latin, paraphrases, and commentaries grew exponentially.[10] Like Livy before him, Tacitus was considered not as a matter of a purely academic interest, but as a handbook of political prudence: to use Michel de Montaigne's words, "ce n'est pas un livre à lire c'est un livre à estudier et apprendre,"[11] while Justus Lipsius, one of the very first and most fervent promoters of Tacitist political

---

[8] Tacitus, *Ann.*, VI.1.
[9] Giuseppe Toffanin. *Machiavelli e il "tacitismo": la "politica storica" al tempo della controriforma*. Padua: A. Draghi, 1921.
[10] Cf. the diagrams in the article by Elena Valery. "La moda del tacitismo (XVI – XVII secolo)." *Atlante della letteratura italiana*, vol. 2, edited by Erminia Irace. Turin: Einaudi, 2011, pp. 256–260.
[11] Michel de Montaigne. *Les Essais de Michel de Montaigne*, edited by Pierre Villey and Verdun-Louis Saulnier. Paris: Presses Universitaires de France, 1978, pp. 718–719.

ideas, considered his works "quasi theatrum hodiernae vitae."[12] The pantheon of Livian heroes, Lucretia among them, could not remain intact in the face of this *décalage*, nor could the European drama remain outside this large-scale discursive event.

It is generally stated that "Lucretia barely plays a role in seventeenth-century Dutch literature," with only two plays by Dirck Pieterz. Pers and Neuyes of Neuye as well as two anonymous dramas dedicated to this topic.[13] Instead of the politically charged image of a heroic woman, Dutch literature, culminating in Jacob Cats, privileged that of a virtuous wife. Still, the above-mentioned connection between crucial historical events and rape accounts was no less valid for Dutch historical and political thought: as Amanda Pipkin has sarcastically observed, the "Dutch republic required stories of rape to create a nation where none previously existed."[14]

Significantly, the two major historical plays of Dutch Golden Age drama that aimed to restage the national past of the city of Amsterdam and corroborate its centrality among the United Provinces – Hooft's *Geeraerdt van Velsen* (1613) and Vondel's *Gysbreght van Aemstel* (1638) – revolved around rape accounts. Hooft's almost obsessive interest in Roman and national history is well known: after *Baeto* (1617), he abandoned drama and dedicated all his efforts to the study of the Dutch past, using Tacitus, whose *History* he read fifty-two times and whose lapidary style he tried to imitate, as an exemplary historical narrative.[15] In his youth, he had been no less eager to imitate the ancient Roman historians and poets, and it was in this context that the figure of Lucretia emerged for the first time. In 1609, Hooft was commissioned to compose the rhymed inscriptions for the so-called *Vertoningen* – *tableaux vivants* celebrating the Twelve Years' Truce between the Netherlands and Spain. Lucretia was chosen as an allegory of the United Provinces. In these verse inscriptions Hooft sticks very closely to the commonplaces of the republican Lucretia myth:

> The holiest thing Lucretia had devoted to her husband,
> The King's son Sextus has stolen out of a stupid passion and envy.
> Lucretia had witnesses of her fidelity:
> Before her husband – her blood, and before God – her spirit.

---

[12] Arnaldo Momigliano. "The First Political Commentary on Tacitus." *The Journal of Roman Studies* 37 (1947), pp. 91–101, p. 91.
[13] Hammer-Tugendhat, *The Visible and the Invisible*, p. 31.
[14] Amanda C. Pipkin. *Every Woman's Fear: Stories of Rape and Dutch Identity in the Golden Age.* New Brunswick: Rutgers University Press, 2008, p. 23.
[15] Simon Groenveld. "Pieter Corneliszoon Hooft en de geschiedenis van zijn eigen tijd." *Hooft als historieschrijver: twee studies*. Weesp: Heureka, 1981, pp. 7–46, pp. 23–27.

> Lucretia's misadventure depressed the people to such an extent,
> That they, on Brutus's admonition, abjured the Kings.
> Brutus esteemed the freedom of his country so highly,
> That he did not spare the life of his own children.[16]

Here we see a kind of a summary or *credo* of the Livian republican myth: Lucretia as a symbol of fidelity; the people who react immediately to oppression by drastically changing the political form of the state; Brutus as a fervent defender of freedom. Two sacrificial deaths – Lucretia's suicide and the killing of Brutus' sons by their own father – are connoted positively and used to impress the audience by an accumulation of bloody acts (two murders in eight lines). This spectacularity was present already in the Livian account. Here Lucretia, a *matrona* molested by the Roman king's son, prepares herself for suicide, but takes great care to have her death observed by the sympathetic and interested public. Ovid, who contributed greatly to the classical image of Lucretia, introduced a very important category to the description of her suicide – that of *honestum*: "even then she took care in dying so that she fell/With decency, that was her care even in falling" ("tunc quoque iam moriens ne non procumbat honeste/respicit; haec etiam cura cadentis erat").[17] In Cicero, the notion of *honestum* meant something morally beautiful and at the same time coinciding with the civilly useful (*utile*). This category is endowed with a great spectacular potential: *honestum* is a revelation of the transcendental in the pagan world, it requires demonstration; otherwise it remains unknown. The demonstration of *honestum* is always linked to a singular person. The pagan hero dies in order to prove that *honestum* exists and that he himself is acting for the sake of *honestum*. In the "honest" deed, spectacularity and publicity go hand in hand with exemplarity; significantly, the main reason for Lucretia's suicide, as she herself states it, is the fear of being a bad *exemplum* if she lived on: "nec ulla deinde impudica Lucretiae exemplo viveret." Considering herself as part – or, rather, a departing point – of the virtuous Roman history, Lucretia is very concerned with founding it upon a righteous *exemplum*. Livy shows us how her admonition – "si vos viri estis" – and death itself weigh as a fatal burden

---

16 "'t Heylighst dat *Lucrees* haer Man had toegewijt, / Rooft *Sextus* 's Koninghs Soon, uyt dulle brandt en nijdt // Van *Lucretias* trouw getuygen zijn geweest, / Haer bloedt voor haren man, en voor de Goôn haer' geest. // *Lucretias* misval 't verdruckte volck soo deert, / Dat het op *Brutus* eysch de Koningen versweert // De Vryheyt van sijn Landt staet *Brutus* voor soo waert, / Dat hy sijn Soons daer voor niet van de doodt en spaert" (Pieter C. Hooft. *Gedichten van P. C. Hooft*, edited by Frederik A. Stoett. Amsterdam: P. N. van Kampen & zoon, 1899, pp. 85–86.)

17 P. Ovidius Naso. *Ovid's* Fasti, edited by James G. Frazer. Cambridge, MA: Harvard University Press, 1933, II.833–834. http://www.perseus.tufts.edu/hopper/text?doc=Perseus%3atext%3a2008.01.0547. Accessed 25 July 2018.

on the shoulders of the spectators. With Lucretia the "age of virtues" (*aetas virtutum*)¹⁸ begins, with myriads of (mainly masculine) heroes seeking the glory of a decorous death for their homeland (Fabii, Curtii, Decii, etc.). Thus Lucretia turns out to be a pivotal figure in the history of Roman liberty: Cicero in *De finibus bonorum et malorum* names her as "a cause of the liberty of the state" ("causa civitati libertatis").¹⁹ Acting like a deity (in Ovid, Brutus states that Lucretia's spirit became a *numen* for him), she breaks the seal of dissimulation, making visible Brutus' hidden virtues ("iam satis est virtus dissimulata diu") – from a stupid brute, derided by the prince and his fellows, Brutus changes into a consul and *pater patriae*.

But this cartoonish image of a heroic sacrifice does not fit the ethics we meet in *Geeraerdt van Velsen*. Hooft's tragedy appears as a kind of a palimpsest, preserving the half-vanished, but still recognizable traces of the 'Lucretia myth,' but at the same time imbued with other motives. The ascent of the Tacitist historiography and post-Machiavellian political rhetoric privileged the rise of new *exempla* and concepts: under monarchy, the virtuous suicide of a republican-minded hero proves to be totally useless. One can find in Tacitus a variety of examples of how harmful heroic behavior may be: these examples were analyzed in detail by sixteenth-century commentators. Thus, in the *Discorsi sopra Cornelio Tacito* (1594) by Scipione Ammirato, one of the most famous and influential Tacitist writers of that time, we find a characteristic gloss on the tragic story of the Senator Publius C. Thrasea Paetus (Book XVI of the *Annales*), a Stoic of impeccable reputation, who scandalized Nero several times – a conduct that resulted in a death sentence in the form of *liberum mortis arbitrium*:

> In spite of the fact that you should never, for whatever reason, and whatever example you want to follow, commit anything wrong, you should nonetheless take into consideration whether your intention, however excellent it may be, may succeed or not, and whether the time allows it. Because otherwise it may prove vain for any living person, and sometimes may even be dangerous and disastrous for one who has undertaken it. Such a story has been narrated about Thrasea: in fact he, with his severe manners, has not been of any use to the Senate, he did not open to others the way to freedom, and to himself caused death.²⁰

---

18 We are referring to Livy's famous expression "nulla aetas virtutum feracior" in *Ab urbe condita*, IX.16.19.
19 II.20.17.
20 "Con tutto ciò come che per niuna occasione, e per niun tempo, & con niuno esempio debba mai alcuno operar male, dee nondimeno in quella cosa, che egli ha in animo di fare, benche ottima, considerare, se è per riuscire; & se i tempi ciò permettono, accioche senza far utile a persona vivente la sua impresa non riesca vana, & talora con pericolo & pregiudicio di chi l'ha tentata, come fu detto di Trasea, il quale con certi modi suoi severi, non fece al senato utile alcuno; a

It was the same Thrasea who stopped his friend, the young tribune Rusticus Arulenus, when he wanted to make use of his *veto* right to block the *senatus consultum* sentencing Thrasea to death – this act would be useless for Thrasea himself and harmful for Arulenus' political carrier ("ne vana et reo non profutura, intercessori exitiosa inciperet,"[21] says Tacitus in the *Annales*). And this in spite of the fact, stressed by Tacitus and repeated by Scipione Ammirato, that Arulenus could hardly do anything less worthwhile than such an intercession. Thrasea's story gives the impression of a sad irony: under the conditions of the principate, his heroic suicide loses its exemplarity and publicity; now it is a *private* choice, but even as such it is conditioned and controlled by the state. In fact, the very terms of the verdict condemning Thrasea point to the fact that the only residue of liberty left to the subject is that of a voluntary death – *liberum mortis arbitrium*.

Thus, the glorious sacrifice is transformed into a useless suicide, the public martyrdom into a private death, perfectly senseless for the *civitas*: in the technical language of rhetoric, this semantic shift was expressed in the figure of *paradiastole*. Quentin Skinner points to the "insidious figure" of *paradiastole*, "the precise purpose of which was to show that any given action can always be redescribed in such a way as to suggest that its moral character may be open to some measure of doubt,"[22] in order to explain the seventeenth-century semantic revolution in political and ethical thought. It was this "rhetorical challenge to the moral science"[23] that the seventeenth-century political theoreticians, such as Thomas Hobbes, had to deal with. By calling a ruler "prudential" rather than "cowardly," we act paradiastolically: in drama, which was a forensic art performing persuasion and fomenting political passions, the use of this *schema* of thought was by no means less in demand than in deliberative oratory. On a par with other key concepts of humanist ethical-rhetorical culture, such as *virtue*, *right reason*, or *natural law*, the Livian exemplary narrative of Lucretia's heroic suicide finds itself involved in the process of the post-Machiavellian paradiastolic revolution. This inversion of the key terms and commonplaces affected drama as well. Let us cite just one example: the way in which Samuel Pufendorf and, later, the brothers Pieter and Johan De la Court interpreted an apophthegmatic verse from Seneca the Younger's tragedy *Hercules furens*: "Cogi qui potest nescit mori" ("Who can

---

gli altri non aperse la via alla libertà, & a se diede occasione di rovinare" (Scipione Ammirato. *Discorsi sopra Cornelio Tacito nuovamente posti in luce*. Florence: Filippo Giunti, 1598, p. 368).
21 Tacitus, *Ann.*, XVI.26.16.
22 Quentin Skinner. "The Study of Rhetoric as an Approach to Cultural History: The Case of Hobbes." *Main Trends in Cultural History: Ten Essays*, edited by Willem Melching and Wyger Velema. Amsterdam: Rodopi, 1994, pp. 17–53, p. 18.
23 Ibid.

be compelled does not know how to die"). In the context of Seneca's text (and for most of his readers), this saying meant a glorification of the heroic ethos, the readiness of the female protagonist of the tragedy, Megara, to die rather than yield to her oppressor. But, paradoxically, both Pufendorf and the De la Courts interpret it as a warning against the impudence of those who despise death and are therefore indifferent to any political or ethical obligation.[24]

In the particular case of Lucretia, it was Machiavelli himself who largely contributed to its paradiastolic rereading with his *Mandragola*. The main problem of Machiavelli's comedy is procreation. The main character's wife – Lucrezia – is sterile, but at the same time she and her elderly husband are obsessed with the idea of having a child. A young scoundrel, Callimaco, in love with Lucrezia, decides to make use of this: with the help of her spiritual father, he convinces her and her husband to accept adultery as the only way to have a child, while the adulterer, as they claim, will die from the miraculous remedy Lucrezia will take in order to become pregnant. At first, the pious and virtuous Lucrezia rejects this abominable idea:

> But of all the things discussed, this seems to me the strangest: to have to submit my body to this shame, to be the cause of a man's death for shaming me. Because even if I was the last woman left in the world and if the human race was to rise again from me, I don't believe that I would be allowed to do something like this.[25]

---

[24] "[R]eligione remota, civitatum firmitas intrinseca in incerto foret, ac ad cives in officio continendos, haud quaquam sufficeret metus temporalis poenae, fides superioribus data, ejusque servandae gloria, et gratitudo, quod ope summi imperii a miseriis status naturalis defendatur. Tunc enim revera locum haberet, QUI MORI SCIT, COGI NESCIT: quippe cum Deum non metuentibus nihil magis quam mors metui possit, huic contemnendae quis sufficeret, in imperantes quaevis futura tentare possit" (Samuel Pufendorf. *De officio hominis et civis secundum legem naturalem libri duo*. Lugduni Batavorum: Sam. et Joh. Luchtmans, 1769, p. 161); "Heeft de onderlinghe vreese voor vernieling, de politie, of tugt bedagt, en uit sich selven voor-gebragt; volgens het oude spreekwoord, *Qui mori scit, Cogi nescit*, die niet vreesd te sterven, kan niet gedwongen, of geregeerd werden. Dewijl ook aan allerhande slag van menschen de tugt genoegsaam even noodsakelik is, so moet hier uit volgen, dat een Natie die best getugtigd is geweest, ook boven de anderen in deugd, en rijkdom, sal uit-steeken: Want uit een wel-gestelde generale politie, moet de Tugt by de menschen in't bysonder, volgen; door dien de selve Wetten, en straffen, tegen alle misdaden stellede, die tot ondergang van het leven, en verlies van goed strekken; so kan de mensch op het geene hy verkregen heeft, sijn staat en reekening machen" (Johan and Pieter de la Court. *Politike discoursen handelende in ses onderscheide boeken van Staden, Landen, Oorlogen, Kerken, Regeringen en Zeeden*. Amsterdam: Pieter Hackius, 1662, p. 244).

[25] Niccolò Machiavelli. *Mandragola*, translated by Nerida Newbigin. 2009, p. 21. http://www.personal.usyd.edu.au/~nnew4107/Texts/Sixteenth-century_Florence_files/Mandragola_Translation.pdf. Accessed 25 July 2018.

One of the arguments set forth by Lucrezia's spiritual father is a reference to the Old Testament story of the incestuous daughters of Lot:

> you have to consider the purpose in all these things. And your purpose is to fill a seat in paradise and make your husband happy. The Bible says that the daughters of Lot, thinking that they were the last women left in the world, lay with their father. And because their intention was good, they did not sin.[26]

Finally, Lucrezia gives her assent and feels happy after the adultery, as do all the characters in *Mandragola*. The parodic inversion of the Livian account of ancient Lucretia's heroic defense of chastity is more than obvious. The characters of *Mandragola* prefer survival and procreation to death for the sake of ethical norms. Machiavelli's play permitted contemporaries to see the link between the author and Tacitus – a historian, who, unlike Livy, exposed the rules of surviving under the conditions of a catastrophe. The diabolic nature ascribed to Machiavelli in the Renaissance and beyond was due to his willingness to look at *honestum* through the lens of sociology, not individual ethics. The multitude of people that constitute the state are supposed to have the wish to live, not to die. Former philosophers sought to dissuade citizens from fearing death; Machiavelli sets himself the goal of recreating in them the sane and natural fear of perishing.

In the Netherlands, we find a characteristic sample of this paradiastolic use of Lucretia's image in Joost van den Vondel's "Amusing introduction" to his *Vorstelijcke warande der dieren* (1617). Here this figure significantly appears in the carnivalesque atmosphere of wandering in the "labyrinth of imagination." In the center of the garden labyrinth, the company of "princes" guided by the author stumble at what they thought was a statue of the dying Lucretia:

> But what is this Lucretia, so well featured, hiding in the green her white naked limbs?
> And threatening death to herself? Not only does she threaten, but stabs!
> She pierces her heart! Look, look, how the blood bursts forth,
> How her blood is pouring out
> Of the wound, and falls down slowly,
> And is collected there by the sculptor's skill.
> Do not be afraid: it is just an appearance:
> It is not woman's blood, it is only red wine
> That Bacchus will serve to Kings
> And others who are resting here, exhausted by the thirst, in the shade.
> [...]

---

26 Ibid.

> Fare well, Lucretia: if someone was a bit too rude
> Or too tyrannical, while sucking your blood,
> Take into consideration that he did it while tormented by the strongest thirst.[27]

This parodic justification of tyrannical 'bloodthirstiness,' this anamorphic transformation of Lucretia, an archetype of republican virtue, into a phantom, a kind of a *simulacrum libertatis*, obviously refers to the burlesque images from the *Ragguagli di Parnaso* of Traiano Boccalini[28]: the Tacitist *occhiali politici*, which allow us to see the hidden thoughts of the rulers; other glasses, which preserve people from seeing horrible and abominable aspects of this world; special pencils, with which the rulers can depict white as black and black as white. As in the case of Boccalini, the use of these tricks is not confined to a simple entertainment or a satirical representation of a political reality that has degenerated through the fault of the Tacitists and Machiavellists. The tragic Lucretia on closer inspection is transformed into a merry Bacchus: the grotesque transforms the *topos* into a *simulacrum*, or, rather, blurs the borderline between them.

In his ethical message based on political irenicism, prudence, and moderation, Hooft exploits the effects of the paradiastolic shift of the 'Lucretia story.'

The affinity between Machtelt and Lucretia has already been underlined by Jan W. Verkaik and, much earlier, by Busken Huet. In addition to the general common frame – the raping of a noble wife by a Roman king's son –, they point to verse 313 of the first act: "Machtelt immediately abandoned her wool work" ("Vrouw Machtelt staeckte' haer naeldwerck knap"),[29] echoing, in their opinion, Livy's image of Lucretia as a virtuous matron, *dedita lanae*.[30] Verkaik quotes Jacob Jansz. Colevelt, the author of the historical drama *Droef-eyndend-spel, tusschen Graef Floris, en Gerrit van Velsen* (1628), where the parallel between Machtelt

---

27 "Maer wat Lucretia, van maecksel wel besneden, / Verberght daer in het groen haer blancke en naeckte leden? / En dreyght haer selfs de dood? Zij dreyght niet, och zij steeckt! / Zij quest haer selven 'thert! Ziet ziet hoe't bloed uytbreeckt: / Hoe't bloed de wonde ontvloeyt, en daelt met groot verlanghen / Benedenwaerts, daer 't word behendelijck gevanghen, / Door s'kunstenaers bedrijf. Verschrickt niet, 'it is maer schijn, / 'Ten is geen vrouwen bloed, 'tis enckel rooden wijn: / Die Bacchus is ghewoon te schenken voor de Vorsten, / En andere die vermoeyt hier inde schaduw dorsten. [...] Vaert wel Lucretia: zoo yemant wat te groff / Of te tyrannig u't bloed heeft afgezoghen, / Denckt dat versmachten dorst tot sulcx hem heeft bewoghen" (Joost van den Vondel. *Vorstelijcke warande der dieren: Waer in de Zeden-rijcke Philosophie, Poetisch, Morael, en Historiael, vermakelijck en treffelijck wort voorgestelt*. Amsterdam: Jan Blom, 1717, s.p.).
28 Arthur Weststeijn. "The Power of 'Pliant Stuff': Fables and Frankness in Seventeenth-Century Dutch Republicanism." *Journal of the History of Ideas* 72 (2011), pp. 1–27, p. 8.
29 Hooft is quoted from the following edition: Pieter C. Hooft. *Geeraerdt van Velsen*, edited by A. J. J. de Witte, 2nd edition. Zutphen: W. J. Thieme & Cie, 1976.
30 Jan W. Verkaik. *De moord op graaf Floris V*. Hilversum: Verloren, 1996, p. 25.

and Lucretia is stated explicitly.[31] In the introductory monologue by Machtelt van Velsen, we may see that some points of the 'Lucretia story' are preserved: for instance, the irreversibility and impossibility of expiating or even attenuating the rapist's misdeed; neither her relatives nor her husband are able to forget the misdemeanor ("Nu is 'er niemandt van mijn Maeghen, noch mijn Man/Die's lasters heughenis, helaes! Af leeren kan").[32] But, obviously, in the crucial point they drastically differ: instead of committing suicide and instigating her relatives and friends to avenge her, she assumes a hesitant, Hamlet-like stance towards death,[33] and tries to mitigate her husband's wrath.[34] Machtelt refuses to follow Lucretia; instead, she advises her husband to give up and to forget her injury for the sake of the common good ("'s Lands welvaart").[35] She tries her best to hide "deep in her breast" any trace of her sorrow. However, she emphatically invokes death several times, first in terms somewhat similar to the ritual of the punishment of Vestals for having lost her chastity ("oh, if only this living corpse could be bricked up by thick walls/in an underground grave").[36] Secondly ("O Vaeder goedt..." etc.), her invocation to death brings on stage two very important

---

[31] "Lucretia wel eer ontsielde selfs haer siel / Beclaeglijck waert dat sy in sulcken saeck verviel." Verkaik also quotes Johannes a Leydis, an early humanist historian of the Netherlands, who described Machtelt's conduct after the rape as similar to Lucretia's (*instar Lucretiae*) (see *De moord*, p. 25).

[32] Hooft, *Geeraerdt van Velsen*, 1.73. – Cf. also another verse: "Wat is het sterffelijck gheslachte swack en broos? / O Godt, hoe licht vergrijpt een uyr, door 't radeloos / Bestaen van moedwil slincx, 't gheen eeuwicheyts verlenghen / Met alle 's wijsheyts Raedt niet weer te recht kan brenghen!" (1.63–66).

[33] "Doch, is de doodt, dien de gheluckighe vervloecken, / Te waerden gast, om my verfoeyde te besoecken? / Soo zijt ghy welkoom my in mynen banghen noot, / O sorchsachtende slaep naemaeghe vande doodt" (ibid., 1.125–129).

[34] "Indien een vrouw betaemt te segghen haer ghevoelen, / Soo bid ick laet den brandt van onse smart bekoelen, / dat onse leedt, en de besondren haet, / Niet boven liefde van 't ghemeene best en gaet" (ibid., 3.813–816).

[35] Setting aside personal offenses in the name of the common good was also a kind of a topos in the Tacitist literature – let us quote the above-mentioned Scipione Ammirato: "Deve dunque un buon cittadino per amor della patria dimenticar l'ingiurie private, il che prudentemente fu ancora da altri avvertito, Et se ciò facciamo per la patria, quando viviamo à Republica, il medesimo habbiamo à fare per lo nostro Principe vivendosi a stato regio, & non solo condonar l'ingiurie, ma la vita, & la riputazione, & tutte le cose più care s'hanno à metter per seruigio di quel, che riconosciamo per nostro capo, col quale va congiunto il bene del regno, & della patria" (Ammirato, *Discorsi*, p. 8).

[36] "Oft waer dit levend' lijck ghemetst, met dicke muyren / In onderaerdtsche tomb' om d'ongheluckighe' uyren / Te brenghen aen een eyndt, en d'overmaet van tijdt, / Die 't straffe noodtlodt my weyghert te schelden quijt" (Hooft, *Geeraerdt van Velsen*, 1.29–32).

categories – Fate (*Noodlodt*) and Providence; according to Jan W. H. Konst,[37] like the later Baeto, she consciously relies upon "a web, spun by the causes" ("'t Web geweven van óórzaaken"), and her passive "Stoic" stance proves to be justified by the god of the river Vecht, "revealing the mysteries of fate" ("verborgentheyt des noodlots")[38] and explaining the necessity of the protagonist's suffering for the future glory of Amsterdam. The real suicide of the historical Machtelt and the quartering of her husband are intentionally omitted from the tragedy, transforming the historical *tragedia* into a *comedia* in the Aristotelian sense of the word. Let us now recall that Machiavelli had intended to teach classically trained people to fear death again – in the name of the common good. In *Geeraerdt van Velsen*, as well as in *Gysbreght van Aemstel* by Vondel, it is women who assume the role of dissuading the classical hero from seeking *honestum* at the expense of his own life – in the former case, Machtelt van Velsen, in the latter Badeloch, Gijsbreght's wife, who is instructed, however, by Machtelt in a dream.

A significant ambivalence affects the notion of revenge: in the 'Lucretia story,' it is represented as a legitimate and laudable affect, the *conditio sine qua non* of true liberty. In *Geeraerdt van Velsen*, the theme of revenge is closely connected to the problem of *Widerstandsrecht* – the right of resistance to tyrannical power.[39] Van Aemstel, the author's spokesperson in the tragedy, adheres to the moderate position,[40] claiming that the right of judging the ruler belongs exclusively to the States, whereas the protagonist, Van Velsen, adopts a radical monarchomachic stance, claiming that every subject has the right to sentence a tyrant ("De minste van het volck is Halsheer des tyrans").[41] In Hooft's tragedy, the private affects clash with the Batavian constitutionalist myth, freshly forged by Hugo Grotius in his *De antiquitate reipublicae Batavicae* (1610), in which the restoration of the Netherlands' true constitution is only possible if the conspirators are not blinded by their thirst for revenge ("verblindt u niet de wraeck").[42] Another vehicle of the author's political views, the Chorus of Amsterdam Maidens (*Rey van Aemstellandsche Jofferen*), also speaks of the resistance to

---

37 Jan W. H. Konst. *Fortuna, Fatum en Providentia Dei in de Nederlandsche tragedie, 1600–1720*. Hilversum: Verloren, 2003.
38 Hooft, *Geeraerdt van Velsen*, 5.1493.
39 For a thorough analysis of this aspect of *Geeraerdt van Velsen*, see Bettina Noak. *Politische Auffassungen im niederländischen Drama des 17. Jahrhunderts*. Münster: Waxmann Verlag, 2002, pp. 101–126.
40 "Wil 't beste deel des volcx verheert zijn van Tyrannen, / Het oordeel staet an haer: des dulden zy, elck een / Die dulde dan met haer, oft geev' hem elders heen" (Hooft, *Geeraerdt van Velsen*, 3.786–788).
41 Ibid., 2.464.
42 Ibid., 3.783.

tyranny in terms of a sacrificial act rather than a regicide.[43] If, in the case of Lucretia, revenge is a political act, directed towards the common good, in that of Machtelt and Gerard van Velsen it is nothing but a subversive and politically dangerous egoistic affect.

But what is the difference between the "blind thirst for revenge" of Van Velsen and Van Woerden and "the laudable revenge" ("het loffelycke wreecken") of Brutus, the male protagonist of the 'Lucretia story'? The name of Brutus is cited twice in the play: the first time, it is recalled by Harman van Woerden, who states that neither Brutus nor Epaminondas nor any other ancient or modern hero would be able to heal a republic in which the supreme power is desperately corrupted.[44] In the second case, Brutus is invoked as an archetype of the avenger, capable of instilling fear into the tyrants and their heirs.[45] The figure of Brutus is profiled against the background of the faded glory of Rome, being at Van Velsen's time nothing but an "unburied corpse,"[46] whose crown is covered with cobweb and his sword with rust; as a part of this antiquarian story, he is nothing but a powerless ghost, whose affects are not convertible to the political language of the modern era. The attempt to imitate Brutus' noble revenge – as well as Lucretia's noble suicide – in the new political context results in damage to the public good: the ancient heroism, to use Giambattista Vico's term, is "civilly impossible"[47] in the post-Machiavellian era.[48]

---

[43] "Den oopenbaeren Dwinghelandt, / Met moed te bieden wederstandt, / En op den harssenpan te treeden; / Om, met het storten van zijn bloedt, / Den vaderlande 't swaerste goedt, / Den gulden vryheyt te bereeden" (ibid., 4.1240–1245).
[44] "Dat konde d'eerste nocht de tweede Brutus niet. / Nocht die in 't vrouwenkleedt als mannelijck bevryder / Zijns Vaederlants hem droech. En waer 't dat het een yder / Soo nauw soud nemen als Epaminond en ghy; / Doen Thebe', en Hollandt nu, bleven in slaverny" (ibid., 3.756–760).
[45] "Och had zy konnen oock de boose lusten breecken / Daer uwer Koninghen gheslacht is toe ghewendt! / En had doch Brutus, met het loffelycke wreecken, / Omsiende vreese den naekoomers ingheprendt! / Soo souden nu ter tydt de vreese wy ontbeeren, / Die ons beleeghert heeft met anxten en verdriet. / Maer, laes! het lichte luck noch trouwe wraeck verleeren / Der grooten kinderen haer woeste moedwil niet" (ibid., 2.649–656).
[46] "Nu zydy immers meer niet, dan een onbegraven / Ghebalsemt lijck, verselschapt met bestoven kleên, / Beraechde Croonen, opghehanghen Scepterstaven, / En waepens uytghedient, en swaerden afghestreên" (ibid., 2.621–624).
[47] On the notion of the "civil impossibility" of heroes in Vico, see Enrico Nuzzo. *Tra religione e prudenza: La "filosofia pratica" di Giambattista Vico*. Rome: Edizioni di storia e letteratura, 2007, pp. 240–255.
[48] The subversive impact of "Machiavellism" *ante litteram* on the ancient Romans and Greeks is described in the monologue of *Bedroch* (ll. 205–217), which uses the famous fox/lion metaphor from *The Prince*.

"Dus wederstreef niet meer uw trouwe gemaelin": this admonition, which the archangel Raphael directs at the male protagonist of Vondel's *Gysbreght van Aemstel* at the culminating moment of the tragedy when the hero firmly decides to die together with his soldiers in the stronghold of Aemstel, rejecting his wife's prudent advice, reveals both the challenge to the Livian republican tradition and the significant change of the position of the female character in Dutch drama. Like the god of the river Vecht in *Geeraerdt van Velsen*, the archangel acts as a *deus ex machina*, justifying the moderate attitude of the female protagonist at the very moment when it seems totally eclipsed by the inflexible word of the man. Being confined to the passive position by her social role, the female protagonist regains power through the intervention of superhuman forces: Stoic/Christian providence/fate, converting disasters and personal catastrophes into the triumph of the whole *civitas*. The rehabilitation of the marginalized feminine voice meant the restoration of the marginalized political position, the triumph of political prudence over the heroic ethos. According to Livy, the immediate outcome of Lucretia's heroic death was the overthrow of royal power in Rome and the establishment of the Republic: *romana libertas*. It seems appropriate to recall that some days before the tragic event, Roman citizens – Lucretia's and King Tarquinius' son among them – organized a kind of competition between married women, and Lucretia was recognized as the best among Roman wives. Immolating the best part is necessary in order to make of the Roman citizens true *viri* capable of taking power and creating a new state which, according to Livy, would be a perfect one. By virtue of Lucretia's voluntary sacrifice, Roman *virtus* managed to outlive the political collapse of the Empire; by virtue of Machtelt's refusal to follow her example, Amsterdam got the chance to become a new Rome. The choice between Lucretia and Livia, between the rejection of political violence and its acceptance as a sort of benevolent policy is now enriched by a third possibility – Stoic providentialism, reconciling the tension between private injuries and the common good in the face of God-guided history.

Ekaterina Boltunova
The Historical Writing of Catherine II: Dynasty and Self-Fashioning in *The Chesme Palace (Chesmenskii Dvorets)*

It is well-known that the emergence of Visual Studies as a research field has encouraged academic interest in the simultaneous appearance as well as coexistence of textual and visual narratives, both of which contribute to social and cultural perceptions of creation. Following the example of some pioneering studies,[1] modern scholars analyze visual and textual semantic references, interpret the way one formal structure gets reflected in another, and engage in a constant search for cases that demonstrate how textual and visual sources correspond and overlap. However, it is hard to get the balance right, as one type of source tends to come into view first and eventually starts to dominate the analysis. It is equally difficult to consider the parallel development of two spheres that do not necessarily synchronize, forcing one to evaluate what might be called a motion in motion.

The historiography of eighteenth-century Russian literature and culture is no exception. A good example here is the scholarly interpretation of the Russian Empress Catherine II's literary work called *The Chesme Palace* (*Chesmenskii Dvorets*), a short text originally written in French at the end of the century[2] and published in Russian only in 1906. Until recently, the text has not drawn much scholarly attention. The current interest is apparently inspired by research into the portrait collection of the eponymous palace,[3] the spot that the empress chose as the setting of her text.

---

[1] Michael Baxandall. *Painting and Experience in Fifteenth-Century Italy: A Primer in the Social History of Pictorial Style*. Oxford: Oxford University Press, 1972; Leo Spitzer. "The 'Ode on a Grecian Urn,' or Content vs. Metagrammar." *Essays on English and American Literature*, edited by Anna Hatcher. Princeton: Princeton University Press, 1962, pp. 67–97.

[2] Ekaterina II. "Le Château de Chesme: L'Entretien des Portraits et Médaillons." *Sochineniya Ekateriny II na osnovanii podlinnykh rukopisey i ob'yasnitel'nymi primechaniyami akademika A. N. Pypina*, vol. 12. St. Petersburg: Im'peratorskaya Akademiya Nauk, 1907, pp. 583–594.

[3] Ekaterina Skvortsova. "Representing Imperial Power in Eighteenth-Century Russian Art: The Portrait Gallery of the Chesme Palace." *A Century Mad and Wise: Russia in the Age of the Enlightenment. Papers from the IX International Conference of the Study Group on Eighteenth-Century Russia, Leuven 2014*, edited by Emmanuel Waegemans, Hans van Koningsbrugge, Marcus

---

Note: The author expresses her gratitude to Vladimir Makarov for his assistance in translating the article.

Open Access. © 2019 Ekaterina Boltunova, published by De Gruyter. This work is licensed under the Creative Commons Attribution-NonCommercial-NoDerivatives 4.0 License.
https://doi.org/10.1515/9783110604276-008

The Chesme Palace was by no means a figment of the empress's imagination. This still surviving building was designed by Yury Felten and erected between 1774 and 1777. It was named after the Battle of Chesme (1770), the most decisive naval victory in the Russian-Turkish War (1768–1774), and the one most glorified in eighteenth-century Russia.[4] The palace stood on the road from St. Petersburg to Tsarskoye Selo with its imperial summer residences. It was often described as one of the empress's *maisons de plaisance*,[5] resembling a medieval castle. Later, in 1780 a church was erected next to it, also designed by Yury Felten. Dedicated to the birth of St. John the Baptist, it was frequently called the Chesme Church. The ensemble was to mark the place where Empress Catherine II presumably received the news of the grand victory over the Ottoman Empire.

In the reign of Catherine II, the interiors of the ceremonial halls of the Chesme Palace featured fifty-nine portraits of monarchs from European royal houses (French, Swedish, Danish, Prussian, English, etc.).[6] Some of these portraits were given to the empress as presents.[7] Beside the portraits on the walls of ten of its rooms, the palace also featured a gallery of bas-reliefs of the Rurikids and Romanovs. Fifty-eight roundels by Fedor Shubin were placed just above almost the same number of monarchs' portraits. The front staircase led into the hall where the portrait of Catherine herself eventually appeared. Thus the empress symbolically opened the Russian dynastic series and was placed at the head of the entire community of European monarchs. Military symbolism was to be found in the marble statue of Catherine II as Minerva, an allegory of her victories.[8]

Interestingly, in Catherine's text, portraits of Russian and European rulers that hang on the walls of the Chesme Palace come to life, judge each other and discuss the role each of their sitters played in history. Thus, there arises the question of a possible interconnection between spatial and textual interpretations.

Levitt, and Mikhail Ljustrov. Groningen: Instituut voor Noord- en Oost-Europese Studies, 2015, pp. 455–469, p. 459.
4 Elena B. Smilyanskaya. "Osvoenie Sredizemnomor'ya vo vremya Russko-turetskoy voyny 1768–1774 gg.: realii i simvoly." *Istoricheskaya geografiya: prostranstvo cheloveka vs chelovek v prostranstve. Materialy XXIII Mezhdunarodnoy nauchnoy konferentsii. Moskva, 27–29 yanvarya 2011*. Moscow: RGGU, 2011, pp. 136–146.
5 Natalia I. Batorevich. *Chesmenskii dvorets*. St. Petersburg: Beloe i Chernoe, 1997, p. 42.
6 Skvortsova, "Representing Imperial Power," p. 465.
7 Batorevich, *Chesmenskii dvorets*, p. 52.
8 Elena V. Karpova. "Skul'pturnye izobrazheniia Ekateriny II (k evoliutsii allegoricheskogo obraza)." *Ekaterina Velikaia: epokha Rossiiskoi istorii. Mezhdunarodnaia konferentsiia "Ekaterina Velikaia: epokha rossiiskoi istorii": Tezisy dokladov. Sankt-Peterburg, 26–29 avgusta 1996*, edited by Tatiana V. Artem'eva and Mikhail I. Mikeshin. St. Petersburg: SPbNTs, 1996, p. 240.

Historians who recognize the significance of the two Chesme Palaces – the imperial residence and the text produced by the empress – typically put the built ensemble and its splendors at the center of their research, whereas the writing is considered as a type of supporting source.[9] Moreover, *The Chesme Palace* is assumed to have been a sort of statement, similar to that of a gallery that aimed to declare the revival of Byzantium,[10] promote the alliance with Austria in the late 1770s,[11] and ultimately proclaim "the high status of the Russian Empire as governed by a legitimate ruler and united by the ties of kinship with other European ruling houses."[12]

However, the history of the text (i.e. the chronological perspective, genre, and context) suggests an alternative interpretation of Catherine II's intentions.

As has been pointed out, the residence was commissioned in 1774; its décor was finalized in 1777. Unfortunately, the precise date of Catherine's written work is unknown. However, there is reason to believe that it was written in the mid-1780s,[13] presumably not later than 1786, since Frederick William II, who became King of Prussia that year, is still called "the Prussian Prince" in the text. Hence, *The Chesme Palace* was created about a decade later than the palace – and a decade and a half after the Battle of Chesme that had given the residence its name.

The genre of *The Chesme Palace* is not easily determined. Even though it has two parts and consists of dialogues and monologues, and despite the author's remarks and references to place and time, it can hardly be a play since, in its time, it would have been absolutely unstageable. One can assume that it was not produced for theatrical production since in eighteenth-century Russia images of the country's real tsars and emperors were prohibited on stage. The most likely interpretation of the genre is provided by Ekaterina Skvortsova, who argues that *The Chesme Palace* is a "dialogue of the dead," a form that "emerged in antiquity and enjoyed great popularity in European[...] literature of the eighteenth century."[14] She discusses the contribution to the genre made by David Fassman (1683–1744), a writer from Leipzig (Saxony) whose book *Gespräche in dem Reiche derer Todten*

---

9 Cf. Skvortsova, "Representing Imperial Power," pp. 455–469, as well as Asen Kirin. "The Edifices of the New Justinian: Catherine the Great Reclaiming Byzantium." *Approaches to Byzantine Architecture and its Decoration: Studies in Honor of Slododan Ćurčić*, edited by Mark Johnson and Robert Ousterhout. London: Ashgate, 2012, pp. 277–298.
10 Thus Asen Kirin in the essay cited in the previous note.
11 Skvortsova, "Representing Imperial Power," pp. 464–465.
12 Ibid., p. 466.
13 Irina V. Babich, Mikhail V. Babich, and Tatiana A. Lapteva, editors. *Ekaterina II: Annotirovannaia bibliografiia publikatsii*. Moscow: Rosspen, 2004, p. 250.
14 Skvortsova, "Representing Imperial Power," p. 466.

(*Dialogues in the Realm of the Dead*) reflected upon the Romanovs' rule in the early eighteenth century.[15] Skvortsova also takes into account the influence of the gothic-novel tradition and suggests Horace Walpole's *The Castle of Oranto* (1764) as a possible source of inspiration for Catherine II's *Chesme Palace*.[16]

It is remarkable that all of the Chesme Palace portraits represented members of European royal houses who were alive when the gallery was created,[17] whereas Fedor Shubin's bas-reliefs of the Rurikids and Romanovs presented the images of Russian princes and emperors who were truly in the realm of the dead. This created two almost equal-sized virtual groups – the dead and the living. Aiming to legitimize her status and her position in the state by acknowledging European kinship, Catherine II turned to the living. Would she be willing to deliver the same message by making the dead speak?

The context of the epoch is of no lesser significance. First, the specific figurative historicism of the Chesme Palace gallery was not unique in the period in question. On the contrary, in the eighteenth century, a special attitude to portraits had arisen, and the tradition of using them in the construction of certain semantic fields was quite current. A portrait always refers to an idea, and a monarch's portrait also has a symbolic meaning. In the early modern period, to possess the monarch's portrait was to possess a symbol, i.e. to have both a claim to an idea and the opportunity to bring it to life. In this "pre-psychological period," to borrow the term of Gennady Vdovin,[18] a portrait would help one stand up to the challenges of self-identification and self-representation.

The data suggest that the use of a portrait as a tool of self-presentation came up in the eighteenth century. During the pre-Petrine period, such manifestations were quite unusual. Yet Prince Vasily V. Golitsyn, the principal minister of state in the late seventeenth century and the favorite of Princess Sofia, stands out. The interior of his Moscow house at *Bolshaya Dmitrovka* was quite unique. On the second floor, there was the so-called Large Table Chamber (*Bolshaya*

---

15 Ekaterina Skvortsova. "Russian Empresses and their Foreign Counterparts: The Validation of the New Title of the Russian Ruler in Illustrations of David Fassman's 'Dialogues of the Dead'." Newsletter of the Study Group on Eighteenth-Century Russia. 2016. http://www.sgecr.co.uk/newsletter2016/skvortcova.html. Accessed 23 July 2018.
16 Ekaterina Skvortsova. "Illyustratsii k 'Razgovoram v tsarstve mertvykh': problema utverzhdeniya titula imperatora Rossii v XVIII veke." *Aktual'nye problemy teorii i istorii iskusstva: sbornik statey*, vol. 5, edited by Svetlana V. Maltseva, Ekaterina Y. Stanyukovich-Denisova, and Anna V. Zakharova. St. Petersburg: NP-Print, 2015, pp. 503–512, pp. 508–509.
17 Skvortsova, "Representing Imperial Power," p. 459.
18 Gennadiy Vdovin. *Persona – Individual'nost' – Lichnost': Opyt samopoznaniya v iskusstve russkogo portreta XVIII veka*. Moscow: Moskva-Traditsiya, 2005, p. 121.

Stolovaya Polata). This red and golden hall was grand in scale, incredibly full of light (46 windows), and refined in its décor. Apart from the pictures of the sun, the moon, the planets, and the signs of the zodiac on its ceiling, it was lavishly ornamented with mirrors and portraits, objects extremely rare at that time.[19] The series of portraits displayed consisted of the images of the Russian monarchs (Prince Vladimir, Tsars Ivan IV, Feodor Ivanovich, and the first Romanovs – Tsars Mikhail, Alexey, and Feodor as well as the reigning Ivan and Peter) as well as Polish and possibly French kings.[20]

For the hundred years to follow, the number of halls and chambers where one could find portraits of members of the Russian dynasties, often together with foreign rulers, increased. Such canvasses formed the décor of royal residences in St. Petersburg, Peterhof, Gatchina, and aristocratic palaces such as Prince Alexander Menshikov's estate house at New Alekseevskoye (*Novoe Alekseevskoye*) and the Sheremetevs' palaces at *Kuskovo* and *Ostankino* in Moscow, to name but a few.[21]

Secondly, Catherine's *Chesme Palace* dates to the second half of the Russian empress's reign, i.e. the 1780s, after the accession of Crimea to Russia (1783), which turned out to be a period in which the empress revised her views on Russian history. She moved away from her interest in Peter I, who for the previous couple of decades had been an absolute example of the Russian ruler and provided a legitimizing ground for those in power during the troubled epoch of the coup d'état. In the 1780s, the figure of Peter the Great began to lose sway

---

19 De la Nevill'. *Zapiski o Moskovii*, edited by Aleksandr Lavrov. Moscow: Allegro-press, 1996, p. 127.
20 Some portraits in the Chamber have not yet been identified. However, Golitsyn is known to have been Louis XIV's passionate admirer and made his son wear a medallion with the French king's image. Cf. Alexander G. Brikner. *Istoriya Petra Velikogo*, vol. 1. Moscow: TERRA, 1996, p. 169.
21 Olga S. Evangulova. *Izobrazitel'noe iskusstvo v Rossii pervoy chetverti XVIII veka*. Moscow: Izdatelstvo Moskovskogo universiteta, 1987, p. 272; Aleksey N. Grech. "Venok usad'bam." *Pamyatniki Otechestva* 32 (1994), pp. 5–190, pp. 110–111. – In the nineteenth century, the special attitude to portraits and the tradition of using them for the construction of specific semantic fields were still very much alive. Dynastic series, for instance, remained quite widespread. In the 1840s, after the reconstruction of the Lesser Hermitage, Emperor Nicholas I approved the creation of the Romanov gallery with the portraits of Russian monarchs in its western wing. The eastern wing at that time housed the monuments of Peter I's reign (including the famous 'Wax Persona,' i.e. a statue of the emperor made of wax by Francesco Rastrelli in 1725), as well as Peter the Great's personal possessions. Thus, Nicholas advanced his own version of dynastic history which differed from the older Catherinian one, as the first Emperor of Russia appeared as a figure of absolute authority. Cf. Vladimir I. Piliavskii and Vladimir F. Levinson-Lessing, editors. *Ermitazh: Istoriia i arkhitektura zdanii*. Leningrad: Avrora, 1974, pp. 192–193.

in the discourse of power. This period was the birth of what might be called 'intellectual Slavophilism,' i. e. the time of seeking inspiration in pre-Petrine Russia.[22]

This was exactly the time when Catherine started studying the history of old Russia and reading the chronicles *(letopisi)*. In 1786, she wrote several dramas whose plots were borrowed from Russian history: *A Historical Scene from the Life of Rurik* (*Istoricheskoie predstavleniie iz zhizni Riurika*, published anonymously), *The Early Years of Oleg's Reign (in Imitation of Shakespeare)* (*Nachalnoie upravleniie Olega [podrazhaniie Shekspiru]*), *Igor* (an incomplete sequel to *Oleg's Reign*), and a comic opera libretto called *Boieslavich, the Bogatyr of Novgorod* (*Novgorodskii Bogatyr' Boieslavich*).

Whereas modern scholars see in Catherine's folk-inspired texts the production of "a daring writer, pulling together elements of history, legend, popular song, and elevated poetry, all in the service of demonstrating Russia's legitimacy while glorifying its culture,"[23] the empress's contemporaries found in these plays quite a number of political references. *Oleg's Reign* was seen as telling the story of the prince's campaign against Byzantium, and thus referring to the empress's plans concerning Constantinople. It was known that Prince Grigory A. Potemkin, Catherine II's military commander and statesman, helped edit the text. *Boieslavich*, the play where Novgorod submits to the strong power of the prince, was considered to express the empress's aim of proving that "strong rule" is preferable to "free" existence.

Catherine's use of the theatrical stage and literary journals to communicate her political and ideological views is no surprise at all. However, what is striking about this set of plays is the fact that the empress here takes a clear stand vis-à-vis her predecessors. This is, in a way, a novel view of the dynastic rule of the country, an expression of the need to address the first Russian royal dynasty, the Rurikids, rather than the Romanovs. It is no surprise, therefore, that in yet another text of the 1780s, Catherine II tries to reassess existing views on outstanding Russian monarchs.

In outward appearance, *The Chesme Palace* is a bitter satire both against most of Catherine's predecessors on the Russian throne and against the lifestyles of contemporary European monarchs. Nevertheless, it can be considered an expression of a different kind, an outstanding example of self-fashioning, to borrow

---

22 Vera Proskurina. *Mify imperii: Literatura i vlast' v epokhu Ekateriny II*. Moscow: Novoe literaturnoe obozrenie, 2006, pp. 135–146.
23 Lurana Donnels O'Malley. *The Dramatic Works of Catherine the Great: Theatre and Politics in Eighteenth-Century Russia*. Manoa: Ashgate, 2006, p. 204.

Stephen Greenblatt's analytical approach, which arose from his studies of authorial self-consciousness in English Renaissance literature[24] and has already been successfully applied to the study of some cases in eighteenth-century Russian history.[25]

In *The Chesme Palace*, the empress brings together historical characters from different eras: a court interpreter witnesses the portraits' conversation and "hastens to write everything down."[26] He "interprets," i.e. deciphers the language of imagery. At first, the empress focuses almost entirely on rulers of Russia. Elizabeth (*Elizaveta Petrovna*) appears simple-minded and carefree, "in manners and feelings much taken after her mother" (i.e. Catherine I) rather than her father (Peter the Great). Catherine I was only a "spouse of the monarch equally respected and feared." In her reign, the "state was administered as if on its own."[27] Emperor Peter II is shown as a young sot in love with his aunt.[28]

Later on, Catherine II delves deeper into history than the eighteenth century: Tsar Ivan, the co-ruler of Peter the Great, was dysfunctional, and Peter's mother Natalia K. Naryshkina (like all her relatives) "of a shallow mind," while Tsar Alexei Mikhailovich appears as the model of a boneless man.[29]

Catherine's European contemporaries from the royal houses of Austria and France are ridiculed as stupid spendthrifts, and the kings of Prussia (Frederick II and Frederick William II) as uneducated boors.[30] For example, Frederick William II (the Prince of Prussia), who was an honorary member of the St. Petersburg Academy of Sciences, says: "How did you end up [...] clueless in the very midst of the session of the St. Petersburg Academy of Sciences? [...] This is nothing. [...] I yawned, covering my mouth with my hat as I am a man of good manners."[31]

In the second part of the text, the irony subsides, however. The conversation moves into the room that features the portraits of Prussian monarchs and the

---

24 Cf. Stephen Greenblatt. *Hamlet in Purgatory*. Princeton: Princeton University Press, 2002. Cf. also his *Renaissance Self-Fashioning: From More to Shakespeare*. Chicago: University of Chicago Press, 2005.
25 Ernest A. Zitser. "The Vita of Prince Boris Ivanovich 'Korybut'-Kurakin: Personal Life-Writing and Aristocratic Self-Fashioning at the Court of Peter the Great." *Jahrbücher für die Geschichte Osteuropas* 59 (2011), pp. 163–194.
26 Ekaterina II. *Chesmenskii dvorets. O velichii Rossii*. Moscow: EKSMO, 2003, pp. 464–476, p. 472.
27 Ibid., p. 467.
28 Ibid., p. 468.
29 Ibid., pp. 470–471.
30 Ibid., pp. 466–468.
31 Ibid., p. 473.

Grand Princes of Russia. Especially when compared to the dimwitted Prussians, the Princes of Vladimir, medieval Russian rulers, form a group of utterly worthy men. Surrounded by his dynastic relatives, Alexander Nevsky appears in this room too.

The Princes of Vladimir are shown as a remarkably unified group. "On my right, you see my father, on my left, my brothers, in front of me is Vsevolod, my grandfather, and two of my uncles," says one of them.[32] The royal author presents them in a positive light: Vsevolod Yurievich is "the founder of the principality of Vladimir"; Vasily Yaroslavich is a relative and peer of most of the monarchs of Europe. Most importantly, the princes of Vladimir "might have known no arithmetic and spelling, but could [...] wage wars."[33]

Alexander Nevsky appears as the direct opposite of the kings of Prussia: he "most valiantly and successfully defended his native land and his allies against Swedes, Lithuanians, and Teutonic knights, founders of Livonia and Prussia."[34] The empress calls Alexander a just, wise, and courageous ruler, also mentioning his sainthood.[35] She concludes that the prince has "nothing in common" with the Prussian dynasty "in this world, or the next."[36]

In *The Chesme Palace*, Catherine II, with her quite dubious hereditary claim to the throne of Russia, also describes several crucial historical figures who, in spite of their own ambitions, did not bring their plans to fruition for a number of reasons. Among the early Romanovs, the empress prefers the "variously gifted" Princess Sofia, Patriarch Filaret, the father of Mikhail, the first tsar of the Romanov dynasty. As a background figure, Tsar Vasily Shuisky appears, who was crowned in 1606 amidst the so-called Time of Troubles, but was then imprisoned and taken to Poland as a prisoner of war.

A special focus is set on the bright personalities of those whose reign was short or ended in a collapse of their power. All of them are presented as capable, yet unfortunate people. There is, for example, Tsar Vasily, who occupied the Russian throne for less than four years. He is said to have been unlucky ("Not everyone has the luck to be [...] well-advised"). Patriarch Filaret, who was *de facto* ruler for quite some time even though he was never crowned, was a man of "great abilities" and "great discretion." His "skill and wisdom" brought Mikhail Romanov to the throne as the first of his dynasty.[37] Tsar Fedor, a gifted man of poor health,

---

32 Ibid., p. 474.
33 Ibid.
34 Ibid.
35 Ibid., p. 473.
36 Ibid., p. 474.
37 Ibid., p. 471.

ruled most peacefully ("While I lived [...] we were at peace").³⁸ Princess Sofia, a regent of Russia from 1682 to 1689, is seen as an extraordinary historical figure who held an almost unthinkable position for a woman of a royal dynasty, and whose stay in power was very much viewed as illegitimate. Her brother and rival emperor, the reformer Peter the Great, describes her as follows: "Had not the circumstances rendered her my enemy, I would be glad to make her my adviser. She was variously gifted, but too inclined to follow her maternal relations, especially her uncle Miloslavsky who had a strong predisposition against the family of my mother."³⁹

The text reveals an attempt to reassess Empress Anna as compared to Elizabeth, Catherine II's godmother and, to a degree, political rival. Having presented Elizabeth as a woman not much engaged in ruling the country, the empress emphasizes Anna's male character-features, stating that she was consequently a better fit for the male-centered political system in Russia. Peter the Great is said to have liked her and to be sad that Anna "was not born a boy." He says to Anna: "I liked you for your masculine and mature mind, presuming thus that you stand further from the inclination to gossip and prattle than other women of our family, who have submitted to slanderous talk."⁴⁰ Furthermore, Catherine II tries to lend additional value to Empress Anna's position in the Romanov family by mentioning that Anna might have been Peter the Great's illegitimate daughter. Peter I says in the text: "Indeed, dear niece, I held you in respect, which is why some slanderously called you my daughter."⁴¹

At the end of the text, Catherine II focuses on the warrior monarchs, such as Peter the Great and Alexander Nevsky. The former, however, does not always appear in the most favorable light, as some researchers suggest⁴²: Peter I, although a "genius endowed with extraordinary talents," is always ready to take sides in family squabbles.⁴³ In the text, the right to talk of higher matters belongs to Alexander Nevsky, a warrior and a saint. As has been mentioned, *The Chesme Palace*, written in the 1780s, should be viewed in the context of the empress's attempt to change the balance between Peter I and Catherine II by downplaying the first Emperor of Russia.⁴⁴ Hence the distribution of roles in the imaginary community of monarchs.

---

38 Ibid., p. 470.
39 Ibid.
40 Ibid., p. 469.
41 Ibid.
42 Skvortsova, "Representing Imperial Power," p. 467.
43 Ekaterina II, *Chesmenskii dvorets*, pp. 469–471.
44 Proskurina, *Mify imperii*, pp. 105–146.

Catherine II herself is conspicuously absent from the text. However, the whole discussion over ruling manners and monarchical virtues aims to fashion the image of one who had mastered rule and embodied the supreme features of an enlightened monarch, that is to say, Catherine II. In *The Chesme Palace*, she highlights features in others (sadly less successful in retaining power) that she herself is believed to possess: a passion for education, no interest in courtly luxury and female gossiping, a sober (masculine) mind and a gentle heart, and the desire to work for the common good. Moreover, we can find certain echoes of her personal success story, or rather hints at the threats she faced: the lack of good advisors (as in Tsar Vasily Shuisky's case), the disruptive behavior of family members (as in Princess Sofia's case), as well as the problem of the succession (as in the case of Peter the Great).

In order to position herself as a dynastic figure among the Rurikids, the Romanovs, and members of the European monarchical houses, the empress, without actually coming into view, created quite an elaborate textual structure based on the notion of a theater-like play and a view of the portrait as a symbolic object. It provided the empress with a tool to shape her ideas by making heroes exist only within certain limitations. The monarchs in *The Chesme Palace* are inside portrait frames, and – in a wider perspective – within the palace, *maison de plaisance* of Catherine II, who appears in this way to be above everyone. The play-like design of the text seems to have been chosen quite deliberately and becomes instrumental for the empress's self-fashioning strategy. It provides freedom within the limits set, encourages interaction between heroes, and so delivers the empress's message in a form accepted in the era of Enlightenment.

Yet, having fashioned herself as a true exception, the empress could not avoid revealing in the text her desire to achieve both legitimacy and her own ruling subjectivity (i.e. to become free of Peter I's patterns, notions, and prescribed roles), and, most of all, to remain on the throne of the Russian Empire. The work concludes with the Russian Prince Vsevolod Yurievich, who claims to have reigned over the principality of Vladimir for thirty-five years.[45]

For Catherine II in the mid-1780s, such a lengthy rule was something to hope for. However, the dream never came true. Having been Russian empress for thirty-four years, she did not beat the record of Vsevolod Yurievich – nor that of Peter the Great, who ruled for more than four decades.

---

45 Ekaterina II, *Chesmenskii dvorets*, p. 474.

Kirsten Dickhaut
History – Drama – Mythology

In early modern times, the culture of drama is closely linked to its founding place: the court. Therefore, the configuration of history, drama, and mythology takes on a specific meaning at the time when drama 'comes on stage,' i.e. when theaters receive a new status in early modern times, which is expressed by the theaterhouses founded throughout Europe – first in Italy (Teatro Olimpico, Vicenza) and then in England (Shakespeare), before France (Richelieu, later Comédie Française) and other courts and countries followed. Once drama has been founded as a courtly genre and a fixed place, i.e. theater, it becomes a model for the court and baroque culture itself; as Jaques puts it in Shakespeare's *As You Like It*: "All the world's a stage/And all the men and women, merely players" (II.7). Establishing drama as an institution of early modern courts was a means of constructing an artful instrument that helped the sovereignty to strengthen its power.[1]

One of the best-known examples of a drama reflecting on itself not only as a means of metatheater, but most of all as a means of self-fashioning[2] and a demonstration of the power of drama, is certainly the 'theater in the theater' featured in Shakespeare's *Hamlet*. It shows us clearly how drama was established as an institution, and that it had the function to reflect the system of power. Drama and courts both wrote and staged history by showing mythological story-telling.[3]

The French court under Louis XIV epitomizes the self-fashioning of the state,[4] not only because it provided a highly influential and much-debated model, but also because it shows how the state worked to conflate history, drama, and mythology. All three components entered what was considered to be a 'natural' relationship. The intertwining of the three elements made them a strong instrument of power, which was a very delicate one nonetheless, since the solidity of the entire system was based on it.

Nowadays we tend to think that the court of Louis XIV was situated in Versailles, but actually the court and the system of state power only moved to

---

[1] Déborah Blocker. *Instituer un "art": Politiques du théâtre dans la France du premier XVIIe siècle*. Paris: Champion, 2009.

[2] Stephen Greenblatt. *Renaissance Self-Fashioning: From More to Shakespeare*. Chicago: Chicago University Press, 1989.

[3] Joachim Küpper. *Discursive Renovatio in Lope de Vega and Calderón: Studies on Spanish Baroque Drama. With an Excursus on the Evolution of Discourse in the Middle Ages, the Renaissance, and Mannerism*. Berlin: de Gruyter, 2017.

[4] Cf. Blocker, *Politiques du théâtre*.

Versailles at the beginning of the 1680s. From 1661 to the 1680s, Versailles was a hunting castle, albeit a very exclusive one, where theater played an important role (the so-called "premier Versailles").

In fact, building a state in such a way that even today we speak of it as the "powerful system of the Sun King" required the mythology of Apollo. The shining sun became almost naturally related to Louis XIV so that previous uses of this myth by the king's ancestors no longer mattered. Louis XIV 'wrote history' in the sense that everything he inaugurated was considered innovative, even if this was not in fact the case. The splendor of the self-fashioned court was impressive. "All the world's a stage" meant for him that his world was the only legitimate one, and, therefore, the king's stage was the world – as Clifford Geertz famously puts it: "Power served pomp, not pomp power."[5] This Eurocentric vision was an effect produced by a court that used drama as a model of state power, and this helped drama to produce in less than twenty years a considerable amount of staged comedies and tragedies which are still today considered the key works of French literary history (cf. Pierre Corneille, Molière).

It is not surprising that Louis XIV played the sun and other allegorical elements himself on stage. In 1651, he danced for the first time on stage in the *Ballet de Cassandre* and in the *Ballet des Fêtes de Bacchus*.[6] In consequence, a Royal Academy of Dancing was founded 1661, even before the Academy of Music was set up. Dancing was not just a means of passing the time, but a duty of courtly practice, and this applied to the king himself, too. The famous "faux pas" was the designation of a false step taken by the dancing king. This already shows just how closely the natural body of the king and the body politic were linked ("the king's two bodies").[7]

In the Louvre as well as in other castles such as Saint-Cloud, Fontainebleau, or Versailles, ballets were shown in which the king performed one or sometimes even two roles. The list of mythological ballets in which the king appeared as the divine Apollo, who also figured as the protector of the arts, is long. This view of kingship is featured and reinforced in Corbiau's film, *Le Roi danse* (2000), with its depiction of the power of courtly dances and the power of the king.[8] The charged

---

[5] Clifford Geertz. *Negara: The Theatre-State in Nineteenth-Century Bali*. Princeton: Princeton University Press, 1980, p. 13.
[6] Marie-Thérèse Mourey. "Der König tanzt – choreographierte Performanzen der Macht." *Die verzaubernde Kunstwelt Ludwigs XIV. – Versailles als Gesamtkunstwerk*, edited by Ute Jung-Kaiser and Annette Simonis. Hildesheim: Olms, 2015, pp. 193–216, p. 195.
[7] Ernst Kantorowicz. *The King's Two Bodies: A Study in Mediaeval Political Theology*. Princeton: Princeton University Press, 1957. See also Louis Marin. *Le portrait du roi*. Paris: Minuit, 1980.
[8] Annette Simonis. "Gérard Corbiau: *Le Roi danse*. Zur medialen Inszenierung des Phaëton-Mythos in der Oper Quinaults und Lullys und seine produktive Aneignung in Corbiaus Film." *Die verzaubernde Kunstwelt Ludwigs XIV.*, pp. 260–270.

image of the dancing king is still very much present in contemporary cultural memory. The film includes a biography of the musician Jean-Baptiste Lully as a framing story in order to parade the splendor and pomp of the Phaethon Myth. More than twelve times at least, Louis XIV was seen on stage[9] after he had danced in the famous *Ballet royal de la Nuit* in 1653. The courtly feasts and ballets alike were documented by the courtly writers so that other courts could be informed of the French 'happenings.' These transmissions in other media were the key to the establishment of the French courtly feasts as a kind of European role model. The royal *Ballet of the Night* remains for us today a precious document, since some drawings show the king being masked as the Sun, which fostered the myth of the king even further.

Right after Tomaso Campanella's *La città del Sole* (1602; the Latin translation, *Civitas Solis*, was published in 1623), the use of Apollo on stage became a means of self-fashioning for the king – but not only for him as a person who had just acquired the trappings of kingship, but most of all for a country that had just recently gone through the crisis of the Fronde. Using the myth of the Apollonian god, Louis XIV could present himself as a victor over darkness and chaos. Whatever he had done in politics, he wanted it documented in history, and therefore he used the ballet as a dramatic means of announcing from the stage freedom and a happy future. Isaac Benserade had written the text for the ballet, and the powerful speech was clearly understood by the court when the king presented himself as a strong hero: "qui ne voudrait pas avouer ma lumière, sentira ma chaleur"[10] – "who does not agree with my light, shall feel my heat," meaning his power. It was more of a threat than a simple saying. The blending of a king representing his power on stage with the representation of the king showing his impact had been accomplished.

The king's self-fashioning as the god Apollo demonstrates how a meaningful myth was successfully reused by a new king in order to appear just like the sun. Yet there is a further twist if one takes into account the so-called Copernican Revolution,[11] which proclaimed that the Earth orbits around the sun. In this view, the Sun King is claiming to rule the world and considers himself a world leader. Louis XIV, then, did much more than just rehearse a myth. Indeed, he produced a new vision of it. Just like the scientists who strove to show that the sun was the center of the universe, Louis XIV wanted to show how the world really 'turns,'

---

9 Mourey, "Der König tanzt," p. 196.
10 Quoted in Véronique Perruchon. *Noir: Lumière et théâtralité*. Villeneuve d'Ascq: Presses universitaires du Septentrion, 2016, p. 37.
11 Hans Blumenberg. *Die kopernikanische Wende*. Frankfurt am Main: Suhrkamp, 1965. See also Küpper, *Discursive* Renovatio.

namely around the Sun King. It is no wonder, then, that the king was a strong supporter of the scientists against the criticism of the Church.

To strengthen his image, to "fabricate"[12] it, he not only took advantage of the myth of the Sun and Apollo, but also integrated the Perseus myth. In the Italian Renaissance, this myth was discussed as providing a role model for a hero and for perfect ethical behavior. Louis XIV wished to be perceived as fulfilling these heroic and ethical ideals. Not only in Italy but also in Spain, the courts had already used myths such as that of Hercules to promote the image of the king.[13] The genre of the *auto sacramental* probably shows best how Christian allegory was presented on stage in seventeenth-century Europe.[14] Taking this allegorical tradition into account, we can clearly see that Perseus and other mythical figures were shown and interpreted on stage according to Christian ethical standards, so that the pagan pattern delivered only the story of how to succeed, while the underlying message remained Christian.

The Perseus myth offers a role model of a hero that made the king not only glorious but also worthy. A story was needed in which a hero was able to overwhelm the enemy, just as Jason fought against the dragon and pulled out its teeth. In France, the Perseus myth was represented again in a volume of the *Métamorphose d'Ovide figurée*, published in 1557.[15] In 1628, when Louis XIII celebrated his victory of La Rochelle, it was again Perseus that had been chosen to represent the king's victory. Henry IV and Louis XIII had also used the heroic model of Perseus rescuing Andromeda from the sea monster.

Just as the Medici had ordered a Perseus from Cellini, Corneille was asked to present a drama that enabled the presentation of a king as a hero. The celebration of Louis XIV begins already in the prologue of Corneille's *Andromède* ("Louis est le plus jeune et le plus grand des Rois") and continues by presenting the figure of Perseus as symbolizing power, justice, prudence, and temperance, i.e. the four central qualities needed to be a hero.[16] Corneille thus wrote a drama that is also, in an allegorical sense, a "speculum principis."[17] That the example of Perseus, both mighty and ethical, also favors drama as an art becomes very clear when

---

12 Peter Burke. *The Fabrication of Louis XIV*. New Haven: Yale University Press, 1992.
13 Sebastian Neumeister. *Mythos und Repräsentation: Die mythologischen Festspiele Calderóns*. Munich: Fink, 1978.
14 Küpper, *Discursive* Renovatio.
15 Bodo Guthmüller. "Henri IV als französischer Perseus: Zur mythologischen Repräsentation fürstlicher Macht in der Renaissance." *Wolfenbütteler Renaissance Mitteilungen* 23 (1999), pp. 53–65, p. 56.
16 Pierre Corneille. *Andromède*, edited by Christian Delmas. Paris: Nizet, 1974.
17 Hélène Visentin. "Oracle et allégorie dans *L'Andromède* de Corneille." *Analecta Husserliana* 42 (1994), pp. 49–60.

we note how Perseus saves the life of Andromède, namely by flying to her on the horse Pégase and carrying her off from the monster. The act of flying was shown as a divine act on stage and was enabled by the machines developed for this theatrical effect. In this way, drama itself became a divine art, too.

What we see throughout these two examples, the French ballet of the king and Perseus as a role model for heroic virtues, is how the three elements discussed here, history, drama, and mythology, strengthen and recalibrate each other: drama becomes the place to show history in an allegorical-mythical way on stage. Drama is used for amusement at the court and at the same time as a means to link history and mythology, i.e. to set up mythology as a panegyric inventory that helps paint the historical Louis XIV as the splendid hero. Drama was a useful means to show history (as fashioned by the powerful), and mythology was useful to legitimize drama. The panegyric system established under Louis XIV not only explained and told history by recourse to mythology, but also allowed this 'mythic history' to be observed by putting its essentials on stage.

To sum up, the dialectical influence of the three elements – drama, history, and mythology – helps forge the configuration of the time. Drama is the key medium for the king's self-fashioning, and for his fashioning of history; it also enables the theater to become a political tool, and therefore one that is no longer banned by the Church. The interaction of history and mythology acts as a guiding line through the king's Sun Empire.

Elena N. Penskaya
Fielding's Farces: Travestying the Historiosophical Discourse

As is well known, the genre of farce, burlesque, and travesty has a long history dating back to ancient times. The history of studying farcical forms in literature and art has a deep-rooted tradition in the humanities. A farce is commonly believed to be a comedy that aims to entertain the audience through situations that are highly exaggerated, extravagant, and hence improbable. Farce is also characterized by physical humor, the use of deliberate absurdity or nonsense, and broadly stylized performances. Farces have been written for the stage and film. Furthermore, a farce is often set in one particular location, where all events occur.

As a rule, a farce is a light comedy with purely exterior comedic techniques. Back in the Middle Ages, the word *farce* was also used to denote a type of folk theater and literature that was widespread around western Europe from the fourteenth to the sixteenth century. Today, there is no essential disagreement among researchers about the genesis and evolution of farce. It is believed that farce matured within mystery plays and, in the fifteenth century, became an independent genre that would in less than one hundred years come to dominate theater and literature. It was not deliberate political satire but everyday urban life – portrayed informally and carelessly, with all its scandals, obscenity, rudeness and fun – that was the true element of farce. Despite its flexibility, plasticity, and changeability from one era to the next, farce has some invariable characteristics. Contemporary farce studies have shed light on the genre, its history, and its treatment by literary critics. In their research, scholars have examined the recurring themes in farcical comedies, including rebellion, revenge, and coincidence.

Farce elicits an immediate, elemental response from all age levels, cutting across national and intellectual boundaries. It dates back to people's first attempts to scoff in public at whatever their neighbors cherished in private: social prestige, eccentricities, virtues that are vices, friendships and enmities. It can be clearly seen how farce retains its properties from the classical Greek stage through English Restoration and French farce, to the young Hollywood of Mack Sennett, Charlie Chaplin, Buster Keaton, and Harold Lloyd, the other silent farceurs of the Jazz Age, and on to W. C. Fields, Mae West, Sid Caesar, Mel Brooks, Woody Allen, and Monty Python – including other luminaries along

∂ Open Access. © 2019 Elena N. Penskaya, published by De Gruyter. This work is licensed under the Creative Commons Attribution-NonCommercial-NoDerivatives 4.0 License.
https://doi.org/10.1515/9783110604276-010

the way, such as Bob Hope and Bing Crosby, Laurel and Hardy, and the Marx Brothers.[1]

"Farce," as the synopsis of Jessica Davis's monograph on the topic puts it provocatively,

> has always been relegated to the lowest rung of the ladder of dramatic genres. Distinctions between farce and more literary comic forms remain cloudy, even in the light of contemporary efforts to rehabilitate this type of comedy. Is farce really nothing more than slapstick – the "putting out of Candles, kicking down of Tables, falling over Joynt-stools," as Thomas Shadwell characterized it in the seventeenth century? Or was his contemporary Nahum Tate correct when he declared triumphantly that "there are no rules to be prescribed for that sort of wit, no patterns to copy; and 'tis altogether the creature of imagination?"[2]

Farcical elements have been incorporated into non-comic drama ever since theater reemerged in the Middle Ages. Already at a very early stage, comic scenes proved to be popular additions to liturgical musical drama and, later, to religious plays in the vernacular. Some scholars believe that the genre of farce developed out of these farcical elements. Some researchers suggest that farces, similar to the stuffing (French: *farce*) of meat or poultry, was added to plays to increase audience involvement. Other researchers see quite different origins for the farce.[3]

It must be added that farce usually accompanies grand genres as a mobile, adjustable commentary. This commentary can perform diverse functions. It can play a deconstructive role vis-à-vis the text with which it enters into dialogue, or it can serve as a screen or mirror that reflects parodied or travestied works of various genres and authors.

The genre of farce developed rapidly in English literature and culture at the end of the seventeenth and during the first third of the eighteenth centuries. It became part of everyday life and of literary and intellectual processes, combining the objectives of artistic play with those of literary polemics and political and social satire. Farce catalyzed the relationships among art-events, history, and politics, its elements erasing the boundaries between the real figures of the historical stage and their parodic duplicates. Farce became a genre in demand, infecting more and more other genres and plots.

---

[1] See Albert Bermel. *Farce: The Comprehensive and Definitive Account of One of the World's Funniest Art Forms*. New York: Touchstone Book, 1983.
[2] Jessica M. Davis. *Farce*. London: Routledge, 2001, back cover.
[3] See Wim N. M. Hüsken, Konrad Schoell, and Leif Søndergaard. *Farce and Farcical Elements*. Amsterdam and New York: Rodopi, 2002.

Thus the political tragedy of the Elizabethan era and its farcical variant in England in the heyday of dramatic theater, from the 1580s and1590s through the 1620s, used real historical events that mattered to contemporaries. In dramatic farce, elements of historical thought and philosophical and historiographical oeuvres receive new theatricalized interpretations and appear in their new 'costumes' of burlesque language.

Theatrical farce and, in particular, its dramatic variant invoked almost the whole available array of genres: epic, lyric poetry, tragedy, comedy, pantomime, etc. All of this shaped a vast field for ironical parallels between aesthetic and social vices, playwrights' 'crimes' against the Art and the abusive practices of politicians (or even social classes) to the detriment of the public good. Meanwhile, the more farce assimilated the potential of literary parody, the stronger its ambition to create a consistent, internally mature travesty model of a specific genre canon became.

While analyzing texts of this type, researchers normally first try to find the source works that were rewritten as farces. For instance, an epic romantic drama of the early seventeenth century provided the source and the paradigm for a tale of the heroic deeds of a grocer's apprentice (*The Knight of the Burning Pestle* by Francis Beaumont, 1607 or 1610/1611), and the adventures of Drawcansir in *The Rehearsal* (1671, by the Duke of Buckingham) represent an ironical parallel to the "heroic poems" by William Davenant and John Dryden.

The Knight of the Burning Pestle describes a derailed theatrical performance: what was originally conceived as a romance illustrating citizens' lives turns into a grotesque epic drama due to the interference of the audience. Francis Beaumont pokes fun at the incompetence of the spectators who decide that they are co-actors and co-playwrights in the play. In another metatheatrical play, the Duke of Buckingham's *The Rehearsal*, the literary defects of a parodic play about two kings of Brentford and the valiant hero Drawcansir reflect the professional and personal vices that concentrated in the grotesque character of the fictional juror and playwright Bayes.

Drama as a self-looped product of a narrow professional environment is the object of mean sarcasm in Buckingham's play, where the protagonist Bayes uses the opportunity offered by the (fictional) creation of a play to demonstrate an array of techniques. These techniques are ironically opposed to the basic rules of Aristotle and Horace.

Many attempts to introduce new elements into the traditional structure of the genre of tragedy (e.g. to create a *proper* classicist tragedy without a love affair storyline, or a national tragedy modeled on the example of Shakespeare) quickly became a cliché at the turn of the seventeenth and eighteenth centuries. For example, in *The Rehearsal,* Bayes mentions a book of drama commonplaces that he compiled ("my book of Drama Common-Places").[4] Indeed, real-life playwrights assimilated such commonplaces rapidly, their plays resembling eclectic collages of clichés. Thus Joseph Addison created his *Cato, a Tragedy* (1713) in accordance with the laws of classicism. His goal was to involve the audience in order to create inner turmoil; the spectator was supposed to weep over the legislative decay. However, the author failed to realize his intention fully and to avoid the love affair storyline: Cato's civil tears were a good basis for rhetoric but not a source of plot development. In line with the tradition, the latter function was assigned to the intrigues of villains – Sempronius and Syphax – and to the self-deception of the young characters – the noble prince Juba and Cato's sons, whose motives are a combination of the bitterness of one-sided love, jealousy, and rivalry. As a result, the enlightening tragedy on republican virtues is shot through by multiple romantic clichés, while the protagonist's stoic courage erodes the baroque passions of the rest of the characters. Similarly, any serious drama has its own set of tragic commonplaces.

A rather paradoxical situation had arisen by the 1720s and 1730s. On the one hand, endless repetition of the same tragic clichés made their conventional, almost mechanical use less meaningful; on the other hand, that very mechanical nature contained a coercive power that had to be considered, whether the authors liked it or not. This conflict reveals one of the important factors of the heyday of farce. One of Fielding's predecessors was John Gay, with his dramatic farce *The What D'Ye Call It* (1715). Most of his plays are farces, including the famous *Beggar's Opera* (1728). Gay's first theatrical burlesque *The Mohocks* (1712), devoted to the then-relevant matter of the crimes committed by a secret club of London revelers, imitated the epic tone of John Milton's poems, while the characters' nicknames (Abaddon, Molock, etc.) parodied the names of Satan's apprentices from *Paradise Lost*. At the same time, farcical tragicomedy as such was ironically called "tragedy" in Gay's sarcastic dedication of his *The Mohocks* to the critic John Dennis.

Using the widespread farce technique of the 'theater inside the theater,' Gay assigns the protagonists of the internal play the typical tragic roles of a maligned hero and a distressed heroine. They are surrounded by high-ranking villains and self-serving plotters, including the 'second heroine' possessed by passions. The plot is driven by fake news about the protagonist's death, the heroine's suicide attempt, a parade of five ghosts, and a wedding finale. Most lines are in Dryden's heroic couplets, which had not yet been completely forced out of English tragedy

---

[4] George Villiers, Duke of Buckingham. *The Rehearsal*, edited by Edward Arber. London: n.p., 1869.

of the early eighteenth century. The characters' words refer the reader to numerous tragedies, from Shakespeare's *Richard III* and *Macbeth* to the plays of John Dryden and Joseph Addison.

The author's irony seeks to travesty the familiar tragic clichés, such as seeing ghosts. Traditionally, ghosts disturb the souls of villainous judicial officials, reminding them of the lives they have ruined. It is not the fates of nations but the daily life of a provincial parish that is the measure of villainy. The victims and their ruined lives fit this small scale perfectly: harassed recruits, the "child unborn," and the mother who never gave it birth (for fear of being sentenced to a severe punishment by lashing). Gay's mockery is ambivalent: rather than degrade the high for no good reason, it distorts the familiar by putting it into a false language and on a false scale, making a 'tragic' caricature out of life. In *The Knight of the Burning Pestle*, the gap between the professional, genre-compliant thinking of actors and the incompetent, canon-breaking mind of the semi-educated apprentice is deflected in the deconstructed structure of the play-within-a-play, where all but one of the scenes involving Rafe (the apprentice) are clearly distinct from those involving Jasper (the merchant's assistant). The choice of the merchant's assistant and the merchant's daughter for the roles of a couple in love in the original actors' play was already an obeisance to shopkeepers. Yet, the 'play of the actors' communicates the familiar flattery to the public in the language of specific theatrical conventionality (dramatic art), which is violated in the scenes with Rafe. In Gay's "tragi-comi-pastoral farce," the author and the 'customer' have the same level of skill in the conventions of drama, yet their interests and goals are different. As Sir Roger bends over backwards to demonstrate all possible dramatic genres "in one play" to his ignorant neighbors (who have never been to a theater), his steward has a contrastingly different concern, that of turning the landlord's caprices to the benefit of his daughter, seduced by the landlord's son Thomas. This results in a classical 'wedding trick,' where the false wedding of Kitty and Thomas on stage turns into a real-life marriage. Theatrical conventionality serves as bait, which the steward uses to catch the simple-hearted landlord. Playing along with the landlord's mania ("Why, what's a Play without a Marriage?"),[5] the steward satisfies all of his theatrical whims in full obedience, only to destroy the illusion later, abruptly and intentionally. Subsequently, Gay's farces keep mixing genres and focusing on the objective grounds as well as the social connotations of the interactions between the high and the low in literature and theater. The techniques used by Gay in his farces (including the generalized model of the genre canon he created by building up parodic

---

5 I.9.21.

quotes from numerous works, the 'theoretical' preface, etc.) are picked up by the farce tragedies of Fielding.

The experience of Fielding, the author of a whole range of farces written in the 1730s and 1740s, appears to be fundamental to, and indicative of, not only his own era but also those that followed. The popularity of farce was higher at the turns of the nineteenth, twentieth, and twenty-first centuries.

Despite his dependence on predecessors, the young Fielding was quick to introduce a number of new subtleties to the long-established method of burlesque travesty. He provided quite unorthodox interpretations of metaphors and analogies typical of burlesque, from the travesty-based model of the theatricalization of life to the parallelism between certain social and historical types and specific roles of dramatic characters.

However, the most important thing is that the genre of farce, in the version developed by Fielding, became an active link in the process of exchange and cooperation between historical thought and theatrical aesthetics in the 1730s. The discourse of historical works began to borrow theatrical metaphors and symbols, and to reproduce the exchange of language and meanings between the everyday environment filled with discussion, debates, collisions, and intellectual conflicts, on the one hand, and theatricalized rituals and stage performances on the other.

The intense dialogue between the baroque and classicism manifested itself most vibrantly in the polemical space of philosophy of history in the second half of the sixteenth and first third of the seventeenth centuries. Even if we analyze only the historical and philosophical conceptions of that period, we see that their basic points were verified through a polemical exchange of treatises and epistles, which often resorted to the vocabulary of farce and theatrical language.

Here we are not attempting to conduct a detailed analysis of the genesis of the ideas and intellectual background of these disputes. What we would like to do instead is to demonstrate the coordinates of the theatrical system, and to represent theater as a place where ἡ κοινὴ διάλεκτος ('*Koine* language') exists as a common theatrical dialect, a lingua franca of the stage that serves as a framework for the exchange of ideas.

In the second half of the sixteenth and the first third of the seventeenth centuries, farces took on the function of a burlesque historiosophic commentary, which can be seen particularly clearly from Fielding's travesty plays. Fielding was not the first to compare "the great people" of history and literature (including tragic characters) to ambitious politicians, nor the first to find personifications for this comparison. However, it was he who sharpened and sophisticated those parallels. In particular, his satirical figures of authors – "the great people" and "the great thinkers" – appear as a blend of genres on stage. Independent characters grow from fragments of famous treatises, quotations, and even stand-alone phrases. A practice like this had already been used in burlesque satire, a mix of genres: *The Author's Farce with a Puppet-Show Called The Pleasures of the Town* (1730–1733), *The Historical Register for the Year 1736*, and *Eurydice Hiss'd* (both dated 1737). One of the characters summarizes the method as follows: "in the first place, my piece is not of a nature confined to any rules, as being avowedly irregular." Thus, "blending" is not only the object, but also a deliberate means of depiction.

The correlations between literary form and real life are stressed by using relevant hints and introducing real historical figures into the dramaturgical fabric. A deliberate conflict of fragments from different genres turned out to be indispensable in the genre of satirical revue, which equated literary realia to extraliterary ones ironically, and turned inside out not a specific style or genre but all popular genres and styles at once. It was, so to speak, a burlesque commentary on literariness as such, on the very historiosophy that had become irrelevant to the aesthetic and meaningful content of its own professional "tools." Tragedy was beyond doubt the easiest target of such "precision" commentary burlesque. Tragic clichés turned out to be absolutely independent of any specific material in that context. From then on, it became possible to extract their quintessence, as Fielding did, for instance, with the historical and philosophical works of his contemporaries and predecessors in *The Historical Register for the Year 1736*.

As a playwright, Fielding consciously elaborated a burlesque tragic canon twice, in *Tom Thumb* and *The Covent-Garden Tragedy*; both were written in the early 1730s and have a relevant ironical genre subtitle describing them as burlesque tragedies. *The Tragedy of Tragedies* was an expanded and rewritten version of *Tom Thumb*; the rewrite was intended to make the satire more obvious. The play was first performed on 24 March 1731, at the Haymarket Theatre in London, with the companion piece *The Letter Writers*. Its printed edition was "edited" and "commented on" by Fielding under the pseudonym H. Scriblerus Secundus, who pretends not to be the original author. It contains a frontispiece by William Hogarth, which serves as the earliest proof of a relationship between Fielding and the painter and printmaker.

The printed edition was available on the opening night, and the notes included in the printed edition served as a way to explain the play. The print version of *The Tragedy of Tragedies* created two versions of the play, one that was performed and another that was to be read, and each contained instances of humor that catered to its respective medium. Fielding referred to these modern works as "laughing tragedies" and claimed that the only difference between his work and the modern tragedies was that his work was intentional in its laughter.

A textological analysis offers a clue to reconstructing the theatrical *koine* in its farce variant. We will give a brief description of the reconstruction process. We compared several revisions of the play: the earlier one (I) and the later one (II), the one designed for stage (III), and the one designed for reading (IV). This allows us to consider the textological features of that farce. The versions differ in the number of real historical figures introduced, the methodology of scholarly commentary, and the volume and nature of incorporated quotes, allusions, and farce-specific historical and philosophical reminiscences. *The Tragedy of Tragedies, or The Life and Death of Tom Thumb the Great* (1731) is considered one of Fielding's most outstanding pieces of burlesque drama. The first part of the name, which appeared only in the print publication of *Tom Thumb* (1731), is crucial for identifying the methodology of building the farce *koine* and the genre-specific features of the play, giving it the status of a "metatragedy" ("the tragedy of tragedies"). Woven from myriads of quotes, both hidden and open, *The Tragedy of Tragedies* was perceived as a grotesque depiction of the very genre of heroic tragedy, which involved characters based on real philosophers, such as Locke, Bacon, Hobbes, etc., who passed from one revision to another. Their presence is felt the most in versions I and IV, as the following list of dramatis personae attests:

- King Arthur – "A passionate sort of King, Husband to Queen *Dollallolla*, of whom he stands a little in Fear; Father to *Huncamunca*, of whom he is very fond; and in Love with *Glumdalca*." He has learnt by heart a fragment of Francis Bacon's *Novum Organum*.
- Tom Thumb the Great – "A little Hero with a great Soul, something violent in his Temper, which is a little abated by his Love for *Huncamunca*"
- Ghost of Gaffar Thumb (Lockehobbes) – "A whimsical sort of Ghost"
- Lord Grizzle – "Extremely zealous for the Liberty of the Subject, very cholerick in his Temper, alter-ego of Francis Bacon, 1st Viscount St Alban and in Love with *Huncamunca*"
- Merlin – "A Conjurer, and in some sort Father to *Tom Thumb*"
- Noodle and Doodle – "Courtiers in Place, and consequently of that Part that is uppermost," *Idola tribus and Idola specus*
- Foodle – "A Courtier that is out of Place, and consequently of that Part that is undermost," *Idola fori*
- Bailiff and Follower – "Of the Party of the Plaintiff"
- Parson – "Of the Side of the Church," again Francis Bacon, 1st Viscount St Alban with his Masques and Triumphs, repeating "Dancing to song is a thing of great state and pleasure"
- Queen Dollalolla – "Wife to King *Arthur*, and Mother to *Huncamunca*, a Woman entirely faultless, saving that she is [a] little given to Drink; a little too much a *Virago* towards her Husband, and in Love with *Tom Thumb*"
- The Princess Huncamunca – "Daughter to their Majesties King *Arthur* and Queen *Dollalolla*, of a very sweet, gentle, and amorous Disposition, equally

in Love with Lord *Grizzle* and *Tom Thumb*, and desirous to be married to them both"
- Glumdalka – "of the Giants, a Captive Queen, belov'd by the King, but in Love with *Tom Thumb*." It is remarked that "If this woman has milk in her breasts, it means she is with child." The sentence is an example of the deductive method (evidence and conclusion) and can originally be found in Sextus Empiricus and elsewhere; it thus forms a contrast to the inductive method of Bacon's *Novum Organum*.
- Cleora and Mustacha – "Maids of Honour, in Love with Noodle Doodle"
- Other characters include Courtiers, Guards, Rebels, Drums, Trumpets, Thunder and Lightning

Fielding turns Tom Thumb, the central fairytale character of his play, into a valiant commander, philosopher, historian, and, on top of that, a gallant heart-throb at King Arthur's court. After defeating an army of giants and killing two dozen giant kings with his own hands, the hero wins the love of three grand ladies at once: the captive giantess Glumdalka, the Queen Dollalolla, and the Princess Huncamunca. Despite the jealousy of the two royal ladies, the machinations of his rival Grizzle, and the ambivalence of the princess's feelings, the hero is confidently approaching his marriage with the princess – only to fall prey, on the day before the event, to the terrible Leviathan (version I), a red cow that devours the brave young man without remorse. The "tragic" resolution is preceded by a clichéd tragedy action – the apparition before King Arthur of the shade of Lockehobbes, Tom Thumb's father (versions I, IV). "The Old Thumb" causes a stir, as befits a theatrical ghost, and confuses the king with his ambiguous predictions, which represent a mash of quotes from historiosophic works by Hobbes, Locke, Bacon, and others.

Meanwhile, the generally accepted conventionality is defamiliarized in a grotesque way: the ghost's "dark" speeches linger on until the break of dawn only to get interrupted at the very beginning of the "practical" part, which nearly brings the monarch to insanity. Arthur has nothing left to do but curse all the philosophers, historians, and poets in the world, including the authors. The final "catastrophe" takes the lives of seven more characters – from the courtier Mr. Noodle, who brings the news of Tom Thumb's death and gets killed by the Queen, mad with grief, to the King, who is the last to stab himself on the pile of aristocratic corpses, not forgetting to compare it to a scattered deck of cards.

The practical rationale of the burlesque effect lies in the conflict of two artistic models of reality: the monumentally heroic one and the playfully private one. In the new context, the characters' "fatal" passions (including the giantess's immeasurable grief over her twenty slain husbands and her desire for their fearless killer) lose their "elaborate irrationality" typical of the baroque, taking up parodically the "natural scandalousness" of rococo. Indeed, Glumdalka's endless grief excites a shade of envy among the other ladies, who have to make do with only one spouse each.

The printed version of *Tom Thumb* deploys the metatextual principle of the *Tragedy of Tragedies* even more consistently than the theatrical revision – thanks to an added burlesque foreword as well as notes that turn the scholarly commentary form inside out. The parodically playful attitude is imparted already in the "publishers's" pseudonym – Scriblerus Secundus, which refers us to the grotesque style of the Scriblerians, the literary fellows of Jonathan Swift.

As a result, the text of *Tom Thumb*, as presented by Scriblerus Secundus, transforms into a "precursor text" and runs back to the era of Elizabeth, the era of the first flourishing of English dramaturgy. The "prototypical" property of *Tom Thumb* is here proved positively by countless in-text patterns echoing the tragedies of English poets of the seventeenth and eighteenth centuries, from Shakespeare to Dryden, from Thomas Otway to James Thomson and Nicholas Rowe.

Of course, the technique of quoting fragments was not at all new to the genre of burlesque, but dates back to Buckingham and Gay. Yet Fielding provided a new, ironic justification for this type of quoting within scholarly commentary, which replaced the former "clues" to burlesque texts. Notes on the tragedy pick up the game initiated in the main text, "accusing" the English playwrights of the previous hundred years of plagiarizing the unknown author of *Tom Thumb*. Scriblerus Secundus argues that the author could be Shakespeare himself, who has become an unshakeable authority for many dramatists and critics – an authority at least as powerful as Aristotle.

In most cases, Fielding finds it vital to emphasize the consistency of borrowing characters and expressions from tragedy authors; for this purpose, he uses a scholarly commentary, which stacks up endless "parallel quotes" to individual phrases from *Tom Thumb*. A sort of moral sentence pronounced by Lockehobbes becomes a worthy ending to the *Tragedy*: "These instances, just like those, teach us/They teach us I don't really know what."[6] This way, the almost compulsory moral instruction becomes meaningless, reduced as it is to the "quintessence" of all final morals ever, but these senseless words are at the same time a quite conscious allusion to the "algorithm" of tragic endings in drama of Fielding's time, as well as to the emptiness of the morals drawn from them.

The "editor's" foreword to *Tom Thumb* performs an independent parodic and satirical function. In earlier burlesques, the figure of the Author often replaced

---

6 Final scene of version II.

volumes of critical commentaries. This critical commentary, on the contrary, is a successful implementation of the satirical figure of the Critic. In this context, the Critic, a character to whom Fielding grants relative independence, continues performing his general functions of burlesque as a form of ironical literary reflection. Not unlike his predecessors, Fielding mediates this reflection through satirical descriptions of the conditions that generate the literary and extraliterary clichés and commonplaces that flood historiosophic treatises. Besides, his reflection is supported even more by parallels between literary and extraliterary processes. It actually played the key role in developing the theatrical *koine* in the waning years of the baroque and throughout the Age of Enlightenment.

Burlesque tragedy was reanimated at the end of the eighteenth century, complemented by everyday social and occupational satire. The genre was resumed in the farce plays *Puss in Boots* (*Der gestiefelte Kater*) and *The Life and Death of Little Thomas* (*Leben und Taten des kleinen Thomas*), written by Ludwig Tieck in the 1790s through 1810s, i.e. in the pre-Romantic era, when the source texts of famous fairytale plots, interpreted by Charles Perrault on stage, underwent a number of metamorphoses and transformations, finally presenting a whole in-built gallery of characters and a panorama of plots. Symbolically, Ludwig Tieck made Fielding – the author of the *Tragedy of Tragedies* about Tom Thumb – one of the central characters in his cycle of fairytale farce commentaries. Meanwhile, the methodology of blending scenes, quotes, figures, and texts into a farce did not need to be rediscovered. It could actually become a powerful tool, which Ludwig Tieck demonstrated skillfully. However, this is a topic for another essay, so we can only mention it in its bare outlines here.

Olga Kuptsova
Ostrovsky's Experience of the Creation of the European Theatrical Canon and Russian Stage Practice

Personal Preferences and General Trends

Alexander Ostrovsky's dramatic heritage has been primarily regarded as 'slice-of-life' plays in the Russian historico-theatrical tradition, due to the detailed descriptions of everyday life and sociopsychological characters/types it represents. The very first (and until recently the only monographic) study of Ostrovsky in a west European language was *Ostrovski et son théâtre de mœurs russes* (1912), by the French Slavicist Jules Patouillet,[1] which gave priority to this point of view among Western historians of literature and theater, too.

However, this perspective is rather one-legged and even incorrect. Studies by Russian philologists of the early twentieth century (Nikolai Kashin, Boris Varneke, Fyodor Batyushkov, Nikolai Piksanov, etc.), who emphasized that Ostrovsky's plays were inscribed in the pan-European theatrical context, were well ahead of their time and hence consigned to oblivion.[2] At the beginning of his anniversary article "Ostrovsky and World Dramaturgy," Alexander Stein wrote: "The topic of Ostrovsky and world culture appears to be much less obligatory than Dostoevsky, Turgenev, Tolstoy, Chekhov – and world culture."[3] Meanwhile, present-day studies in this field, though largely compelling in their hypotheses

---

[1] Jules Patouillet. *Ostrovski et son théâtre de mœurs russes*, 2nd edition. Paris: Plon-Nourrit et Cie., 1912.

[2] See Nikolay Kashin. *Etyudy ob Ostrovskom* [*Essays on Ostrovsky*]. 2 vols. Moscow: Kushnerev & Co., Typography of the Literary Fellowship Consolidated by the Imperial Court, 1912; Nikolay Kashin. "Ostrovskiy i italyantsy" [Ostrovsky and the Italians]. *Teatr i dramaturgiya* 4 (1933), pp. 29–35; Boris Varneke. *Zametki ob Ostrovskom* [*Notes on Ostrovsky*]. Odessa: Ekonomicheskaya tipografiya, 1912; Fyodor Batyushkov. "Bytovoy teatr Ostrovskogo v osveshchenii frantsuzskogo uchenogo. Rets.: J. Patouillet. *Ostrovski et son théâtre de mœurs russes*. Paris, Plon, 1913" [Ostrovsky's Theater of Everyday Life from the Perspective of a French Researcher. A Review of J. Patouillet...]. *Zhurnal ministerstva narodnogo prosveshcheniya* 9 (1913), pp. 163–169; Nikolay Piksanov. *Ostrovskiy: literaturno-teatral'ny seminariy* [*Ostrovsky: Literary and Theatrical Seminar*]. Ivanovo-Voznesensk: Osnova, 1923.

[3] Alexander Stein. "Ostrovskiy i mirovaya dramaturgiya" [Ostrovsky and World Dramaturgy]. *Novye materialy i issledovaniya. Kn. 1. Literaturnoe nasledstvo. T. 87.* [*New Materials and Studies*, book 1. *Literary Heritage*, vol. 87.] Moscow: Nauka, 1984, pp. 43–74, p. 43.

and observations, usually lack a general perspective or consistent position, being unable to dispel the established literary 'myth.'[4]

Ostrovsky's personal library materials kept at the Pushkin House in St. Petersburg demonstrate that he was engaged in thorough research into the history of theater (from ancient times to the present day), not only in Russian but also in several European languages. According to the surviving evidence from Nikolay Luzhenovsky, a university friend of the playwright's son Sergey, Ostrovsky's personal library contained about 3,000 volumes by the end of his life:

> You can find works from all Western stages, all centuries and countries here: Greek tragedies translated into Russian, original Aristophanes translated into Latin; original works by Plautus and Terence, Calderón and Shakespeare, Cervantes and Gozzi, Corneille and Metastasio, Racine and Goldoni, Scribe and Molière, all the pseudo-classicists, playwrights of romanticism, all or nearly all the new French dramatists, such as Augier, Sardou, Feuillet, and a lot more – bad and good, mediocre and profound. Russian-language, translated, and foreign drama is represented here to its fullest, from *scenes* of the eighth century, through *Rossiyskiy Featr*, to our most recent productions. [...] A separate cabinet is occupied by critical works, studies in the history and exegetics of theater and its literary luminaries, complemented with a collection of Russian chronicles, songs, fairytales, proverbs, etc.[5]

As we know, Ostrovsky got tired of theater more than once during his life and wanted to quit playwriting, choosing an alternative among lexicography (he dreamed of building a vocabulary of the Russian language, similar to that of Vladimir Dal, amended and upgraded), history, and translation.

It seems that Ostrovsky's translations have been studied fairly well.[6] He translated from five foreign languages: he was taught Latin and French at *gymnasium* (French remained his favorite and the most common one: he had plays of virtually all world classic authors that had not yet been translated into Russian not only in the original but also always in French), while he mastered English, Italian, and Spanish independently. In addition, he spoke German, and he could read Polish and Czech.

Ostrovsky became concerned about repertoire in the late 1860s, and so he plunged into translations, eager to enrich the Russian stage with the best playwrights,

---

4 Cf. Stein, ibid., as well as Irina Ovchinina, editor. *Alexander N. Ostrovsky: Entsiklopediya* [A. N. Ostrovsky: Encyclopedia]. Kostroma: Kostromaizdat/Shuya: Shuya State Pedagogical University, 2012.
5 F. V. Il'ina, editor. *Biblioteka A. N. Ostrovskogo: Katalog* [Alexander Ostrovsky's Library: A Catalogue]. Leningrad: Nauka, 1963.
6 Vasily Malikov and Roman Tomashevsky. "Ostrovskiy-perevodchik (1850–1886)" [Ostrovsky the Translator]. Alexander Ostrovsky. *Polnoe sobranie sochineniy* [*Complete Works*], vol 9. Moscow: Iskusstvo, 1978, pp. 599–614.

according to his opinion. Investigating the problem of Russian theater reform in the 1870–1880s, Ostrovsky often wrote about the need to develop the repertoire consciously and consistently (including its European segment).

However, all of these well-known facts still in a way exist independently of Ostrovsky's literary reputation. Without at all trying to deny Ostrovsky's merit in building the national (local, purely Russian) theater, I suggest approaching his works in the light of a search for theatrical universals and identifying at least approximately his range of interests in the history of world theater. This article is based not only on Ostrovsky's translations – an important part of his enlightenment mission in theater – but also on the clues to his connection with the pan-European tradition that are embedded in his own plays.

Literary and theatrical reminiscences are most abundant in the comedy *The Forest (Les)* and the spring fairytale *The Snow Maiden (Snegurochka)*, written one after the other in the early 1870s, one of the critical periods in the dramatist's life. In 1870, Ostrovsky created his most 'theatrical' play *The Forest*, which is a concentration of all the previous history of both west European and Russian theater. This effect is provided first of all (though not entirely) by the characters of two actors, the tragedian Gennady Neschastlivtsev (Unlucky) and the comedian Arkashka (Arkady) Schastlivtsev (Lucky). They both behave theatrically in real life, and their theatricality is the sum of all the roles they have ever played. For Neschastlivtsev, these include, first of all, Shakespeare (Hamlet), Schiller (Karl Moor), and Cervantes (the non-dramatic role of Don Quixote). Meanwhile, Schastlivtsev, who acts as Sganarelle, the role once played by Molière himself, with its roots in French *théâtre de la foire* ('fair theater') and Italian *commedia dell'arte*, impersonates the tradition of all the 'comic unfortunates.'

The Snow Maiden, in its turn, was a reminder of dramatic fairytale, féerie, comic opera, and fantastic comedy traditions (in particular, those underlying *A Midsummer Night's Dream*). *Repertoir i panteon* was a literary and theatrical journal published in St. Petersburg in the 1840s and 1850s that aimed to cultivate an idea of the best specimens of European and Russian dramaturgy in Russian readers and spectators. Ostrovsky was building a pantheon of European theaters of his own throughout his creative career – consciously and consistently, sometimes following the common trends and sometimes digressing from them and being guided by his own preferences.

It is definitely no coincidence that Ostrovsky would often be called the "Russian Shakespeare" by his contemporaries and successors (and not always metaphorically). There can be no doubt that Shakespeare was the most important European literary author for Ostrovsky as well as for the rest of his generation, i.e. the '40ers. Indeed, that late-Romantic generation grew up with *Hamlet*, first played by the Moscow tragedian Pavel Mochalov in 1837, and was the one that discovered Shakespeare for Russian culture.

It is revealing that Shakespeare was assimilated through German and French translations in addition to the original English at that time. However, this intricate path of learning from the English playwright introduced the pan-European context right away, providing an opportunity to compare translation strategies: literal, German/'free' (translating the 'spirit,' not the words), and French. In addition, translations were usually accompanied by a detailed philological commentary, facilitating the process of getting to know the alien culture and the remote era.

Enthusiasm for Shakespeare not only permeated theater and theater lovers – it also became a broader cultural phenomenon. In particular, this resulted in the so-called Russian Hamletism, i.e. imitating the Prince of Denmark's appearance and behavior in real life. The '40ers, in their turn, fell victim to the Shakespeare-mania they themselves had initiated.

All of Ostrovsky's translation activities were, in a way, framed by Shakespeare's texts: his first ever experience of translation was Shakespeare's comedy *The Taming of the Shrew* in the early 1850s (he translated it again later, in 1865 and 1886, and left two versions, one in prose and another in verse), and his final piece of translation at the end of his life was *Antony and Cleopatra*, which he did not complete.

Ostrovsky also used *Hamlet* and *A Midsummer Night's Dream* – the two pivotal Shakespeare texts for Russian Romanticists – as a basis for a cross-cultural dialogue in his own plays. His Russian Hamlets are always lowered in tone and often comic (in various modifications of the comic, from tragicomedy to almost farce): these are the "goosey" Kapiton Bruskov in his early comedy *Hangover at Somebody Else's Feast (V chuzhom piru pokhmelye)*, the tragic Neschastlivtsev in *The Forest*, and Paratov in *Without a Dowry (Bespridannitsa)*. All of them illustrate the evolution of Ostrovsky's attitude towards the '40ers' creative 'Hamlet' life–model, which they never digested critically (thus, he would often talk about the morbidity of spectators' exaltation that was developed by Shakespeare's passions). The key component of Ostrovsky's attitude toward the image of the Russian Hamlet was his irony over the romantic air surrounding the character, as he highlighted the "degeneration" of Russian Hamlets (both on stage and in real life). Ostrovsky's perception of Russian Hamletism is one of many manifestations of his intense personal life-long dialogue with the Romantic era.

A Midsummer Night's Dream was made part of *The Snow Maiden* as a specifically built-in narrative plot line in the argument over the "nature of love" (one of the points of disagreement between Romanticists and the subsequent generation of Realists) – not only and not so much with the English dramatist as with the authors of Russian adaptations and translations, from Alexander Veltman to Apollon Grigoryev. Another aspect is Shakespeare's example of historical chronicles, which is reflected (through Alexander Pushkin's *Boris Godunov* as well) in Ostrovsky's historical plays, first of all in *The False Dmitry and Vasily Shuisky (Samozvanets Dmitry i Vasily Shuysky)*.

Friedrich Schiller was another iconic figure for Ostrovsky's generation along with Shakespeare, even echoing him in some way. Ostrovsky never actually translated German plays, except his poetic translation *From Schiller (To an Artist)* composed to congratulate Ivan Samarin, actor of the Moscow Imperial Theater, on his birthday in 1884. The playwright remained almost untouched by the passion for German idealist philosophy typical of his era, however. On the whole, he was rather distant from German culture, which was obviously not in harmony with his own nature.[7] However, his plays refer repeatedly to Schiller's *The Robbers* as if to a specific sore point that reanimates the idols of youth and knocks off their crowns in their smugness (*The Forest, An Ardent Heart [Goryacheye Serdtse], In a Busy Place [Na boykom meste]*, the historical drama *Voyevoda*). Of course, this was not only about Schiller as such but also largely about the Russian actors Pavel Mochalov and Pyotr Karatygin, who developed a convincing scenic character of Karl Moor as a righteous avenger in the 1830s. In particular, Ostrovsky parodies the romanticization of "high-souled robbers" in the characters of the tragic Neschastlivtsev and comic Schastlivtsev, who play to a virtual Schiller scenario in the Penki Mansion (thus, Neschastlivtsev delivers Karl Moor's incriminating monologue as his own at the end).

As we can see, Shakespeare and Schiller were 'model' playwrights for Ostrovsky's generation. However, there is another, more subjective and personal part of Ostrovsky's theatrical pantheon. French dramaturgy of the seventeenth and eighteenth centuries was an object of Ostrovsky's thorough research; French books on dramaturgy and theater of that time formed the bulk of his foreign library. He studied plays by Alain-René Lesage, Pierre-Augustin Caron de Beaumarchais, Pierre de Marivaux, and his nineteenth-century successor Alfred de Musset, as well as dozens of less popular authors (such as Nolant de Fatouville, Florent Carton Dancourt, Charles Simon Favart, and many others) with a pencil in his hand: there are numerous marginal notes. He traced back and analyzed carefully the continuous chains of adapted plays (a common practice among dramatists of the seventeenth and eighteenth centuries) as a centuries-old European tradition. Contrary to common belief, Ostrovsky never searched for original plots (on Vissarion

---

[7] See Nikolay Kashin. "Ostrovskiy i Shiller (posvyashchaetsya akademiku A. N. Veselovskomu)" [Ostrovsky and Schiller (to the Academician A. Veselovsky)]. *Russkiy vestnik* 3–4 (1917), pp. 1–137.

Belinsky's advice). Instead, he consciously combined the pre-established plot lines in his plays and introduced previous characters, following and developing the theatrical tradition of cross-national adaptations, imitations, and paraphrases. For instance, some hints of Fatouville and Lesage (Fatouville's comedy *Le Banqueroutier* and, related, Lesage's *Turcaret, ou Le Financier*) can be seen in the plot of his 'financial comedy' *The Bankrupt* (*Bankrot*); of Beaumarchais, in *Enough Stupidity in Every Wise Man* (*Na vsyakogo mudretsa dovolno prostoty*); and of Musset, in *Sin and Sorrow Are Common to All* (*Grekh da beda na kogo ne zhivet*). The list could go on and on. In the 1860s to 1870s, Ostrovsky's quest for 'nomadic plots' and 'timeless characters' received historical and theoretical support from representatives of the so-called mythological school (Alexander Afanasyev) and the comparative historical school (in particular, in Alexey Veselovsky's works on Molière).

To avoid distorting the idea of Ostrovsky's dramatic heritage, I should note in parentheses that the timeless nonetheless did acquire a pronounced local flair in his adaptations. He localized foreign works mainly by adding some concrete everyday-life ingredients (e.g. by describing the lifestyle of a specific class, the merchants, which also received a precise geographic localization, living not just in Moscow but in the specific district of Zamoskvorechye), and a zesty, grassroots language.

Full of well-known names, French dramaturgy nonetheless had a climax for Ostrovsky, namely Molière's tradition of high comedy, assimilated by the Russian theater in the eighteenth century and reanimated later by Nikolai Gogol. Ostrovsky never got the chance to translate Molière, although he dreamed of it all his life. A year before his death, he mused in a letter to Anna Mysovskaya, a writer from Nizhny Novgorod, despite the recent first ever publication of complete plays of Molière in Russian: "You and I, we will translate all Molière plays, you'll take the verse and I'll do the prose, and we will make a luxurious publication. It will be a most precious gift to the public, and we will raise ourselves a monument forever."[8] Ostrovsky was first of all interested in the structure of Molière's comedy, his dramaturgical methods and techniques. Not only did he read Molière's plays, but he also studied a vast amount of secondary literature on the playwright and the theater of his time (in French first of all). Molière's 'code' is present both everywhere and nowhere in Ostrovsky's plays, being vaguely perceived (as was also mentioned by Patouillet, who referred to Ostrovsky as the "Russian Molière") but still elusive. There have been numerous observations and

---

[8] Alexander Ostrovsky. *Polnoe sobranie sochineniy* [Complete Works], vol. 12. Moscow: Iskusstvo, 1978, p. 374.

hypotheses on correlations between Molière's and Ostrovsky's characters.⁹ Yet, unlike the Shakespeare component, which is highlighted by the dramatist in many ways, the Molière aspect looks deliberately blurred and concealed. It only manifests itself once in *The Forest*, in the recurring name of the comic Arkashka Schastlivtsev. The latter is forced to play the role of an alleged servant in real life, so he presents himself as Sganarelle to Karp, a real servant in Landlady Gyrmyzhskaya's house. The mention of the mask of Sganarelle created by Molière evokes the whole European tradition of comic servants, from the cunning slave in *comoedia palliata* (Ostrovsky translated Terence and Plautus) to Italian *commedia dell'arte* and Spanish *graciosos*. This Schastlivtsev-Sganarelle plotline may be dubbed 'the Harlequin line' and Arkashka's behavioral model a 'Harlequinade,' if we understand Harlequin as a broader figure, according to the Silver Age interpretations. Alternatively, in the terms of Vsevolod Meyerhold (who also drew on Aleksey Veselovsky's works), Schastlivtsev demonstrates the opportunities of a trickster character when playing Sganarelle.¹⁰

Ostrovsky's interest in Spanish dramaturgy of the Golden Age (Lope de Vega, Calderón de la Barca, Cervantes) began to rise in the early 1860s. However, in the end he only translated nine interludes by Cervantes. The work took a long time, was interrupted for a few years, and then resumed (amending, editing, double-checking), lasting until the dramatist's death. In his unfinished review of *The Best Mayor, the King (El mejor alcalde, el rey)*, Ostrovsky draws parallels between Lope de Vega, author of this drama, and Cervantes. The plot of the play followed the dramatic principles, provided enough space for character development, and all in all had an all-human value, but the author, in Ostrovsky's opinion, "approached it from an exclusively national perspective, creating an interesting and even moving play for [...] the Spanish of the seventeenth century." He continues: "We are interested in what all people are like, not what the Spanish wanted to be like [...].".¹¹ Meanwhile, Cervantes, a contemporary of Lope de Vega, "involved hidalgos and graciosos but made them look like universal people, not

---

9 See, for example, Moisey Kagan. ""Meshchanin vo dvoryanstve" Molyera i "Bednost' ne porok" Ostrovskogo" [Molière's *Le Bourgeois gentilhomme* and Ostrovsky's *Poverty Is No Vice*]. *Filologicheskie zapiski* V–VI (1914), pp. 776–792; Nikolay Kashin. "Ostrovskiy i Molyer" [Ostrovsky and Molière]. *Slavia* (1926), pp. 107–135; Jules Patouillet. *Molyer v Rossii* [*Molière in Russia*]. Leningrad: s.n., 1924; Vladimir Rodislavsky. "Molyer v Rossii" [Molière in Russia]. *Russky vestnik* (1872), pp. 38–96.
10 Vsevolod Meyerhold, Valery Bebutov, and Ivan Aksenov. *Amplua aktera* [Typecasting]. Moscow: State Higher Director Workshops, 1922, pp. 6–7.
11 Alexander Ostrovsky. "Luchshiy al'kal'd korol'" [The Best Mayor, The King]. *Polnoe sobranie sochineniy* [Complete Works], vol. 10. Moscow: Iskusstvo, 1978, pp. 529–532, p. 530.

Spanish ones."[12] The latter short quotation probably explains why Ostrovsky resorts to Cervantes' interludes (and not to any other texts by Spanish dramatists) as his specimen of classical Spanish theater.

It should be noted that Ostrovsky made a historical and realia-commentary to Cervantes' interludes. A lot of value (in historical and theatrical terms) can also be found in his observations on the 'nomadic plot' that Cervantes used as the basis for his *The Cave of Salamanca* (*La cueva de Salamanca*). Ostrovsky traced the sequence of theatrical transformations from the fabliau *Le pauvre clerc* to the comic operetta *Soldat magicien*, and then to *Moskal-charivnyk* (*Muscovite Wizard*), an operetta by the Ukrainian playwright Ivan Kotlyarevsky, in which Mikhail Shchepkin played a successful part. However, Ostrovsky's interest in Cervantes was not limited to all of the above. According to the testimonies of his contemporaries, he was going to translate some chapters from *Don Quixote* and a couple of Cervantes' short novels.

Besides, Ostrovsky's own Don Quixotes are at least as curious as his Hamlets. One of the examples is the same tragic Neschastlivtsev from *The Forest*, who is a Hamlet and a Don Quixote in one.[13]

The Italian segment of Ostrovsky's European theatrical pantheon is represented first of all by Carlo Goldoni (translations of *La bottega del caffè*, *Raggeratore*, and *Il vero amico* – the latter two were lost and remained unpublished) and – quite unexpectedly – Carlo Gozzi. In January 1883, Ostrovsky wrote to Pyotr Veinberg, editor of *Izyashchnaya literatura*, who specialized in literary translations:

> Finally, after twenty-five years of futile search all over the Italian libraries, I have found a copy of the complete works by Carlo Gozzi. This curious dramatist is completely unknown in Russia, and even in Europe he is more known for his memoirs than for his plays. Schiller translated one or two, and there are also five or six prosaic translations into French – meanwhile, he is author to fourteen volumes.[14]

In the letter to Anna Mysovskaya mentioned above, Ostrovsky compares Gozzi's talent to that of Molière.[15] Gozzi's fantasies accorded with Ostrovsky's interest in dramatic fairytales (*The Snow Maiden*, *Ivan-Tsarevich*). He translated at least one of Gozzi's *fiabe*, of which he notified Pyotr Veinberg in one of his letters, but literary historians have not reached a consensus as to which of Gozzi's plays he

---

12 Ibid., p. 532.
13 For an overview of critical comments on the Quixotic Neschastlivtsev, see Vsevolod Bagno. *"Don Kikhot" v Rossii i russkoe donkikhotstvo* [Don Quixote *in Russia and Russian Quixotism*]. Saint Petersburg: Nauka, 2009, pp. 123–124.
14 Ostrovsky, *Polnoe sobranie sochineniy*, vol. 12, p. 148.
15 Ibid., pp. 373–374.

was talking about; no finished translation of Gozzi was preserved in Ostrovsky's archives. Pieces of translation can be found in *Il re cervo* and *La donna innamorata da vero* from the collection of Gozzi's plays preserved in Ostrovsky's personal library. More importantly, Russian theoreticians of literature and theater attribute the discovery of Gozzi's dramatic heritage to Vsevolod Meyerhold's circles (in the magazine *Lyubov k trem apelsinam*), dating it back to as late as the 1910s. However, we can see now that Ostrovsky was a step away from this discovery thirty years before that, and only "embarrassment," as he wrote to Veinberg, kept him from publishing an imperfect, in his view, translation of a dramatic fairytale by Gozzi.

To sum up, I should say that the theatrical pantheon Ostrovsky created in his translations, articles, and plays embraces virtually all the eras of European theater from ancient times to the present day, and involves all national schools. His point of view was close to the contemporary understanding of the classical heritage. European dramatists selected by Ostrovsky form the basis of the so-called classical repertoire of modern Russian theater. Being the foundation of the Russian national repertoire, Ostrovsky's plays at the same time represent a method, or form, of digesting the pan-European theatrical heritage.

Natalia V. Sarana
The *Bildungsdrama* and Alexander Ostrovsky's Plays

The term *Bildungsroman* is generally used in the theory of the novel to designate a text that contains a story exploring the formation of a hero. My research works with an understanding of the *Bildungsroman* (or 'novel of formation') as the genre associated with the Golden Age of the European novel in the nineteenth century: a biographical novel, the subject and the content of which is the story of the formation of a character in the process of his interaction with society. The story of this formation reflects the topical moral quest of the time in which the hero lives.[1]

Having studied a corpus of novels written from the 1840s to the 1880s as one megatext of the Russian *Bildungsroman*, I have argued that the *Bildungsroman* was one of the key genres in the Russian literary context of that time, synthesizing European and Russian traditions, shifting and adjusting to the topical issues in Russian society, and possessing a particular pattern, a formula that was perceived by the authors of that time. Building on this previous research,[2] I now wish to approach the question of whether it is possible to apply the notion of *Bildung* to the study of a theatrical work. In other words, I would like to discuss whether one could use the term *Bildungsdrama* when analyzing Russian plays of the nineteenth century in particular. This question remains overlooked in modern literary studies. Nevertheless, there have been attempts to approach the issue of *Bildungsdrama*'s presence (or absence) in literary contexts, and its legitimacy as a concept. In 1976, during the period of revival in *Bildungsroman* theory, Margaret

---

[1] See, for example, the following two studies: Todd Curtis Kontje. *The German Bildungsroman: History of a National Genre*. Columbia, SC: Camden House, 1993; Karl Morgenstern and Tobias Boes. "On the Nature of the '*Bildungsroman*'." *PMLA* 124 (2009), pp. 647–659.
[2] Cf. Natalia V. Sarana. "Russkaya 'Dzhenni Ir': Retseptsiya tvorchestva Sharlotty Bronte v romane YU.V. Zhadovskoy 'Zhenskaya istoriya' (1860)" [The Russian "Jane Eyre": The reception of Charlotte Brontë in Yulia V. Zhadovskaya's novel *Women's History* (1860)]. *Vestnik Moskovskogo universiteta*, seriya 9, *Filologiya* (2018), pp. 173–181; "Angliyskiy 'sopernik' romana Goncharova: obyknovennaya istoriya ili prostaya?" [An English "rival" to Goncharov's novels...] *Vestnik Tverskogo gosudarstvennogo universiteta*, seriya: Filologiya (2017), pp. 262–267; "Angliyskiy 'repertuar' kak element polemicheskoy retseptsii A. F.Pisemskogo" [English "repertoire" as a factor in the polemical reception of Alexey Pisemsky]. *Russkaya filologiya 27: Sbornik nauchnykh rabot molodykh filologov*. Tartu: Tartu University Press, 2016, pp. 82–92; "Anna Karenina, the 'English Novel.': Towards the Study of Anglomania in Leo Tolstoy 's Novel *Anna Karenina*." *ENTHYMEMA* 11 (2014), pp. 58–63.

ⓐ Open Access. © 2019 Natalia V. Sarana, published by De Gruyter. This work is licensed under the Creative Commons Attribution-NonCommercial-NoDerivatives 4.0 License.
https://doi.org/10.1515/9783110604276-012

Scholl was, to our knowledge, the first English-speaking scholar to approach the question why the word "Bildungsdrama" had never been used as a literary term. Her answer is more or less obvious for scholars of the *Bildungsroman*:

> Perhaps that is because of the seeming contradiction in the word itself. "Bildung" implies time, time necessary for a person to mature, and most drama takes place in a matter of hours or at most, days. Even drama that covers a longer period of historical time is limited in stage time. It therefore seems unlikely that the dramatic hero could undergo anything as complex as a "Bildungsprozess" in the short time span covered by the drama.[3]

While pointing out this contradiction, she notes that it should not stop scholars from investigating this genre which, according to Scholl, appeared at the same time as the *Bildungsroman*, in the last part of the eighteenth century. For my research, I am most interested in Scholl's ensuing remark that, paradoxically, the contrasting aspect of time in a novel and in a theatrical work gives the latter the opportunity for just as powerful an idea of *Bildung* as the *Bildungsroman*. Scholl states that "the authors [of drama] intentionally place their heroes in a situation where they must eventually accept the superiority, and the righteousness, of a reality outside themselves."[4] One may say that this "ethical tendency" described by Scholl is almost congenital in Alexander Ostrovsky's plays. Therefore, the purpose of this article is to isolate the idea of *Bildung* from the theory of the novel and to demonstrate that the story of one's development can be told by means of drama. Moreover, it has its precedent in the history of Russian drama from the 1850s to the 1880s.

This article will analyze several plays by Alexander Ostrovsky, among them *Groza* (*The Storm*; 1859), *Zhenit'ba Belugina* (*Belugin's Marriage*; 1877), *Bespridannitsa* (*Without a Dowry*; 1879), and *Bez viny vinovatye* (*Guilty Innocents* or *Innocent as Charged*; 1884). Comparing them will provide insights into the dramatic possibilities of the hero's formation story.

Olga Kuptsova has recently published an article entitled "To Study or to Marry?," in which she uses the term 'educational comedy' when referring to Ostrovsky's comedies that explore the different modes of education that Ostrovsky's heroes receive, as well as the problems of fathers and sons arising from this. While this approach is invaluable for the study of Ostrovsky's idea of education, which he defined within the broader context of educational debates in Russian society of that time, it is proposed within the framework of the current article to shift the focus from the educational system and the debates associated

---

[3] Margaret Scholl. *The Bildungsdrama of the Age of Goethe*. Bern: Lang, 1976, p. 11.
[4] Ibid., p. 12.

with it to the study of a classic hero of a *Bildungsroman* and his/her formation and development.

In analyzing the theories of *Bildung* within the context of drama, one sometimes finds oneself on the borderline between literary studies and drama theory. It could be argued that drama theory may also be of use in the current research. For example, in an article entitled "Exploring the Notion of Bildung in Theatre Work: Conversations with Actors Rehearsing Brecht's *Fatzer*" (2014), Stig A. Eriksson cites the work *Bildning och teater* [*Bildung and Theater*] (2005) by the Swedish theater researcher Alexandra Ahndoril, in which it is hypothesized that the *Bildung* possibilities are endless when it comes to the theater. *Bildning och teater* is Ahndoril's essay on her own experience as a professional actress and author. It provides "a set of deliberations about theater as an educative force."[5]

Eriksson argues that Ahndoril's work provides valuable insights into the educational potential and characteristics of theater which convert it into a force capable of creating the notion of *Bildung*, including appreciating, and engaging in, the experience of others, accepting new circumstances, embracing shifts in perspective, etc. In order to frame the notion of story and exemplification, Ahndoril uses Sophocles' *Oedipus the King* and discusses Oedipus' journey as a form of *Bildung*. Thus, drama theory and practice can provide an additional framework within the context of current research on the notion of *Bildung* in theater works.

Conversely, reference should be made to the Russian drama from the 1860s to the 1880s in order to research the topic of drama and *Bildung* in correlation with the Russian literature of that time. During this period, Ostrovsky was himself researching the psychological and educational possibilities of drama. The ideas of the French Enlightenment and the broader context of the European theory of *Bildung*, including the European *Bildungsroman*, may have had an influence on the educational aspect of Ostrovsky's works.

Several plays by Ostrovsky will now be discussed, to argue that Ostrovsky's works present the key elements of a study of the hero's formation story through dramatic means. The first play I would like to discuss in relation to the aesthetics of *Bildung* is *Zhenit'ba Belugina* (*Belugin's Marriage*). In *Zhenit'ba Belugina*, written in 1877, the process of formation occurs through marriage. Marriage, whether it be the concluding chapter in a story of a woman's life or the challenge she is or is not willing to undertake, always plays the crucial role in the narration of female experience in literary works of the 1800s. Hence, in my view, this play should be

---

5 Stig A. Eriksson. "Exploring the Notion of Bildung in Theatre Work: Conversations with Actors Rehearsing Brecht's *Fatzer*." *Drama Australia National Journal (NJ)* 38 (2014), pp. 8–24, p. 12.

analyzed within the broader process of feminine *Bildung* and its representation in literary works of that time, as actively present in the Russian literary context. In my other work relating to the feminine *Bildungsroman* in the Russian literary context,[6] I have argued that its presence in Russian literature is derived from similar processes occurring in the British literature of that time. In Elaine Hoffman Baruch's article "The Feminine *Bildungsroman*: Education through Marriage," the author argues as follows:

> If the central theme of the *Bildungsroman* is the education of the hero, who is brought to a high level of consciousness through a series of experiences that lead to his development, then many of the great novels that deal with women treat similar themes. From *Emma* to *Jane Eyre* to *Madame Bovary* to *Middlemarch* to *Anna Karenina* to *Portrait of a Lady* to *Lady Chatterley's Lover* and beyond, the novel presents a search for self, an education of the mind and feelings. But unlike the male *Bildungsroman*, the feminine *Bildung* takes place in or on the periphery of marriage. In some cases, the heroines of these novels seek successful marriage, sometimes, as Jane Eyre, they long for 'expanded experience'.[7]

Elena, the bride and wife in *Zhenit'ba Belugina*, agrees to marry Belugin solely for the sake of money, while being persuaded by her lover, Agishin, to start the life of an adulteress. Over the course of the five acts, Elena undergoes a dramatic transformation from a frivolous and greedy young lady to a woman who not only realizes that her not-so-educated merchant husband is far wiser than she is, but also refuses the path of an adulterous lover, saying that, while a mind can be persuaded to do almost anything, the will cannot:

> *Агишин*. Ну, да как хотите рассуждайте; а вы сделали ошибку большую! Задумали-то хорошо, а исполнить – характера не хватило. Вот плоды сентиментального воспитания.
>
> *Елена*. Да, то есть ум-то вы успели во мне развратить, а волю-то не умели – вот вы о чем жалеете! Помешали вам мои хорошие природные инстинкты. А я этому очень рада...[8]
>
> *Agishin*. Well, think as you may; but you made a big mistake! The idea was good, but you lacked the character to carry it out. These are the fruits of sentimental education.
>
> *Elena*. Yes, well you have managed to spoil my mind, but you didn't succeed with my will – this is what you regret! My strong natural instincts didn't let you do it. And I am very happy about it...[9]

---

6 Cf. n.2.
7 Elaine Hoffman Baruch. "The Feminine *Bildungsroman*: Education through Marriage." *The Massachusetts Review* 22 (1981), pp. 335–357, p. 339.
8 Alexander Ostrovsky. *Polnoe Sobranie Sočinenij* [Complete Works], vol. 8. Moscow: s.n., 1950, pp. 213–214.
9 Translations from Ostrovsky's plays are mine.

The topic of feminine *Bildung* is also addressed in plays such as *Groza* (*The Storm*) and *Bespridannitsa* (*Without a Dowry*). These two plays are invaluable to the study of Russian *Bildung* in the context of drama. In these texts, the key conflict results from the necessity of marriage as women's only option to complete their formation. In *Bespridannitsa*, the heroine, Larisa Ogudalova, is forced to get married not only by the social norms of the time, but also by her mother. She is deprived of the right to "the expanded experience," and so the only experience she can afford is that of a marriage:

> Разве мне самой такая жизнь нравилась? Мне было приказано, так нужно было маменьке; значит, волей или неволей, я должна была вести такую жизнь. Вы видите, я стою на распутье; поддержите меня, мне нужно ободрение, сочувствие; отнеситесь ко мне нежно, с лаской! Ловите эти минуты, не пропустите их![10]

> Do you think I liked this sort of life? I was told to live it by my mother, so, whether I want it or not, I have to lead a life like this. You can see I am standing at the crossroads; support me, I need compassion, reassurance; treat me with care and love! Catch these moments, do not miss them!

Unable to break free, or to come to terms with marrying a person who might give her a peaceful life, Larisa's life ends dramatically. In *Groza*, by contrast, the story of the heroine, Katerina, illustrates the future Larisa Ogudalova could have, if she were to enter into marriage willingly:

> *Катерина*. Такая ли я была! Я жила, ни об чем не тужила, точно птичка на воле. Маменька во мне души не чаяла, наряжала меня, как куклу, работать не принуждала; что хочу, бывало, то и делаю [...]. Ничего мне не надобно, всего у меня было довольно. А какие сны мне снились...[...].А то будто я летаю, так и летаю по воздуху. И теперь иногда снится, да редко, да и не то.[11]

> *Katerina*. How different I used to be! I lived without a care in my heart, as free as a bird. Mother adored me, dressed up like a doll, and never forced me to work; I could do just as I liked [...]. I wanted nothing, I had enough of everything. And what dreams I used to have... [...] Sometimes I seemed to be flying, simply flying in the air. I dream sometimes now, but not often, and never dreams like those.

Katerina begins to realize that she cannot live under her present circumstances. Although she appears to be fond of her husband, she is not granted the opportunity to embrace her own development:

---

[10] Alexander Ostrovsky. *Polnoe Sobranie Sočinenij* [Complete Works], vol. 10. Moscow: s.n., 1951, pp. 169–170.
[11] Alexander Ostrovsky. *Polnoe Sobranie Sočinenij* [Complete Works], vol. 2. Moscow: s.n., 1950, pp. 222–223.

> *Катерина*. Сделается мне так душно, так душно дома, что бежала бы. И такая мысль придёт на меня, что, кабы моя воля, каталась бы я теперь по Волге, на лодке, с песнями, либо на тройке на хорошей, обнявшись...¹²
>
> Katerina: I am stifled, stifled at home, I should like to run away. And the fancy comes to me that if I were my own mistress, I would float down the Volga now, in a boat, to the singing of songs, or I would, I would drive right away clasped close...

When discussing the key *Bildung* features present in Ostrovsky's plays, it may be argued that *Bez viny vinovatye (Guilty Innocents)* serves as the most elaborate example of theatrical works constructed around the notion of *Bildung*. As opposed to the plays discussed earlier in this paper, *Bez viny vinovatye* not only follows the idea of a hero's formation, but also uses methods that bring it closer than any other play by Ostrovsky to a classic *Bildungsroman*.

The play follows the story of a heroine called Otradina, who later appears in the text as Kruchinina. Ostrovsky depicts the full story of the heroine's formation, paralleling the key element of a *Bildungsroman*. The readers first meet Otradina as a young girl who is on the verge of a personal drama: she is soon left by her lover and has to suffer through the death of their child. It is worth noting that money as the root of all evil (here, Otradina's inability to marry the man she loves) is perceived in this context, as well as in many other Ostrovsky plays, as the misfortune that sets the hero's formation story in motion. The story of Otradina then breaks off for seventeen years, up until the moment when she returns to her hometown disguised as the famous actress Kruchinina. She has already gone through the key stages in the classic story of a hero's development.

In his study *The Way of the World: The Bildungsroman in European Culture*,¹³ Franco Moretti hints that the *Bildungsroman* follows the structure of a fairytale, the morphology of which was developed in a fundamental work by Vladimir Propp. Applying Propp's definition of a fairytale to the story of Kruchinina's life clarifies the patterns of her development. She has undergone the journey, characterized in a Russian idiom as a journey through "fire, water, and brass pipes," in which the brass pipes stand for fame or flattery. Having first been cheated on by her lover, having then lost her child, she has become a successful actress, yet she continues to be a humble and generous woman. Seventeen years later, her story of development is nearly completed. This sequence of events culminates in a dramatic moment in which the heroine of the story finally receives her reward. It comes in the form of divine providence, namely in the figure of her son who was hitherto thought to be dead. Neznamov, one of the actors in

---

12 Ostrovsky, *Polnoe Sobranie Sočinenij*, vol. 2, p. 223.
13 London: Verso, 1987.

the local theater, turns out to be her son. Although the main function of that character in Ostrovsky's play is that of rewarding Kruchinina with the return of her child, he is also described as a hero in his own right, having gone through a classic story of development. Neznamov's story is told to Kruchinina by one of his fellow actors:

> *Дудукин.* Я изложу вам краткую биографию его, как он мне сам передавал. Ни отца, ни матери он не помнит и не знает, рос и воспитывался он где-то далеко, чуть не на границах Сибири, в доме каких-то бездетных, но достаточных супругов из мира чиновников, которых долгое время считал за родителей. Его любили, с ним обращались хорошо, хотя не без того чтобы под сердитую руку не попрекнуть его незаконным происхождением. Разумеется, он их слов не понимал и разобрал их значение только впоследствии. Его даже учили: он бегал в какой-то дешевенький пансион и получил порядочное для провинциального артиста образование. Так он прожил лет до пятнадцати, потом начались страдания, о которых он без ужаса вспомнить не может. Чиновник умер, а вдова его вышла замуж за отставного землемера, пошло бесконечное пьянство, ссоры и драки, в которых прежде всего доставалось ему. Его прогнали в кухню и кормили вместе с прислугой; часто по ночам его выталкивали из дому, и ему приходилось ночевать под открытым небом. А иногда от брани и побоев он и сам уходил и пропадал по неделе, проживал кой-где с поденщиками, нищими и всякими бродягами, и с этого времени, кроме позорной брани, он уж никаких других слов не слыхал от людей. В такой жизни он озлобился и одичал до того, что стал кусаться как зверь. Наконец, в одно прекрасное утро его из дому совсем выгнали; тогда он пристал к какой-то бродячей труппе и переехал с ней в другой город. Оттуда его, за неимение законного вида, отправили по этапу на место жительства. Документы его оказались затерянными; волочили, волочили его, наконец выдали какую-то копию с явочного прошения, с которой он и стал переезжать с антрепренерами из города в город, под вечным страхом, что каждую минуту полиция может препроводить его на родину.[14]

> *Dudukin.* I am going to present a short biography of him, as he told it to me. He remembers neither his father nor mother, he was raised somewhere far away, almost on the borders of Siberia, in the house of a childless but quite wealthy couple from the class of officials, whom he took for his parents for a long time. He was loved, he was treated well, although not without being reproached for his illegal origin on occasion. Of course, he did not understand their words until later in his life. He was even educated; he went to some cheap boarding school and got a decent education for a provincial actor. In such a way he spent his last fifteen years, then sufferings began which he cannot recall without horror. The officer died, and his widow married a retired surveyor who would drink, quarrel, and fight endlessly. He, Neznamov, bore the brunt of the situation. He was sent into the kitchen to live together with the servants; at night, they often threw him out of the house, and he had to spend the night on the streets. And sometimes, tired of abuse and beatings, he went away of his own

---

14 Alexander Ostrovsky. *Polnoe Sobranie Sočinenij* [Complete Works], vol. 9. Moscow: s.n., 1951, pp. 168–169.

volition and vanished for a week, living here and there with the day laborers, beggars, and all sorts of vagrants. And from that time on, he heard no words from other people except for shameful swearing and cursing. Because of this life, he became embittered and got so wild that he could bite like an animal. Finally, one morning he was kicked out of the house for good; then he joined some wandering troupe and moved to another city. From there he was, for lack of a legal residence-permit, sent under escort to his place of residence. His documents turned out to be lost; he was dragged and dragged about, until he was finally given [the required papers], with which he began to move [...] from city to city, under the perpetual fear that at any moment the police might transmit him to his homeland.

Neznamov's development is subsequently presented in more detail in the text. He starts to travel with a theater troupe from town to town. This part of Neznamov's journey resembles the story of the classic *Bildungsroman*, namely Goethe's *Wilhelm Meister*. Neznamov's journey, recounted in one passage by his fellow actor, corresponds to the most basic plot of a *Bildungsroman*. The only point lacking in his story of development is the end. Oppressed and disappointed throughout his journey, he finally receives a hero's reward, namely the "mother's touch," the reunion with his biological mother, which brings not only his own story of formation, but also Kruchinina's journey to a close.

In conclusion, I would like to emphasize that the drama of *Bildung*, or the *Bildungsdrama*, the term I would propose in this context, can be analyzed from an educational point of view as a dramatic debate on the contemporary educational system. In the present paper, an attempt has been made to demonstrate that the textual analysis of a hero's upbringing and formation can be illustrated and achieved by dramatic means, thus contributing to the debate on whether the idea of *Bildung* is only present within the context of a *Bildungsroman* or may also be achieved in other literary genres. I would argue that the texts by Ostrovsky discussed above prove the latter claim correct.

Gautam Chakrabarti
"Sail[ing] on the Pathless Deep": Michael Madhusudan Datta's Dramatic Entanglements

Michael Madhusudan Datta (1824–1873) was a pioneering Indian dramatist who wrote in both English and Bengali, and the first great canonical poet of modern Bengali literature. Datta's was a fluid, flamboyant, and rather scattered personality and he was a polyglot, being fluent in English, Bengali, Sanskrit, Tamil, Greek, Latin, Italian, and French. Bankim Chandra Chatterjee, India's first great novelist, said that "to Homer and Milton, as well as to Valmiki, he is largely indebted, and his poem [*The Slaughter of Meghnad*] is on the whole the most valuable work in modern Bengali literature."[1] Datta's major works, written mostly between 1858 and 1862, consist of prose drama, long narrative poems and lyrical poetry. As a nineteenth-century classicist, he handled the mythological narratives that formed his intellectual inheritance with a vigorous methodological freshness: *Meghnād Badh Kābya* (*The Epic on the Slaughter of Meghnād*, 1861), a tragic epic in nine cantos, is deemed to be his masterpiece and is path-breaking in Bengali literature both stylistically and content-wise. Though the story of its publication and reach is anything but smooth and it took some years for its nationwide recognition, Datta, with its eventual acceptance, earned for himself acknowledgment as a serious practitioner of an entirely new form of heroic poetry, which was both Homeric and Dantesque in technique and style, and yet, thematically, so fundamentally Indian, something Sri Aurobindo does in the next century with *The Life Divine*. In the words of Lord Byron, who appears to have deeply influenced

---

[1] This quote is taken from Sri Chinmoy (*Mother India's Lighthouse: India's Spiritual Leaders*). Jamaica Agni, 1971). Cf. http://www.srichinmoylibrary.com/books/3004/1/11/index.html. Accessed 23 July 2018.

Note: All translations, unless it is mentioned otherwise, are by the present author.
The quote in the title is taken from Act I, Scene 1 of *Sermista*, the English version, done by Datta himself, of his Bengali play *Śarmiṣṭhā* (1859): "When a merchant, noble Sovereign, sails on the pathless Deep with his argoise laden with priceless gems and gold and silver [...]?" (Michael Madhusudan Datta. *Madhusudan Racanābalī* ["Collected Works of Madhusudan"], edited by Kshetra Gupta. Kolkata: Sahitya Samsad, 2012, p. 666.)

Open Access. © 2019 Gautam Chakrabarti, published by De Gruyter. This work is licensed under the Creative Commons Attribution-NonCommercial-NoDerivatives 4.0 License.
https://doi.org/10.1515/9783110604276-013

Datta – personally and stylistically – and was often quoted by him: "I awoke one morning and found myself famous."[2]

He also wrote beautiful poems about the sufferings and travails of love as articulated by women, making him one of the first writers anywhere to 'gender' the representation of feeling. His lyrics on the mythopoeic love of Radha and Krishna are considered a significant improvement, both structurally and in content, on the medieval corpus of Bengali *Vaiṣṇava*[3] poetry. He has also bequeathed to Bengali literature a cluster of one hundred and two sonnets and provides the modern reader with a rather disarmingly opinionated glimpse on nineteenth-century Calcutta through his countless letters, mostly to friends and well-wishers, which he wrote in English. As a playwright, he laid the foundations of modern Bengali dramaturgy, not only through the introduction of Europhone generic and technical novelties but also through the reconfiguration of classical Sanskritic mythopoeic constellations as tropes of the socio-cultural regeneration of colonial Bengal and India. Though an exhaustive research design, which could do justice to the immense versatility of Datta's oeuvre, is beyond the scope of the current essay, one would like to indicate – admittedly in a rather prolegomenous fashion – the depth and fecundity of Datta's interweaving of the 'historical' with the 'mythological.' Thus, it could be possible to theorize his dramaturgical

---

2 This quote is taken from Byron's "*memoranda*," as attributed to the poet by Thomas Moore (*Life of Lord Byron: With His Letters and Journals*, vol. II. London: John Murray, 1854. http://www.gutenberg.org/files/16570/16570.txt. Accessed 23 July 2018). Byron was referring to the critical acclaim, which was not unlike that received by Datta for the *Meghnād Badh Kābya*, accorded to the first two cantos of *Childe Harold's Pilgrimage*, a work quite popular in Datta's intellectual circle.
3 The word *vaiṣṇava* means "adherent and worshipper of Viṣṇu," one of the so-called Hindu Holy Trinity, who is supposed to be the upholder of the Cosmic System, being its preserver and protector: "Vaiṣṇavism has developed the most variegated and richest mythology of all the schools of Hinduism. At the core of Vaiṣṇavism, however, is Lord Viṣṇu as Savior, a belief that, again, has found expression in countless myths" (Klaus K. Klostermaier. *A Survey of Hinduism*. Albany: State University of New York Press, 2007, p. 228). The *vaiṣṇava*-s, cutting across their sectarian dogmatic specificities, believe in the primacy of the divine love between Śrī Viṣṇu, as Himself and in his various *avatāra*-s (quotidian/mortal reincarnations) like Rāma and Kṛṣṇa, and His Divine Consort, Śrī Lakṣmī, as a determinant of the love between the Deity and humanity. Hence, *vaiṣṇava*-s, throughout the history of Indian literature, have come up with considerable works of lyrical poetry and verse-drama that locate amorous love, especially between divine and semi-divine figures, within the normative discourse of religiosity. Eastern India had seen a number of major epics, like Jayadeva's twelfth-century text *Gitagovindam*, being composed in the medieval period. Datta, despite his conversion to Christianity, appreciated the immense literary value of this poetic inheritance and used and reworked the rich poetic techniques and metaphoric and metonymic schemes handed down through it. At the same time, he also introduced new Europhone literary forms in Bengal, like the blank verse in his play *Sermista*.

and broader literary-cultural contributions to the process of canonical consolidation in post/colonial India through the prism of cultural historiography. In this context, his work in reconfiguring classical Sanskritic myths and other literary narratives into 'vernacular' canonical texts in early-colonial Bengal is significant both in terms of the development of what may be called 'colonial modernity' and the gradual evolution of national/ist cultural expression/s. Datta's plays and his dramaturgical praxes, thus, serve as discursive models for the entangled process through which history and drama permeate each other.

Datta's education had started at an old village mosque, where he was taught Persian, as was the custom of the time. He was a brilliant and creative student, who was reputed to be "a precocious child with a gift of literary expression."[4] An early exposure to English education and European literature at home and in Calcutta molded his literary tastes on Anglophone lines, making him take on English tastes, manners, and intellectual attitudes. His teachers at Hindu College, Calcutta, the cultural incubator of the Western-educated Bengali middle class, especially Captain David Richardson (1801–65), a Professor of English and an active Freemason and Utilitarian, were a significant formative influence, and Datta adopted his support of Thomas B. Macaulay's "Minute upon Indian Education" (1835) without, apparently, understanding its full significance. Capt. Richardson seems, as Sivanath Sastri notes, to have become "so intoxicated while discussing Shakespeare that his students came to believe firmly that there was no poet equal to Shakespeare and no literature equal to that of the English."[5] Datta, though belonging to the Hindu landed aristocracy – having been born to an esteemed lawyer and his wife – converted to Christianity in 1843 at the Fort William Church, despite staunch family-opposition and social opprobrium, and the resultant alienation, and took the added first name Michael.

Datta dreamt of immense fame if he went abroad to England, to the part of the planet that, from his adolescence, he was convinced he belonged to, not least due to what he – and many others like him – saw as the spirit of fresh intellectual and cultural inquiry. He drew the conclusion that conservative Hindu society in early nineteenth-century Bengal and, by extension, India had not yet evolved sufficiently to understand and appreciate a spirit of rationalistic inquiry and intellectual eclecticism. This, he opined, would hinder his chance of public appreciation in India. He, initially, firmly believed that the 'free thinking' and post-Enlightenment West would be more appreciative of his talents and composed his

---

4 Zinia Mitra. *Indian Poetry in English: Critical Essays*. New Delhi: PHI Learning, 2012, p. 35.
5 Sivanath Sastri. *Rāmtanu Lāhiḍi o Tatkālīn Banga Samāj* ["Ramtanu Lahiri and the Contemporary Bengali Society"], edited by Barid Baran Ghosh. 1904. Calcutta: New Age, 2009, p. 113.

early works – both poetry and drama – almost entirely in English. Given their lack of success, he later shifted, though with initial reluctance, to Bengali. This shift could have been influenced by, among other things, his second partner Henrietta, "a Frenchwoman deeply enamored of Bengal and the Bangla language."[6] Also, when one of his friends had presented *The Captive Ladie*, Datta's best-known English narrative poem, to John E. Drinkwater Bethune, the then Secretary for Education in Bengal, this is what the latter had commented:

> he could render far greater service to his country and have a better chance of achieving a lasting reputation for himself, if he will employ the taste and talents, which he has cultivated by the study of English, in improving the Standard and adding to the stock of the poems of his own language [...].[7]

This seems to have produced a lasting impression on him, as he was already asking a friend, on 14 February 1849, to send him "a copy of the Bengali translation of the Mahabharut by Casidoss as well as a ditto of the Ramayana,– Serampore edition."[8] He began to consider the scope of expanding and enriching his literary tastes with the study of major European and Indian languages, ancient and modern, and wrote to his friend, on 18 August 1849: "[...] I devote several hours daily to Tamil. [...] Here is my routine; 6 to 8 Hebrew, 8 to 12 School, 12–2 Greek, 2–5 Telugu and Sanskrit, 5–7 Latin, 7–10 English. Am I not preparing for the great object of embellishing the tongue of my fathers?"[9]

Datta studied at the Bishop's College, in Calcutta, after he converted and could no longer continue at the Hindu College. However, despite an added emphasis on Classical Greek, Latin, and Hebrew in the former, both these pioneering institutions had curricula, taught mostly by British educationists, that were deeply rooted in the Europhone tradition. It is also necessary to point out that though his intense passion for European literature and culture and undying aspiration towards 'Englishness' may have driven him towards Christianity, he genuinely did not, as he wrote to his friend Gour Dass Bysack on 15 May 1860, seem to have "care[d] a pin's head for Hinduism,[despite] lov[ing] the grand mythology of our ancestors."[10] One could argue, with Amit Chaudhuri, that, "in India, such

---

6 Sheldon Pollock. *Literary Cultures in History: Reconstructions from South Asia*. Berkeley: University of California Press, 2003, p. 228.
7 Datta, *Racanābalī*, p. xv.
8 Ibid., Letter 36, p. 510.
9 Ibid., Letter 42, p. 516.
10 Ibid., Letter 58, p. 525.

journeys and disquiets [with cultural and linguistic inheritances] largely begin"[11] with Datta. He calls Datta "the first figure to give literary history in India, in effect, a sense of theatre," with "his life and practice form[ing] a parable of inner and actual exile, a negotiation between the 'civilized' and the 'barbaric.'"[12]

However, it may be useful to take another look at the extent to which this exteriorized negotiation between the 'old,' Hindu patrimony of the early-colonial, western-educated, bourgeois Indian elites and the 'new' life they clearly aspire to is, in fact, a function of their pre-configuration of the discourses of secular Indian nationalism, as Chaudhuri seems to suggest. The remarkable processes of, at first, "a rejection, or disowning, of the polytheistic, idolatrous aspects of Hinduism" and, then, "of the intermittently comic, but nevertheless seminal, radicalism of Young Bengal, of the breaking of dietary and religious taboos, of social reform," could not have – as they seem to have done, almost without much ado – led to the effective crystallization of what Chaudhuri calls "a relationship between identity, rebellion, creativity, and the subconscious."[13] It does seem that, in this tussle between "public acts of disowning and recovery,"[14] the categorical reassertion of the older, more traditional modes of religious and cultural self-expression, though nuanced through their often, though not always, adversarial engagement with the new ideas of Europhone radicalism, points more towards the 'old' picking and choosing from the 'new,' to address the need to reinvent itself in keeping with the demands of the times. This is nowhere more self-evident than in the manner in which classical Indian drama was, in early- and mid-nineteenth century Calcutta, considerably enriched by cross-fertilization with the floating cultural material of Europhone dramatic techniques and theatergrams that had come calling with British ascendancy.

In his poetry, too, Datta takes his themes mostly from classical Indian texts, mostly Sanskrit epics like the *Rāmāyaṇa*, but often inverts the creative perspective, so as to focus on the marginalized and peripheral figures and narratives in those texts. In his best-known work *Meghnād Badh Kābya*, the first 'modern' Bengali epic, he takes the secondary tale of Meghanāda, the favorite son of the demon-king Rāvaṇa and an accomplished warrior, and makes him and his father the heroic figures. Meghanāda, in the original Sanskrit epic, died in battle with Rāma due to an unethical – according to epic battle-conventions – maneuver by

---

[11] Amit Chaudhuri. *Clearing a Space: Reflections on India, Literature, and Culture*. Oxford: Peter Lang, 2008, p. 39.
[12] Ibid., p. 40.
[13] Ibid.
[14] Ibid.

Rāma's soldiers, who were normatively seen to be fighting for T/truth and J/justice and, therefore, traditionally seen as the epic heroes despite their occasional lapses from the code of heroic conduct. According to Ashis Nandy, Datta was led to do this by his clear admiration of Rāvaṇa's "masculine vigor, accomplished warriorhood, and his sense of *realpolitik* and history; he accepted Ravana's 'adult' and 'normal' commitments to secular, possessive this-worldliness and his consumer's lust for life."[15] Nandy interprets this as – in the contemporaneous context of British governmental power still being "a manageable vector within India"[16] – Datta's "attempt to explain the West in Indian terms and to incorporate it in the Indian culture as an unavoidable experience."[17]

Thus, Datta's 'rebellion,' though clear and even abrasive, is one that seems to be more integrative than disruptive, if one does not view subversion as, necessarily, ever disruptive and a corollary to a total negation of the traditional. One sees the rebellion that Chaudhuri identifies, as mentioned above, but feels that the frames of reference, within which the romantic, even Byronic, heroism of Meghanāda is depicted, are decidedly classical Indian. If one were to venture a deconstructive reading of Datta's subtextual self-identification/s, Meghanāda, whatever be his un/just causes and actions, remains, like the poet himself, though "Christianize[d]," "Hindu".[18] His prism, however, was certainly not that of a traditionalist Hindu "or at least a person treating the tradition respectfully."[19] Inspired by his rebellious instincts, Datta effects numerous plot- and character-inversions in order to subvert the religious aspect of the traditional narrative, "depriving Rāma and Lakṣmaṇa of any divine halo and changing Rāvaṇa and his beloved son Meghanāda into real heroes."[20] In this, his work was of pioneering significance, especially in the contested domain of the secularization of the Hindu literary-mythopoeic canon "and its liberation from the traditional bonds with religion."[21] He veritably blazed a trail for his numerous antecedents, who were shown

---

15 Ashis Nandy. *The Intimate Enemy: Loss and Recovery of Self under Colonialism*. New Delhi: Oxford University Press, 1983, p. 20.
16 Ibid.
17 Ibid., p. 22.
18 Datta asserts, in the last paragraph of his long speech *The Anglo-Saxon and the Hindu*, "It is the glorious mission, I repeat, of the Anglo-Saxon to renovate, to regenerate, or– in one word, to Christianize the Hindu" (*Racanābalī*, p. 608).
19 Dušan Zbavitel. *Bengali Literature: A History of Indian Literature*, vol. IX, edited by Jan Gonda. Wiesbaden: Otto Harrassowitz, 1976, p. 233.
20 Ibid.
21 Ibid.

the exciting mimetic possibilities in the literary-cultural narratives of India's past and, crucially, how to deploy them in the modern post/colonial context.

Another theory, which needs to be engaged with before considering Datta's plays, especially points out his aversion towards "caste-based endogamous marriage"[22] and ascribes his decision to convert to a move by his parents to arrange a custom-sanctioned match for him. This is, perhaps, understandable in view of his avid enthusiasm for European culture and the socio-cultural openness it had begun to generate at the time. He married Rebecca McTavish, the daughter of an indigo planter of Scottish origin, and had four children with her, as he wrote to Bysack on 20 December 1855.[23] Later, he separated from her and married Henrietta Sophia White, who is said to have been of French origin and was the daughter of a professor at the Madras Presidency College. This marriage lasted till the end of his life, even in times of dire and ceaseless poverty, often caused by his endemic insolvency, in London, Paris, Versailles, and Calcutta. This forced him to seek the support of his Calcutta-based friends and well-wishers, most notably Īśvar Candra Vidyāsāgar, the eminent Bengali Sanskritist, educational and social reformer and philanthropist.[24] From very early on, he had Anglophone

---

22 Mitra, *Indian Poetry in English*, p. 33.
23 "Yes, dearest Gour, I have a fine English Wife and four children" (Datta, *Racanābalī*, Letter 44, p. 517). Vinay Dharwadker writes that she was "a Scottish inmate of the girls' hostel at the [Church of England's Madras Male and Female Orphan] Asylum" and "[d]uring the next eight years [they] had four children and lived on his limited income," which came from teaching at the boys' free day-school in the Asylum and journalism, since his father had, earlier, stopped his allowance (Pollock, *Literary Cultures*, p. 228). – This and other biographical details have been sourced from Dharwarker's essay "The Historical Formation of Indian-English Literature" (see Pollock, pp. 226–230). See also John B. Alphonso-Karkala. *Indo-English Literature in the Nineteenth Century.* Mysore: Literary Half-Yearly, University of Mysore, 1970; Amalendu Bose. *Michael Madhusudan Dutt.* New Delhi: Sahitya Akademi, 1981; Kshetra Gupta. "Madhusudan Datta: Life-Story." *Racanābalī*, pp. xi–xxiv.
24 Īśvar Candra Bandopādhyāy (1820–91), better known by his honorific *upādhi* (title and/or surname earned by a display of major educational aptitude and merit, especially in the field of traditional Sanskrit Studies in India) *Vidyāsāgara* (meaning "Sea of Knowledge"), was one of – often the only one – of Michael Madhusudan Datta's consistent benefactors. As their ample correspondence – between London, Paris and Versailles, where Datta had stayed at various times, and Calcutta, where Vidyāsāgar was based – shows, the latter took a personal and engaged interest in the material subsistence of Datta and his family. This was born out of Vidyāsāgar's great personal love for Datta and appreciation of the work he was doing for Bengali literature and culture, given the former's vigorous and steadfast interest in social and educational reform in India. In his personal life and belief-systems, Vidyāsāgar was a confirmed rationalist and even something of a sceptic, despite his Brahminical and traditionalist upbringing and education, and tried, throughout his life, to reconcile classical Hindu noetic and theological frameworks

socio-cultural aspirations but, later in life, he regretted this attraction to the Occident and even attempted to arrive at a stylistic balance. Many intensely emotional sonnets and other poems date from this period and he even goes on to write: "If there be any one among us anxious to leave a name behind him, and not pass away into oblivion like a brute, let him devote himself to his mother tongue. That is his legitimate sphere, his proper element."[25]

Datta was one of the pioneers of Bengali drama and, arguably, the most important, having played what some historians have called a 'historical' role in its growth and evolution. Kshetra Gupta credits him with the "establishment of the occidental dramatic idiom"[26] in India, with interventions in the form of introducing the first historical play, significant tragedy, and Europhone farce. His early works, including *Śarmiṣṭhā* and another play called *Ratnāvali*, literary translations like that of the *Nīl Darpaṇ* by Dinabandhu Mitra and – not to overlook his primary creative self, that of a poet – poems like the *Captive Ladie*, which was written about the mother of his close friend Bhudev Mukhopadhyay, demonstrate immense intellectual sophistication. This creative achievement was not always effortless and uncomplicated, especially in the delicate negotiations that had to be carried out between the demands of Sanskritic dramaturgy. These stylistic maneuvers were, occasionally, forced upon him by considerations of audience-responses and the tastes and limitations of his patrons, notably the Belgāchiā Theatre,[27] which was managed by people who did not always appreciate Datta's overt Occidentalism. In fact, in his own words, "he was too early for the age"[28] and his extensive introduction of European stage-techniques and generic specificities in his plays, were, more often than not, frowned upon and even derided as irreverent.

---

with the demands of Europhone modernity. In Bengal, his name is almost a byword for boundless philanthropy – despite great personal poverty or financial limitations – erudition, selflessness, and strength of character. Datta, in many of his letters to Vidyāsāgar and others, appears beholden to him. On 2 June 1864, he writes to the latter: "You are the only friend who can rescue me from th[is] painful position... and in this, you must go to work with that grand energy which is the companion of your genius and manliness of heart" (Datta, *Racanābalī*, Letter 95, p. 555).
25 Arabinda Poddāra. *Renaissance in Bengal: Quests and Confrontations, 1800–1860*. Shimla: Indian Institute of Advanced Study, 1970, p. 216.
26 Datta, *Racanābalī*, p. xlvii.
27 The so-called "Belgāchiā Theatre," which was located in a neighbourhood still called Belgāchiā, was one of Calcutta's first suburban garden-house stages, which was patronized by Iśvar Chandra Singha, the Rājā (King) of Pāikpārā, who became one of Datta's staunchest friends.
28 Datta, *Racanābalī*, p. xlviii.

His first play, *Śarmiṣṭhā* (1859), first written in Bengali, apparently in 1858,[29] though performed and "also translated into English by the author himself"[30] as *Sermista* in 1859, is based on an episode from the ancient Sanskrit epic, the *Mahābhārata*. It was first performed at the Belgāchiā Theatre on 3 September 1859, with the English version of the play being distributed to the European visitors, and "[t]he audience on the first night gave a very cordial reception to the play."[31] The play presents the story of a tussle between two women, one sacerdotal and the other aristocratic, against the backdrop of the rivalry between the Gods and Datta's Titans. It was replete with contextualized rhetorical embellishments and Datta's encoding of the same sort of assertive valorization into the demonic characters – the so-called "Asuras or Titans"[32] of his English translation – in it as in the *Meghnād Badh Kābya*. It develops the well-known legendary narrative, recurring in the *Mahābhārata* and various *Purāṇa*-s,[33] of the mythical king Yayati (Yayāti, son of Nahuṣ), who was forced to age prematurely by the sage Sucracharya's (Śukrācārya) curse, and the crisis that was caused in his kingdom by his love for his wife Devayani (Devayānī), the sage's daughter, and his passion for and relationship with Sermista (Śarmiṣṭhā),[34] a princess of the Asuras, given an old quarrel between the two women. Datta seems to emphasize the personal

---

29 According to Kshetra Gupta, "it appears, after reading a letter[, dated 16 July 1858,] from Jatindramohan Thākur to Gaurdās Basāk, that the play had been completed" on that date. Thākur (Anglicized: Tagore) writes, in this letter, that he is "very anxious to have a perusal of your friend's manuscript drama, for I am pretty sure that he who wields his pen with such elegance and facility in a foreign language may contribute something to the meagre literature of his own country, which cannot but be prized by all" (Datta, *Racanābalī*, p. xlviii).
30 Zbavitel, *Bengali Literature*, p. 232.
31 Prabhucharan Guha-Thakurta. *The Bengali Drama*. 1930. London: Routledge, 2000, pp. 78–79.
32 In the literary traditions of Sanskritic demonology, *asura*-s, *rākṣasa*-s and *daitya*-s, despite being generically categorizable as demons, refer to different levels of monstrosity and antagonism to the Vedic Gods. While only *daitya*-s, being usually of large, even gigantic proportions, could be compared to the classical European Titans, Datta seems to use these terms rather freely and interchangeably in his translation.
33 The *Purāṇa*-s (= "of ancient times") are ancient post-Vedic and even early-medieval Sanskrit texts, which are widely accessible through culturally-significant medieval translations in almost all the major vernacular languages of the Subcontinent. They deal with the genealogies of the various Hindu Deities, semi-divine monarchs and heroic figures, along with their respective families and clans, sages, and savants, for which they have been called "the true Bibles of Hinduism" (Klostermaier, *Survey*, p. 15). They also serve as compendia that structure ancient and medieval knowledge of Hindu cosmogony, philosophy, and sacred geography.
34 *Sermista* is the Anglicized form, as used by Datta in the English version of the play, of Śarmiṣṭhā.

rivalry, leading to intense animosity, between the two main female characters; but he does so with considerable sensitivity.

The play begins with Vakasura (Vakāsura), a heroic demon-warrior, informing another demon, who is serving as a border-guard and spying on the city of the Gods, the sworn enemies of the Asuras, about the terrible news that was shaking their kingdom. The king's beloved daughter Sermista, while engaged in a juvenile argument with her friend Devayani, pushed the latter into a dark pit (a "well" in the Bengali version); she is rescued from there by Yayati, who was passing by during a royal hunt. Devayani's father Sucracharya, who is the supreme spiritual guide or *guru* of the Asuras, was so enraged by this humiliation of his daughter that he demanded, from the Asura-King, whom he bullied into abject submission by threatening to desert them – something that would certainly lead to their decimation by the Gods – that Sermista become Devayani's slave. Though the King is loath to banish his daughter to such a fate, he is pressurized by his Minister and his sense of his royal duties to agree to this demand. Sermista accepts her lot and joins Devayani's household in her new state of abject servitude. Devayani's earlier humiliation seems to have changed her destiny: having been saved from the dark pit by the mighty king Yayati, she fell in love with him the moment she saw his face. However, Devayani has no legitimate hopes of marrying him as a union between a Brāhmaṇa girl and a Kṣatrīya king would, normally, be unacceptable. Her father, nevertheless, gladly agrees to give her in marriage to Yayati, as he perceives him to be a spiritually gifted ruler, who, more than once, proved himself to be a true defender of Dharma, the code of Righteousness and Justice that is central to Indic socio-religious thought. The King is also happy to make Devayani the Queen of Prātiṣṭhāna, as he has also fallen deeply in love with her.

However, after marrying Devayani, Yayati spotted the princess of the Asuras among her maids, who constituted her dowry, and her beauty made him fall in love with her. Sermista reciprocates and becomes Yayati's second wife and they even have three children together. Their almost idyllic relationship, kept a secret from the Queen, lasts for many years, but one day the truth is revealed to her accidentally. Hurt, devastated, and craving for revenge, Devayani leaves the palace and begs her mighty father, the sage Sucracharya, to curse Yayati with premature old age. Consequently, the King becomes decrepit and ill, which brings his kingdom to near chaos. This is the occasion for Devayani to reconsider her actions and responses: she is remorseful for her ill temper and asks her father to recall the curse. However, as curses like this one are irreversible, Sucracharya is unable to oblige her and can only modify it: the King will be given his youth back only in case any of his children agreed to bear the curse, for a thousand years, in his place. None of Devayani's progeny agrees to do this and it is left to the youngest of Sermista's children, Puru, to offer to save his father. Sucracharya realizes the events that have been leading to this moment are not random, but have been arranged by Fate, for Puru is destined to become the king of the world. Eventually, the King recovers his youth and the sage releases Sermista from her bondage to his daughter and both Devayani and she reign as Queens beside Yayati.

In his "Reminiscences of Michael Madhusudan Dutta," Gour Dass Bysack attributes the origin of the play to a conversation between Datta and himself about the paucity of good Bengali plays worthy of the Belgāchiā Theatre:

> I laughed at the idea of his offering to write a Bengali play, and chaffingly asked if it was his wish to see us introduce a wretched Vidya Sundar on our stage. Conscious of the dearth of really good plays in language [sic], he could not but feel the sting of my remark as a home-thrust and simply muttered, "we shall see, we shall see." [...] [I]n the course of a week or two [he] read to me the first few scenes of his Sarmishta which struck to me as having the ring of true metal.[35]

Thus, it does appear that Datta did have a pioneering motivation in writing this play and went about it with the hands-on approach of a literary apprentice, having borrowed "a few Vernacular and Sanskrit books, dramas specially"[36] from Bysack and resolved to give the Bengali-speaking stage its hybrid bridge to the future of the past.

One of the key thematic constellations in *Śarmiṣṭhā* is that of the rivalry and ill-feeling between two powerful female characters that seem to be locked in what are, basically, ego-clashes. From this perspective, one European play that parallels, in this thematic orientation and also in the dramatic resolution in its *dénouement*, is Friedrich Schiller's *Maria Stuart* (1800), a play consisting of five acts, each of which is sub-divided into numerous scenes. The first English translation of the play seems to be that of Joseph Mellish, "who appears to have been on terms of intimate friendship with Schiller."[37] He made his translation, apparently, from the pre-publication prompt-copy and, as Samuel Taylor Coleridge had done with Schiller's *Wallenstein* trilogy, made a number of his own interpolations while omitting a number of passages from the German original. Mellish's own creative interventions, in the English version of the play, as with the Coleridgean ones in the *Wallenstein* trilogy, were not without a certain degree of accomplished craftsmanship and a sensitive appreciation of his friend's artistic proclivities. It is quite possible, even to a degree of certainty, that Datta had familiarized himself with this English version of Schiller's *Maria Stuart* during his voracious engagement

---

35 Bysack quoted in Datta, *Racanābalī*, p. xlviii.
36 Ibid.
37 This reference is from the *Project Gutenberg* edition of Mellish's translation of the play, which is accessible at http://www.gutenberg.org/files/6791/6791-h/6791-h.htm. Accessed 23 July 2018.

with Europhone literature, primarily but not always in English translation, at the Hindu and Bishop's Colleges. In fact, given the *leitmotif* of feminine rivalry and an asymmetric power-distribution between the leading female characters – putting one at the utter mercy of the other – Datta's conceptualization of the relational gradient between Sermista and Devayani, the two rival characters in *Śarmiṣṭhā*, seems to have noteworthy parallels with that of Schiller's treatment of the asymmetric relationship between Mary, Queen of Scots, and Elizabeth I.

Mary is in an English prison, ostensibly for having had her husband Darnley murdered but, in reality, due to her claim to the English throne, which was held by her cousin Elizabeth I. While the latter prevaricates – or pretends to, as is closer to the historical facts – over signing the warrant of Mary's death, the Queen of Scots swings between despair and hope about a possible reprieve or escape. Upon coming to know that Mortimer – an imagination of Schiller's – the nephew of her custodian, is favorably disposed to her cause, she puts her hopes in his efforts to free her by interceding with Robert Dudley, the Earl of Leicester, who, despite his unwillingness to see Elizabeth have Mary's blood on her hands, seems well-disposed towards the English Queen. When Mary, ultimately, is given an audience with Elizabeth – again a figment of Schiller's imagination – her hopes for a reprieve are dashed after a rather bitter altercation breaks out between the two, given Mary's unreadiness to surrender completely to her cousin's wishes. Mortimer's ill-starred plans of freeing Mary, which are based upon the historical Babington Plot, lead to his suicide and – under the rubric of popular demand – Elizabeth's signing of Mary's death sentence, which is passed to Lord Burleigh, in confirmation of the order, by Sir William Davison. This allows Elizabeth to transfer the culpability for Mary's execution to these two members of her court and the play draws to an end with the former left completely alone, with both the Earls of Shrewsbury and Leicester leaving her retinue forever. The intensity of relational angst and political competitiveness between Mary and Elizabeth does resonate – both historically and dramatically – with the fraught relationship between the two female protagonists of *Sermista*; thus, the personal becomes the political in the latter, too.

In the case of his *Śarmiṣṭhā/Sermista*, this constant code-switching between the often-colliding lexical-metaphorical worlds of Sanskritic Bengali and Romantic and/or early-Victorian English led to an intense polysemy between various mythopoeic, semantic, discursive, and metonymic fields. This polysemic engagement would, of course, trigger off a cultural-metaphysical revolution in mid-nineteenth-century Bengal, through the asymptotic operation of competing, though, quite often, collaborating socio-cultural trajectories. Datta's life and work do seem to fulfil the discursive patterns enumerated by Pascale Casanova in her characterization, following Goethe, of the notion of *Weltliteratur* as a self-regulating function of the interplay of the "competitive nature" of international literature and "the paradoxical unity that results from it."[38] The complex processes through which Sanskritic paradigms of classical Indic dramaturgy were adapted to work with their Europhone counterparts, along with the travel of the results of this cross-cultural formal dialogue to Europe in the mid-twentieth century, deserve a separate paper. For the time being, it should suffice to bear in mind the various interesting commonalities and divergences between semantic and staging-structures in the two dramaturgical paradigms, as seen in the way Datta's plays – especially *Śarmiṣṭhā* – were fashioned, especially at the textual level. Specialists in early modern European dramaturgy do not seem, till date, to have managed to envision and analyze the holistic scheme through which the complex interweaving of early modern theatergrams, plays, dramatists, actors – both rooted and peripatetic – generic and theoretical debates and staging-technologies, through transcontinental travel, reconfigured Europhone theater into a multifaceted transcultural platform.

It is interesting to note, in this context, that one of the most significant plot-defining aspects of Datta's play was the operation of a spatio-temporal 'deferral,' in keeping with Jacques Derrida's formulation of the concept, that serves as a powerful challenge to "the possibility of an identity, sameness, or inside that could be conceived of independently of the altering power of its difference, its other, or its margin."[39] This deferral oscillates with "affirmation [... in a manner Hélène] Cixous makes productive especially in her autobiographical feminist texts of the 1970s."[40] Further, as in Datta's play, it seems to encapsulate "the systematic play of differences, of the traces of differences, of the spacing by means of which elements are related to each other"[41] that is an important aspect of the dramaturgical scheme through which Datta sought to adapt classical Sanskritic mythopoeic and socio-cultural motifs and tropes to the demands of early-modern European norms of theatrical stage-production. This rather intuitive configuration and concatenation, on Datta's part, of thematic and dialogic similarities and material-contextual asymmetries between a neo-classical Sanskritic mythopoeic landscape and early-modern European theater culture creates an interstitial pattern of alternating transformations, through structural negotiations and

---

[38] Pascale Casanova. *The World Republic of Letters*, translated by Malcolm B. DeBevoise. Harvard: Harvard University Press, 2004, p. 40.
[39] Irene Rima Makaryk, editor. *Encyclopedia of Contemporary Literary Theory: Approaches, Scholars, Terms*. Toronto: University of Toronto Press, 1993, p. 585.
[40] Ibid., p. 275.
[41] Jacques Derrida. "Interview with Julia Kristeva." *Positions*, translated by Alan Bass. Chicago: University of Chicago Press, 1982, p. 27.

content-acculturations. This does seem analogous to Derrida's categorical identification of "[d]ifferences [as] the effects of transformations," and his deduction of the incompatibility of the concept of *différance* "with the static, synchronic, taxonomic, ahistoric motifs in the concept of structure."[42] In this very structural fluidity of dramaturgical borrowings and thematic adaptations, Datta's Śarmiṣṭhā embodies noteworthy parallels with, for example, southern German folk-drama,[43] especially in the context of their expressions of a pastoral, even bucolic ideal of romantic love. In fact, the dialogue between the Vidushaka and the King, in the former (Act II, Scene ii), especially when the Nati sings what can doubtlessly be described as an attempt at configuring an Indic bucolic idyll, may be read through the prisms of speech-act theories and perception-analysis and construed to be attempts at the retrospective nationalization of bucolic descriptive modes. This is quite apparent when the Nati sings for the King at the behest of the Vidushaka:

> Hark to the herald kokila – [...]
> How loud it swells – that sylvan lay –
>   Above the air-born minstrelsy!
> Lo! Incense-like o'er grove and bow'r,
>   O'er forest-glade, and green-rob'd vale,
> Floats the soft perfume of each flow'r,
>   Borne gaily by the winged gale.[44]

Along with the above-mentioned section, one could also characterize the opening scene of the play, containing the stage-setting dialogue between the Asura-guard and Vakasura, as attempting to create a bucolic milieu. Especially significant from this perspective is the Asura's opening monologue, where he talks of "this wild mountain solitude... [and] this lone and vast valley, [where] a thousand birds people the air with the softest melody and myriads of sweet flowers bloom and smile around"[45] him. However, it ought also to be noted that this Indic approximation of the bucolic includes certain unnerving non-bucolic elements: "I hear the deafening roar of the lion; the thunder growl of the tiger; and the hoarse and angry voice of the mountain-torrent ceaselessly struggling to leap down its

---

42 Makaryk, *Encyclopedia*, p. 275.
43 This was initially pointed out to the present writer by a colleague on the ERC Project "Drama-Net," Toni Bernhart.
44 Datta, *Racanābalī*, p. 676.
45 Ibid., p. 665.

cloud-cradle."⁴⁶ The fact that the Asura finds the juxtaposition and even simultaneity of the bucolic semi-domesticity of his vantage-position with natural and animal presences and phenomena that can only be described as constitutive of the '*raudra*'⁴⁷ or '*furioso*' should indicate that Datta's configuration of the bucolic ambience followed the more eclectic formal and content-related conventions of the Sanskritic theoretical paradigm, where the pastoral/bucolic idyll coexisted and collaborated with the more tumultuous aspects of Life and Nature.

Thus, the term 'bucolic' should, perhaps, be used in any discussion of Datta's work in a rather qualified manner, so as to acknowledge the tonal and formal distinctions between it and, for example, Torquato Tasso's *Aminta* (1573), one of the most significant examples of the use of bucolic elements in early-modern European drama, the poetry of the German Baroque-era *littérateurs* Georg Philipp Harsdörffer and Sigmund von Birken, the essays published in *The Spectator* and *The Tatler* by Joseph Addison and Richard Steele in the early eighteenth century. Here, it should be useful to point out that Datta, from an early age, must have been familiar with, at least, Addison's work given that the latter had written the preface to John Dryden's 1697 translation of Virgil's *Georgics*. Given that world literature is seen, to a considerable extent, as a function of paradigm-shifting socio-cultural and politico-economic developments, one could connect Datta's theatrical evocations of bucolic idylls to the configurations of landscaped civility, through the design and maintenance of elaborate gardens and garden-houses – in affluent early-colonial Indian households – following the British model. Thus, Datta's Asura was not only admiring the ethereal beauty of his vantage-post outside the City of the Gods but also addressing the urbane angst of the leisured absentee landlords, who would, largely, constitute his audience, at the overwhelming transcontinental psycho-social footprint of the British Industrial Revolution. The felicity with which *Weltliteratur*, as both an aspirational framework to emancipate literary-cultural texts from the boundaries of language and a global portal for noetic and aesthetic consumption, enters the domain of the subaltern stage shows the parallelism between anthropological and rhetorical-discursive evolution. The need of the hour was to formulate new thematic frames for a new *Zeitgeist*.

---

46 Ibid.
47 *Raudra* (= furious) refers to one of the nine *rasa*-s (= functions/categories of aesthetic/poetic pleasure and appreciation) that constitute the core of Indian aesthetic/poetic theories. Cf. Satya Dev Choudhary. *Glimpses of Indian Poetics*. New Delhi: Sahitya Akademi, 2002, p. 67.

Hence, it does appear that the "value of *Śarmiṣṭhā* is not as literary as it is historical."[48] Though Datta had talked of the "foreign air"[49] of the play, the play seems to be an affirmation of the normative frameworks of classical Sanskritic dramaturgy. This is, according to Kshetra Gupta, apparent in different aspects of the play, namely, "the configuration of the jester's character, the predominance of the descriptive mode in the dialogues, the lack of complexity and individualism in characterization, the style of dramatic creation based on *ménage à trois* romances like that seen in *Ratnāvalī*, *Vikramorvaśī* and *Mālavikāgnimitra*."[50] All of these, along with Datta's adherence to the linguistic practices of Kālidāsa, only reflect Sanskritic dramaturgical ideas much more than the Europhone. One could, in keeping with some mid-twentieth century critics and literary historians, like Kshetra Gupta himself, call *Śarmiṣṭhā* a 'romantic comedy' that belonged more to the realm of classical Sanskrit dramaturgical norms, which privileged evocative descriptions of locale and mood over the dynamic directness of action. This would, then, highlight the clashes between human inclinations and moral/ethical conflicts – in the play – that were considered to be rather European. In the matter of characterization, too, one can only categorize the play as rather unremarkable, with characters often following the preset trajectories that had been stereotypically assigned to them as per the conventions of Sanskritic dramaturgy. Thus, Yayati comes across solely as having a weak-minded, licentious, and loose personality, Sermista is the picture of serene, all-suffering, benevolent, and dignified *noblesse*, and Devayani is portrayed as "a character with a strict personality,"[51] in what has been identified with the stock conventions of classical Sanskritic dramaturgy. However, one feels that critics like Gupta have been somewhat harsher to this play than it deserved, especially given the prescriptive nature of the influence of Datta's patrons at the Belgāchiā Theatre. He does seem to have been successful in effecting a tenuous negotiation and even reciprocity between the 'West' and the 'East' in this play, even if the creative orientation did stay somewhat formulaic Sanskritic.

If, as Stuart Blackburn and Vasudha Dalmia say, "[e]ver since Clifford Geertz transformed the drama of Balinese cock-fighting into a text, and new historicism made the complementary gesture of returning culture to the center of literary studies,"[52] there has, indeed, been a conceptual, methodological, and referential

---

48 Datta, *Racanābalī*, p. li.
49 Ibid., p. 1.
50 Ibid., p. li.
51 Ibid.
52 Stuart Blackburn and Vasudha Dalmia, editors. *India's Literary History: Essays on the Nineteenth Century*. New Delhi: Permanent Black, 2004, p. 1.

convergence between literary and cultural historiography, one can be sure that one area in which this development should be of significant help is that of researching Datta's work. As seen earlier, Datta's personal and literary biographies often coalesce into a composite narrative, which is not bereft of its bipolar surprises. He did show himself to be acutely sensitive to both positive and negative criticism of his work, as seen often in his letters, especially after Bethune's lukewarm response to *The Captive Ladie*. This, along with the manner in which he responds to traditionalist critiques of *Śarmiṣṭhā* – "I have no objection to allow a few alterations and so forth, but recast all my sentences – the devil !! I would sooner burn the thing."[53] – shows that it is imperative to look very closely at the critical histories of both the Bengali and English texts of the play, keeping the cultural context always in the foreground. If one returns, briefly, to the "zone of conversion,"[54] as a factor in framing creative choices, one should note the argument put forward by Vinay Dharwadker about this protean space, that, "when placed on a continuum with the zone of interracial marriage and family, [it] produced a high proportion of the Indian-English writers of the nineteenth century."[55]

Thus, one could argue that, in the case of Datta's creative output, the personal is conflated with the literary, and his defense of Europhone dramaturgical innovations, especially when those were challenged by the more traditional critics, could have been characterized by a sense of cultural otherness, even if 'borrowed.' This, however, assumes an interesting dimension when the 'borrowed' elements are stylistic and semantic and do not have much or even anything to do with thematic and structural continuities and ruptures. There, Datta is very clear in his stand: "In matters literary, old boy, I am too proud to stand before the world in borrowed clothes. I may borrow a neck-tie, or even a waist coat, but not the whole suit."[56] In this letter, he also makes it clear, in no uncertain terms, that he is aware of his readership: "I am writing for that portion of my countrymen who think as I think, whose minds have been more or less imbued with Western ideas and *modes of thinking* [italicized by Datta]; and that it is my intention to throw off the fetters forged for us by a servile admiration for everything Sanskrit."[57] This championing of the linguistic subaltern could also be linked to "the strong long-term effect on the transmission of the English language and its culture to

---

53 Datta, *Racanābalī*, Letter 49, p. 519.
54 Pollock, *Literary Cultures*, p. 214.
55 Ibid.
56 Datta, *Racanābalī*, Letter 49, p. 519.
57 Ibid.

Indians"[58] that European and, with the arrival of the first significant educated gentlemen-converts like the Rev. Krishna Mohan Banerjee on the scene, Indian missionary activity had in early-nineteenth century Calcutta, whatever may have been its evangelical success.

Nevertheless, one should not be oblivious to the potential implicit in pre-colonial literary-cultural forms and tropes to leverage dynamic articulations of protean normativities in narratives of identity-formation. One cannot deny, to paraphrase Indira Viswanathan Peterson, "[t]he ability of traditional scholars to transform literary genres in response to new patrons and worldviews."[59] In an essay on a nineteenth-century Tamil Christian poet and playwright, Vedanayaka Sastri, Peterson demonstrates how transitional and interstitial literary personalities can adapt "prevailing poetic and performance conventions for new ritual and devotional roles."[60] Sastri had used a traditional form of dance-drama, the *kuravanci*, to praise European scientific rationalism and privilege Christianity; this hybrid mode of literary-theological syncretism, after multiple vicissitudes over the centuries, is still in use today. Datta's plays, though largely shorn of theological and even metaphysical approximations, retain a strong sense of the traditional, as in Sastri's case above. Thus, despite the strength of its Europhone component, *Śarmiṣṭhā* retains an Indic core that defies the dilution of the fact of its secure location within the frames of reference of traditional content-specifications. This dramatic entanglement is, therefore, not bereft of rootedness.

---

58 Pollock, *Literary Cultures*, p. 214.
59 Blackburn and Dalmia, *India's Literary History*, p. 9.
60 Ibid.

Toni Bernhart and Janina Janke
The Crystallization of Early Modern European Drama in the Folk-Theater Tradition in Tyrol

The Marienberg *Griseldis* from 1713, Staged in 2016

Since the Late Middle Ages, the southern part of the German-speaking area – Bavaria, the German-speaking lands of the Habsburg Empire, especially the County of Tyrol and the capital Vienna, and Swabia – have been extremely vibrant and vivid spaces for popular drama and theater.[1] This area might serve as a principal background for understanding the so-called folk-poetry tradition, as Johann Gottfried Herder in his "theology of folk poetry"[2] pointed out: "If, all of a sudden, a *Macpherson* were to arise in Tyrol or Bavaria and sing some German *Ossian*, this might suffice, so far would we let ourselves be carried away" ("Wenn da auf einmal ein *Macpherson* in Tyrol oder in Baiern aufstünde, und uns da so einen deutschen *Ossian* sänge, ginge es hin, so weit ließen wir uns etwa noch mitziehen.")[3] The idea of folk literature, as Werner Michler states, doubled each existing literary genre: *folk* theater, *folk* literature, *folk* poems, and so forth

---

[1] For Tyrol, see, e.g., Ellen Hastaba. "Theater in Tirol: Spielbelege in der Bibliothek des Tiroler Landesmuseums Ferdinandeum." *Veröffentlichungen des Tiroler Landesmuseums Ferdinandeum* 75/76 (1995/1996), pp. 233–343, p. 233; Bernd Neumann and Hannes Obermair. "Tiroler Spiele." *Killy Literaturlexikon: Autoren und Werke des deutschsprachigen Kulturraumes*, edited by Wilhelm Kühlmann et al., vol. 11, 2nd edition. Berlin: de Gruyter, 2011, pp. 546–548, p. 546. – For Vienna, see, e.g., Otto Rommel. *Die Alt-Wiener Volkskomödie: Ihre Geschichte vom Barocken Welttheater bis zum Tode Nestroys*. Vienna: Schroll, 1952; Herbert Zeman. "Die Alt-Wiener Volkskomödie des 18. und frühen 19. Jahrhunderts: Ein gattungsgeschichtlicher Versuch." *Die österreichische Literatur: Ihr Profil von den Anfängen im Mittelalter bis ins 18. Jahrhundert (1050–1750)*, edited by Herbert Zeman, vol. 2. Graz: Akademische Druck- und Verlagsanstalt, 1986, pp. 1299–1333; *Volkskomödie und Volkstheater in Wien. Ein literarhistorisches Handbuch*, edited by Wolfgang Neuber. Graz: Styria, 1989; Jürgen Hein. *Das Wiener Volkstheater*, 3rd edition. Darmstadt: Wissenschaftliche Buchgesellschaft, 1997; Johann Sonnleitner, editor. *Hanswurstiaden: Ein Jahrhundert Wiener Komödie. Joseph Anton Stranitzky, Joseph Felix Kurz, Philipp Hafner, Joachim Perinet, Adolf Bäuerle*. Salzburg: Residenz, 1996.
[2] The term is that of Robert T. Clark. "Herder, Percy, and the Song of Songs." *PMLA* 61 (1946), pp. 1087–1100, p. 1095.
[3] Johann Gottfried Herder. "Von deutscher Art und Kunst. Einige fliegende Blätter." *Schriften zur Ästhetik und Literatur 1767–1781*, edited by Gunter E. Grimm, vol. 2. Frankfurt: Deutscher Klassiker Verlag, 1993, pp. 443–562, p. 555. The translation is ours.

Open Access. © 2019 Toni Bernhart and Janina Janke, published by De Gruyter. This work is licensed under the Creative Commons Attribution-NonCommercial-NoDerivatives 4.0 License.
https://doi.org/10.1515/9783110604276-014

Audience in the library of the Benedictine Abbey of Marienberg during the *Griseldis* performance in 2016. Photo by Maria Gapp.

began to be identified alongside any general, conventional, or canonical theater, literature, and poems.[4] Folk-lore was born.

It seems, however, rather difficult, if not impossible, to identify folk plays empirically and to distinguish them conclusively from 'ordinary' plays. Nevertheless, the existence of folk plays continues to be tenaciously asserted. The only criterion seems to be the sum of assertions stating that a certain play was a folk play. This sum is, indeed, huge, and has been amassed over and over again during the last two centuries. A further, somewhat more reliable criterion could be that folk plays are written in vernacular languages, though this is not an exclusive criterion. A certain marginality, however, in terms of language (the text was often written down in local dialect), place of performance (far from cultural or political centers), and poetics and aesthetics (far from canonical literature and 'high' culture) constitutes one of the main characteristics and qualities of folk plays.[5]

For the rise of folk poetry from the late seventeenth to the nineteenth century, several causes may be considered. On a more practical level, debates on folk poetry have been connected to the idea of a broader, more popular audience. On a more political and philosophical level, such debates aimed to construct a German identity against cultural otherness or, more precisely, against French literary otherness, which was widely experienced as invasive in German culture in the late seventeenth century. The emphasis on a supposedly essential German character has also been strongly connected to emerging patriotism and national identity-building processes during early German Romanticism. Furthermore, debates on folk poetry demonstrate an awareness of *poetae minores* as well as canonical poets, and clearly show a fascination with 'nature' and 'natural life' as a reaction to industrialization and urbanization, and, as a result, with traveling to the Alps, especially from Britain and Germany. On the whole, the attraction of folk literature expresses a cultural discomfort and societal unrest and tends to promise an identitarian vanishing point.

In folk literature, dramatic genres were considered last and only after lyric and epic genres had been collected, published, and discussed.[6] With respect to

---

4 Werner Michler. *Kulturen der Gattung: Poetik im Kontext, 1750–1950*. Göttingen: Wallstein, 2015, p. 174.
5 For a summary of different viewpoints, see Toni Bernhart. *Volk – Schauspiel – Antivolksstück: Genese einer kulturgeschichtlichen Formation*. Habilitation thesis, University of Stuttgart, 2017, forthcoming.
6 This can clearly be deduced from an analysis of nineteenth-century folk-play collections. At a certain point in the first half of the nineteenth century, students of literature became interested in dramatic texts that within the previously prevalent context of folk poetry had been overlooked and neglected. See, e.g., Franz Horn. *Die Poesie und Beredsamkeit der Deutschen, von Luthers*

The Benedictine Abbey of Marienberg seen from the construction site of the library in 2015. Photo by Janina Janke.

myths, themes, and motifs, folk theater is strongly based on the early modern dramatic and literary tradition, and especially on the Bible, including the tradition of passion plays, Ancient Greek and Roman myths and literature, and Christian legends and tales. Folk theater also, if to a lesser extent, adopts works from canonical literature. Favorite characters in folk plays were Genovefa, Hirlanda, Perpetua, Griselda, Mary Stuart, Absalom, Saint Eustace, and Saint George. Transmitted works of this type have been documented in several catalogues.[7] Folk plays and the folk theater tradition can thus be seen as a late – perhaps the last – crystallization of early modern drama in Europe.

The 'Griselda Myth,'[8] which is the basis of the play under scrutiniy in this article, draws on the final novella from Giovanni Boccaccio's *Decameron* (around 1350). After its translation into Latin by Petrarch, Griselda became one of the most seminal characters in European literatures. In his impressively in-depth, detailed bibliography, Raffaele Marabito reports the reception of the plot throughout global literature.[9] All the same, he does not touch upon the Griselda reception in the German folk-play tradition, which is quite far from canonical reception.

Zeit bis zur Gegenwart, vol. 2. Berlin: Enslin, 1823, pp. 254–304; Heinrich Lindner, editor. *Karl der Zwölfte vor Friedrichshall: Eine Haupt- und Staatsaction in vier Actus, nebst einem Epilogus.* Dessau: Karl Aue, 1845, pp. 5–81; Karl Weinhold, editor. *Weihnacht-Spiele und Lieder auß Süddeutschland und Schlesien.* Graz: Damian & Sorge, 1853, pp. III-VI; Heinrich Pröhle. *Weltliche und geistliche Volkslieder und Volksschauspiele: Mit einer Musikbeilage.* Aschersleben: Fokke, 1855, pp. XIX–XLIV.

7 Adalbert Sikora. "Zur Geschichte der Volksschauspiele in Tirol." *Zeitschrift des Ferdinandeums für Tirol und Vorarlberg* 50 (1906), pp. 339–372; Karl Konrad Polheim. *Katalog der Volksschauspiele aus Steiermark und Kärnten: Nebst Analekten aus Bayern, West- und Ostösterreich.* Tübingen: Niemeyer, 1992; Hastaba, "Theater in Tirol." – For the tradition of the passion play, see Michael Henker, Eberhard Dünninger, and Evamaria Brockhoff, editors. *Hört, sehet, weint und liebt: Passionsspiele im alpenländischen Raum.* Munich: Süddeutscher Verlag, 1990; Jaša Drnovšek. "Early Modern Religious Processions: The Rise and Fall of a Political Genre." *Poetics and Politics: Net Structures and Agencies in Early Modern Drama,* edited by Toni Bernhart, Jaša Drnovšek, Sven Thorsten Kilian, Joachim Küpper, and Jan Mosch. Berlin: de Gruyter, 2018, pp. 215–224.

8 The term was coined by Madeline Rüegg. *The Patient Griselda Myth in Late Medieval and Early Modern Literature,* forthcoming.

9 Raffaele Marabito. "La diffusione della storia di Griselda dal XIV al XX secolo." *Studi sul Boccaccio* 17 (1988), pp. 237–285. On Griselda's reception in particular vernaculars, see Achim Aurnhammer and Hans-Jochen Schiewer, editors. *Die deutsche Griselda: Transformationen einer literarischen Figuration von Boccaccio bis zur Moderne.* Berlin: de Gruyter, 2010; Rinaldo Comba and Marco Piccat, editors. *Griselda: Metamorfosi di un mito nella società europea. Atti del Convegno Internazionale a 80 anni dalla nascita della Società per gli Studi Storici della Provincia di Cuneo, Saluzzo, 23–24 Aprile 2009.* Cuneo: Società per gli Studi Storici, Archeologici ed Artistici della Provincia di Cuneo, 2011; Madeline Rüegg, *The Patient Griselda Myth.*

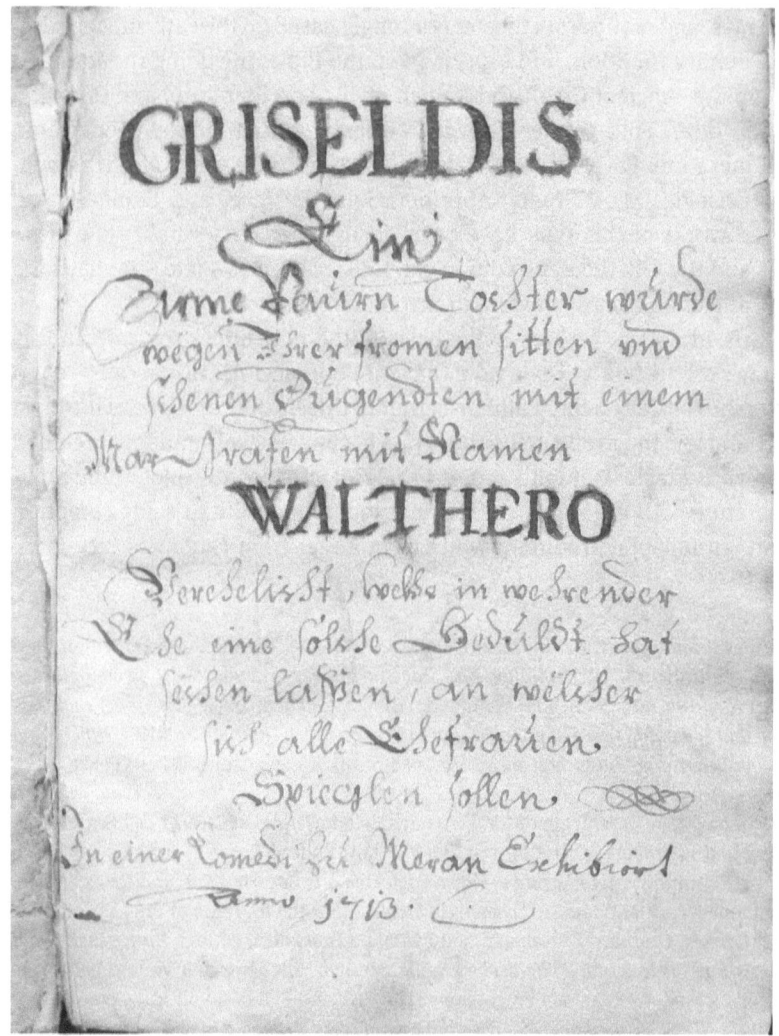

Title page of the Marienberg *Griseldis* (1713). Photo by Toni Bernhart.

Considering the great success the character achieved, it is little surprise that Griselda was adopted eagerly also in the folk-theater tradition of the southern German-speaking area. These adaptations may be reconstructed through catalogues of regional archives.

In his paper on the history of folk plays in Tyrol from 1906, Adalbert Sikora reports a dozen performances of Griselda plays in different places in

Tyrol during the period from 1750 to 1800.[10] Furthermore, three hand-written Griselda plays in vernacular German have been transmitted to the present day. Two of them are preserved in the Tiroler Landesmuseum Ferdinandeum in Innsbruck and are briefly described by Ellen Hastaba in her commented bibliography of play manuscripts in the Ferdinandeum[11]; the third one is the Marienberg *Griseldis* of 1713.

In the context of a research project on folk-theater history conducted within the DramaNet framework,[12] we searched for manuscripts of folk plays in regional archives. In January 2014, we visited the archive of the Benedictine Abbey of Marienberg in South Tyrol, which was founded in the eleventh century, and discovered several manuscripts of school plays that were written in Latin or German and that had, until then, been completely unknown to scholarship.[13] One of the manuscripts is a Griselda play by an anonymous writer, entitled *GRISELDIS Ein Arme Paurn Tochter wurde wëgen Ihrer fromen sitten und schenen Dugendten mit einem Margrafen mit Namen WALTHERO Verehelicht, welche in wehrender Ehe eine solche Geduldt hat sëchen lassen, an wëlcher sich alle Ehefrauen Spieglen sollen* (Griseldis: a poor peasant's daughter, for her pleasant modesty and beautiful virtues, was married to a count named Waltherus; during her marriage, she demonstrated such an abundance of patience that it shall be a mirror for all wives).[14] The title page indicates the place and year of a staging: Meran in 1713. In 1724, the Benedictine monks of Marienberg established a school in the town of Meran, which is about 60 km from the abbey and was, at the time, the

---

10 Sikora, "Zur Geschichte der Volksschauspiele in Tirol."
11 Untitled. Incipit: *Wo wirdt sie abzuhollen sein | ohne brauth Kan ia Kein hochzeit sein*. Manuscript, fragment, eighteenth/nineteenth century. Tiroler Landesmuseum Ferdinandeum, Innsbruck, shelfmark FB 32118; *Schau Spiel Von der Gräffin Griseldis*, manuscript, nineteenth century. Tiroler Landesmuseum Ferdinandeum, Innsbruck, shelfmark FB 32134. See Hastaba, "Theater in Tirol," no. 360 and nos. 453–457.
12 See http://www.geisteswissenschaften.fu-berlin.de/we03/forschung/drittmittelprojekte/dramanet/Team-_-Topics/index.html#bernhart. Accessed 25 September 2018.
13 For a more detailed theatrical history of Marienberg, see Toni Bernhart. "'Griseldis' (1713): Ein Neufund aus dem Stiftsarchiv Marienberg und die Geschichte des Schultheaters am Benediktinergymnasium Meran." *Nestroyana* 37(2017), pp. 175–187, pp. 176–183.
14 *Griseldis*, Meran 1713. Archive of the Benedictine Abbey of Marienberg, Mals/Vinschgau (Italy), no shelfmark. – We profoundly thank Markus Spanier OSB, Abbot of Marienberg, as well as the archivists Ulrich Faust OSB and David Fliri for permission to reproduce the title page of *Griseldis*.

Waltherus (Christian Mayer) and Griseldis (Judith Abart). Photo by Maria Gapp.

capital of the historical County of Tyrol. The manuscript's history is unknown. However, it can be assumed that the *Griseldis* manuscript found its way to the Benedictine school of Meran, from where it was brought to the abbey after the school was closed in 1986.

The play consists of four acts, each of them of five scenes. Two funny interludes have been inserted: one after I.1, the other after III.1. In its original form, *Griseldis* apparently included four choruses: "Chorus 1mus" after I.2, and "Chorus 4tus" after III.5; the second and third choruses are missing, as are a few pages of the text. The manuscript also lacks a musical score. With respect to music, it was a quite usual practice in folk-play manuscripts that only the texts of sung parts, often referred to as either 'Aria' or 'Recitativo,' were recorded, but no score.[15]

The dramatic text derives from a scholarly context. The language is German, but some quotations from Latin literature are included in the characters' speech. Stylistically, the dramatic text is a rather typical mixture of literary language and local dialect. Some Middle German also emerges throughout the text, which leads to the assumption that the play was based on pre-existing versions.

The diction, register, and style of the characters' speech are class-specific. Such poetic differentiation leads one to assume a certain erudition on the part of the author. While Waltherus, his confidant Vigilius, and the counts and courtiers make use of a rather elevated diction and style, peasants and working people use an informal, occasionally vulgar language. Everyday work life is portrayed at length, with farmers' tasks and merchants' duties described in detail. The advantages and disadvantages of marriage are discussed, too.

We were fascinated with this play at first sight and developed the idea of performing it on stage. In scholarly, artistic, and organizational terms, it was a long trajectory from discovering the manuscript in 2014 to staging the play in the Benedictine Abbey of Marienberg in 2016. Ten performances were finally put on stage, all of which were fully booked and had great public resonance.

From the very beginning, it was obvious to us that the staging of such an 'unstageable' play would be a challenge. From a contemporary perspective, *Griseldis* seemed 'unstageable' because of the play's not very fashionable choice of a humble and obedient wife as its protagonist. Griseldis puts all her faith and fortune in God's hands and for this she suffers injustice and mental torture from her husband, who claims to be testing her loyalty.

The first step on our way to the play's performance was to find the right coordinates in space and time. We approached Markus Spanier, the abbot of the

---

15 For music in folk-play history, see Franz Gratl. "The Role of Music in Folk Drama: An Investigation based on Tyrolean Sources." *Poetics and Politics*, pp. 185–198.

Start of rehearsals in the library. Photo by VinschgauDesign.

Griseldis (Hermina Asam) with child. Photo by VinschgauDesign.

Marienberg Benedictine Abbey, who was impressed by our endeavor and instantly decided to support it. Since theater has been a constant activity in Benedictine history and school tradition, Abbot Markus became enthusiastic about our plan and came up with the idea of showing the play in the context of the 200th anniversary of the re-foundation of the Marienberg Abbey in 2016. As a suitable space he suggested the new library building, an underground structure in the monastery garden, which at that time was under construction, and therefore still empty and not yet filled with books.

The abbot introduced the idea to the monastery *conventus*, which approved the project. Thereafter we met with amateur theater groups from the surrounding villages in the community of Mals/Vinschgau. Amateur theater is very common in Tyrol; it looks back on a long tradition, and nearly every village has its own theater group. In the end, eight of these groups were eager to participate, appreciating the opportunity to work with professional theater makers and – as the occasion had never arisen before – to form one ensemble out of the eight local groups. In 2015 and 2016 we conducted two workshops to introduce the play and try out some first readings and possible stagings of the text. Finally, twenty-five local amateurs, who ranged from eight to eighty years of age, formed the cast. Everybody who wanted to play was invited to play. This, as a consequence, forced us in our capacity as directors to find roles for every willing actor and set the first paradigm for the scenic concept: Griseldis was to be represented by five actresses of three generations. This multiplication of the main character formed the crucial point in the play's dramaturgy. Through her being mirrored in five actresses, the personage of Griseldis loses her individuality and is transformed into an allegorical phenomenon. In conclusion, we worked with the multiplication of people, space, and voices as the artistic guiding line throughout the whole piece. In a four-week period of reading-rehearsals, the local actors got used to the historical language of the play; their common local dialect facilitated the pronunciation of the characters' speech.

Some of the costumes were made out of rag paper, which is the same material the play's manuscript is written on. This paper consists of textiles, mostly hemp and linen, which are ground, dissolved in water, and drained through a screen. This sort of paper is very strong and flexible. A local tailor sewed coats and skirts out of rag paper, while a group of volunteers assisted in painting the fabric with colorful patterns.

Finally, the scenic rehearsals began in October 2016, in the newly built library designed by the architect Werner Tscholl, winner of the Italian Architect of the Year Award 2016. Tscholl is renowned for his sensitivity in dealing with historic monuments. He constructed the subterranean library under the cloister garden of

Two counts on the left (Vivienne Gapp and Barbara Strobl), Waltherus (Christian Mayer) and Vigilius (Hannes Warger) on the right. Photo by Maria Gapp.

the monastery and integrated the existing rocks and Romanesque stone walls of the eleventh century into his modern concrete architecture. This unusual space formed the set and stage design for the *Griseldis*. Its special acoustic and spatial defaults had a huge impact on the performance. The walls, consisting of concrete and stone, sharply reflect every sound and spoken word, creating echoes and delays. We worked with these acoustic phenomena and tried to create a musical atmosphere through the voices of our actors.

A conventional stage-audience theater setting would have been impossible in this particular architectural layout. We found a solution by placing the audience-platform along a diagonal in the center of the room: half the audience faced a Romanesque stone wall, while half was looking towards a newly built concrete wall. Throughout the whole performance we played with the fact that half of the audience could see one scene on their side of the stage but hear the other one from behind their backs, and vice versa. As a result, a strong focus lay on the characters' speech and the voices of the performers, which became very present and prominent in the space, differentiating scenes on the two stages on either side. From time to time, the performers' voices connected and formed choral songs, which were based on the text of *Griseldis* and had been composed by the local musician, composer, and folk music expert Ernst Thoma.

It was a long, adventurous, and intensive rehearsal period, bringing together individuals of different cultural and educational backgrounds. In the end, the whole process led to a unique experience for every single person involved: the monks, the architect, the local inhabitants of the villages, the members of the DramaNet project, and finally the actors and the audience. Ten fully booked performances were shown in November 2016 and the media response was overwhelming. This experience has encouraged us to continue interweaving artistic with scholarly approaches to early modern theater and drama and placing apparently 'unstageable' plays in a contemporary cultural context, creatively confronting one with the other.

DS Mayfield
Rhetorical Ventriloquism in Application

we must make another speak in our place.
Aristotle[1]

et voluptate ad fidem ducitur[.]
Quintilian[2]

In Book VIII of his *Confessions*, at the crucial moment of the entire endeavor – as regards the literary composition, the life and self it is to reflect – Augustine introduces "Chastity ['continentiae']" personified as having "appeared ['aperiebatur']" to him.[3] Twice the orator ventriloquizes in writing what she

---

1 Aristotle. *The 'Art' of Rhetoric*, edited and translated by John Henry Freese. Cambridge: Harvard University Press, 2006, 1418b.
2 Quintilian. *Institutio Oratoria / The Orator's Education*, edited and translated by Donald A. Russell. 5 vols. Cambridge: Harvard University Press, 2001, 4.2.119.
3 Aurelius Augustine. *Confessions: Books 1–8*, edited and translated by Carolyn Hammond. Cambridge: Harvard University Press, 2014. In a context referring to a (previously) prodigal use of his God-given "intellectual ability" ("de ingenio meo, munere tuo," I.17.27), Augustine refers to performing a *prosopopoiía* during his student years, detailing the resp. rhetorical process as follows: "A task ['negotium'] was assigned to me [...]. It was to perform the speech of Juno when she was angry and hurt [...], words that I had never heard Juno utter. Instead we were obliged to go astray by following the footsteps of poetical inventions ['figmentorum poeticorum'], and to declaim in prose something similar to what the poet [sc. Virgil] had written in verse. The one who was displaying a

---

Acknowledgments: The author is grateful to Prof. Hoxby (asking about layered *sermocinationes* and generic specificities in this regard), Prof. Dickhaut (stressing the significance of the *aptum*), Prof. Küpper (commenting on the import of differentiating factual and fictional figures with respect to *sermocinatio*), Dr. Sven Thorsten Kilian (inquiring about collective voices personified), and Prof. Gasan Gusejnov (adducing a nexus with *ratiocinatio* and mentioning the Theophrastan *Characters*) for their questions and comments following the talk. Thanks go to the chair, the general audience, and particularly to the conference's international respondents Profs. Jan Bloemendal, Kirsten Dickhaut, Susanne Friede, Blair Hoxby; as well as to Lena Maria Hein for assisting in proofreading an earlier version. Above all, the author wishes to express his gratitude to Prof. Kathy Eden (Columbia U., NYC) and Prof. Küpper for reading and commenting on drafts of the essay at hand.

Note: For an extended version of this article, detailing its theoretico-conceptual foundation and discussing *sermocinatio* and related concepts in the *Rhetorica ad Herennium*, Cicero, Dionysius of Halicarnassus, and Quintilian, see the publisher's website: https://www.degruyter.com/view/product/505530

ϴ Open Access. © 2019 DS Mayfield, published by De Gruyter. This work is licensed under the Creative Commons Attribution-NonCommercial-NoDerivatives 4.0 License.
https://doi.org/10.1515/9783110604276-015

might say ("quasi diceret," iterated) – and is then careful to clarify (in forensic terms): "ista controversia in corde meo non nisi de me ipso adversus me ipsum" ("[t]his debate took place within my heart; it was myself arguing against myself").[4] That envisioned *prosopopoeia* with interior *sermocinatio* causes

---

more realistic ['similior'] impression of anger and hurt in defending the honor of the character being delineated ['adumbratae personae'] (using appropriate words to clothe the ideas ['verbis sententias congruenter vestientibus']) was the one whose speech won the most praise" (ibid.). Cf. Carol D. Lanham. "Writing Instruction from Late Antiquity to the Twelfth Century." *A Short History of Writing Instruction: From Ancient Greece to Modern America*, edited by James J. Murphy, 2nd edition. Mahwah: Hermagoras Press, 2001, pp. 79–121, here p. 85. The young Augustine outperformed everyone – an accomplishment for which the mature writer has only contempt, albeit rather ostensively so (cf. *Confessions*, I.17.27). Seeing that the basic procedure outlined for the Greek goddess is here repeated in the personification of an abstract entity equally 'inexistent' from the Church Father's perspective, it is not the technique itself that is at issue, but the (intended) use to which it is put – with *Continentia* personified serving a moral, and (more importantly) Christian purpose, here; in terms of motive, Augustine's craving for personal glory is reallocated to disseminating the Deity's.
4 Augustine, *Confessions*, VIII.11.27. – Cf. p. 406n. Concerning the Church Father's relationship to rhetoric, including as to passages under consideration here, see Wendy Olmsted. "Invention, Emotion, and Conversion in Augustine's *Confessions*." *Rhetorical Invention & Religious Inquiry: New Perspectives*, edited by Walter Jost and Wendy Olmsted. New Haven: Yale University Press, 2000, pp. 65–86, passim, spec. 79–80. See Arnaldo Momigliano (referring also to Augustine): "this effort of explaining oneself and one's own purposes to a personal audience, if not to one's own direct accusers, may well have been a decisive contribution to the recognition of the self as a person with a definite character, purpose and achievement. After all, in so far as they express a relation to gods or God, confessions have an element of self-defence which links them to judicial speeches" ("Marcel Mauss and the Quest for the Person in Greek Biography and Autobiography." *The Category of the Person: Anthropology, Philosophy, History*, edited by Michael Carrithers et al. Cambridge: Cambridge University Press, 1986, pp. 83–92, p. 90, cf. p. 91). Cf. "It is Christians who have made a metaphysical entity of the 'moral person' (*personne morale*), after they became aware of its religious power. Our own notion of the human person is still basically a Christian one" (Marcel Mauss. "A category of the human mind: the notion of person; the notion of self," translated by Wilfred D. Halls. *The Category of the Person*, pp. 1–25, p. 19). The rhetorico-dramatic view of the *persona* is at variance therewith. As to the Christian refunctionalization, see Manfred Fuhrmann. "Persona, ein römischer Rollenbegriff." *Identität*, edited by Odo Marquard and Karlheinz Stierle, 2nd edition. Munich: Fink, 1996, pp. 83–106, spec. pp. 102–104; Peter L. Oesterreich. "Person." *Historisches Wörterbuch der Rhetorik*, vol. 10 [*Nachträge A–Z*], edited by Gert Ueding. Tübingen: Niemeyer, 2012, pp. 862–872, here p. 865; Jean Yves Boriaud and Bernard Schouler. "Persona," translated by Martin Steinrück and Thomas Zinsmaier. *Historisches Wörterbuch der Rhetorik*, vol. 6 [*Must–Pop*], edited by Gert Ueding. Tübingen: Niemeyer, 2003, pp. 789–810, spec. p. 799; Christopher Gill. "Particulars, selves and individuals in Stoic philosophy." *Particulars in Greek Philosophy*, edited by Robert W. Sharples. Leiden: Brill, 2010, pp. 127–145, here p. 129; generally thereto, see DS Mayfield. "Interplay with Variation: Approaching Rhetoric and Drama." *Rhetoric and Drama*, edited by DS

emotional upheaval (a form of auto-*movere*, to be experienced vicariously by the reader), the tension of which the speaker feels he must "let [...] all pour out, in words as well ['cum vocibus']" – wherefore he leaves his silent ("tacitus") interlocutor Alypius, sensing "that the business ['negotium'] of weeping was better suited ['aptior'] to solitude."[5]

In an even "remotius" place – somewhere (albeit inevitably "sub quadam fici arbore") and "somehow" (the speaker stresses his ignorance, "nescio quomodo") – he addresses himself to the Deity twice, thus paralleling the structure of the utterances put in Chastity's mouth moments ago.[6] In this case, however, the qualification differs: given his spatial isolation, the speaker writes that he actually voiced himself "non quidem his verbis, sed in hac sententia" ("not in these actual words, but along these lines").[7] After having imagined a personified *Continentia* address-

---

Mayfield. Berlin: de Gruyter, 2017, pp. 3–52, p. 21n. https://www.degruyter.com/downloadpdf/books/9783110484663/9783110484663-002/9783110484663-002.xml. Accessed 25 July 2018.
5 Augustine, *Confessions*, VIII.12.28.
6 Concerning 'fig trees' as familiar settings, vivid mental (and nominal) anchors in various parables and related encounters within the *New Testament* (partly of highly significative import), see, e.g., the narrative of Jesus 'cursing a fig tree' (*Mt* 21:18–22; *Mk* 11:12–14, 20–24; the analogous parable in *Lk* 13:6–9), with its (figurative) foci both on 'bearing fruit' and on 'faith alone'; the tree's leaves are also referred to as a seasonal indicator, and functionalized as an anticipative sign of coming things (*Mt* 24:32; *Mk* 13:28; *Lk* 21:29–31); finally – and arguably most importantly for Augustine's case (from his point of view) – see the fig tree's (apparently incidental) nexus with men (and sinners) being called into the Lord's service (*Lk* 19:4–5, plus context; especially also *Jn* 1:48–50).
7 Augustine, *Confessions*, VIII.12.28. Petrarch – emulating Augustine in many matters literary – also uses the device of putting words into his own mouth: "and [I] addressed myself in words like these" (Francesco Petrarca. "The Ascent of Mount Ventoux," translated by Hans Nachod. *The Renaissance Philosophy of Man*, edited by Ernst Cassirer et al., 9th edition. Chicago: Chicago University Press, 1965, pp. 36–46, here p. 39), "talibus me ipsum compellabam verbis" (Francesco Petrarca. *Epistole*, edited by Ugo Dotti. Turin: Unione Tipografico-Editrice Torinese, 1978, p. 122, 9*[IV, i]); the following also features an embedded *sermocinatio* ("they say," "ut aiunt"), with the added piquancy that he is here quoting *Scripture*, while treating beatitude nominalistically: "The life we call blessed" ("Mount Ventoux," p. 40), "vita, quam beatam dicimus" (*Epistole*, pp. 122–123, 9*[IV, i]). The process of auto-*sermocinatio* (metapoetically speaking) is repeated further down: "and I said to myself" ("Mount Ventoux," p. 42), "Dicebam [...] ad me ipsum" (*Epistole*, p. 126, 9*[IV, i]) – with the ensuing remarks featuring an embedded citation from Augustine (cf. "Mount Ventoux," p. 42; *Epistole*, p. 126, 9*[IV, i]); again: "and asked myself" ("Mount Ventoux," p. 43), "et querebam ex me ipse" (*Epistole*, p. 128, 9*[IV, i]). Then, of course, he reenacts the Augustinian '*tolle lege*' scene in a sort of intertextual *mise en abyme* (explicitly so: "The same had happened before," "Mount Ventoux," p. 45; "Quod iam ante [...] acciderat," *Epistole*, p. 130, 9*[IV, i]) – and from on high, Petrarch being on a mountain at this (at least physical, temporal) turning point (the imposing setting might be part of the

ing him in the interiority of his mind with words he attributes to her, Augustine here confesses to be 'writing words into his own mouth' (so to speak).[8] The envisioned interlocutor is silent.[9]

Then – accentuated by the crucial indicator "ecce,"[10] by a change to the present tense ("audio") for purposes of vivid immediacy (*evidentia*), and couched in ignorance ("nescio") once again – the decisive *sermocinatio* occurs, which everyone knows:

> et ecce audio vocem de vicina domo cum cantu dicentis et crebro repetentis, quasi pueri an puellae, nescio: 'tolle lege, tolle lege'. statimque mutato vultu[.]
>
> And look! – From the house next door I hear a voice – I don't know whether it is a boy or a girl – singing some words over and over: 'Pick it up and read it, pick it up and read it!' Immediately my expression transformed.[11]

---

aemulatio, given the trouble taken to describe it in vividmost detail, while Augustine is just 'out there in the nowhere under some fig tree'): "I thought it fit to look into the volume of Augustine's *Confessions* [...]. I opened it with the intention of reading whatever might occur to me first" ("Mount Ventoux," p. 44, cf. p. 45; cf. *Epistole*, pp. 128–130, 9*[IV, i]); "Aperio, lecturus quicquid occurreret" (*Epistole*, p. 130, 9*[IV, i]). Before the passage is read out, Petrarch's brother is said to stand "beside" him, "intently expecting to hear something from Augustine on" the speaker's "mouth" – the Humanist envisions himself as, writes himself into the role of, the Father's mouthpiece ("Mount Ventoux," p. 44): "per os meum ab Augustino aliquid audire" (*Epistole*, p. 130, 9*[IV, i]). As to the persistence of the aforesaid reading *praxis*, cf. Hans Blumenberg. *Arbeit am Mythos*, 6th edition. Frankfurt a. M.: Suhrkamp, 2006, pp. 587–588 and 587n.

8 This being possible or plausible due to the temporal (and notional) distance between the narrating (and refining) *persona* – the *auctor* called 'Augustine' – and the protagonist of the *Confessiones* (by the same name), whose previous experiences are said to be rendered in narrative form. As to chronology, Hammond suggests "AD 354–386" in terms of the events referred to in the *Confessions* overall, "AD 397" as "the time when Augustine composed this account," while it was not until "AD 426 or 427" that "he looked back [...] at what he had written and evaluated it" (Carolyn Hammond. "Introduction." *Confessions: Books 1–8*, pp. xiii–xl, here p. xv).

9 Cf. "vides haec, domine, et taces [...] numquid semper tacebis" (Augustine, *Confessions*, I.18.28) – see *Ps* 82:2 (*Vulgate*; i.e. *Ps* 83:1; *NIV*); "habitans in excelsis in silentio, deus" (*Confessions*, I.18.29); cf. the gloss: "A[ugustine] repeatedly associates silence with God" (*Confessions*, p. 52n.). Regarding Petrarch's *Secretum*, and the 'silence of Truth personified,' see Joachim Küpper: "die Allegorie der Veritas, hinter der sich niemand anderes als der christliche Gott selbst verbirgt, jener Gott, der zu Zeiten des fiktiven Interlokutors [sc. Petrarch's 'Augustinus'] noch gesprochen hatte ('tolle, lege'), schweigt in diesem von Anfang bis Ende kontroversen Gespräch" (*Petrarca: Das Schweigen der Veritas und die Worte des Dichters*. Berlin: de Gruyter, 2002, p. 52).

10 See *Jn* 19:5; *Vulgate*.

11 Augustine, *Confessions*, VIII.12.29. Cf. Küpper, *Schweigen der Veritas*, pp. 32 and 52; as well as *Discursive* Renovatio *in Lope de Vega and Calderón: Studies on Spanish Baroque Drama. With an Excursus on the Evolution of Discourse in the Middle Ages, the Renaissance, and*

The face turns first – owing to the outward sign – quasi 'prefiguring' the inner conversion resulting from the perusal of the message within the book subsequently opened.[12] Standing in for the tacit Deity, a child – see "parvulos,"[13] "pueros,"[14] and "pueri"[15] (in the plural, hence no matter which gender) – is heard to utter the above, with the writer (decidedly) putting them into the mouth of those with respect to whom it is written that "talium est enim regnum Dei."[16]

Mannerism. Berlin: de Gruyter, 2017, pp. 174 and 285. https://www.degruyter.com/viewbooktoc/product/491780. Accessed 25 July 2018. Given the context – it being a passage from Paul's *Letter to the Romans* ("codicem apostoli") that effects Augustine's 'conversion' (*Confessions*, VIII.12.29) – a comparison with the words that bring about Saul's volte-face is meet: "Saule, Saule quid me persequeris" – the situation having been specified as "audivit vocem dicentem" (*Acts* 9:4; *Vulgate*; resp. "audivi vocem dicentem" in *Acts* 22:7, "loquentem" in 26:14). For the expediency (hence durability) of this pattern in the Christian tradition, see Küpper on Constantine's 'conversion' as per Eusebius and Lactantius (*Discursive* Renovatio, pp. 171–176, spec. 173–174). Augustine not only accommodates his own version to the intentional structure and significance of the situation that is to prefigure his own, but also 'ties in with' (sc. *hypólepsis*) the precise wording ("audio vocem"), and even with the 'tonality' of the prefiguring statement – the iterated vocative "Saule, Saule" being comparable to the twofold imperative repeated ("tolle, lege"). As a bilingual *sýnkrisis* will render patent, the translation here is likely to seem infelicitous; there appears to be no (linguistic, grammatical) reason for not rendering the dictum (trochaically) as 'take it, read it' – or even (less gently and euphoniously, while entirely in line with the imperative): 'take! read!' The formula is repeated and varied (as per the resp. rhetorical precept) in the following paragraphs: "ut aperirem codicem et legerem quod primum caput invenissem" (*Confessions*, VIII.12.29); "arripui, aperui, et legi in silentio capitulum quo primum coniecti sunt oculi mei" (ibid.) – here a paronomastic tricolon, featuring a (continued) density of ‹i›. As to the above semiotic marker ('*ecce*'), see Hammond, "Introduction," p. xxxvii. Concerning references to 'not knowing', cf. that the writer takes care to intimate his being unable to remember what his earlier self had done precisely at that point in time: "Then I put my finger ['aut digito'], or some other marker ['aut nescio quo alio signo'], into the book and closed it" (*Confessions*, VIII.12.30); in the next sentence, Augustine describes his not having known at the time ("quod ego nesciebam") what had been going on in Alypius all the while the aforesaid was taking place with(in) himself (ibid.). On the concept of '*hypólepsis*' ('taking up and tying in with'), see DS Mayfield. "Variants of *hypólepsis*: Rhetorical, Anthropistic, Dramatic (With Remarks on Terence, Machiavelli, Shakespeare)." *Poetics and Politics. Net Structures and Agencies in Early Modern Drama*, edited by Toni Bernhart et al. Berlin: de Gruyter, 2018, pp. 233–274. https://www.degruyter.com/view/product/486170. Accessed 25 July 2018.

12 See the parallelism with the above: "Immediately ['statim quippe'], the end of the sentence was like a light of sanctuary poured into my heart; every shadow of doubt ['dubitationis'] melted away" (*Confessions*, VIII.12.29). The translation does not render the emphatic "quippe."

13 *Mt* 19:14, *Mk* 10:14.

14 *Lk* 18:16.

15 *Confessions*, VIII.12.29.

16 *Mk* 10:14, *Lk* 18:16; *Vulgate*. Cf. *Mt* 19:14, which has "caelorum" in lieu of "Dei." Consistent with his gestures signaling doubt, uncertainty regarding knowledge prior to the 'conversion' – "nescio,"

It seems entirely unlikely that the 'momentaneous evidence' effectuated by this Augustinian *sermocinatio* could have escaped anyone living in a prevalently Christian community pertaining to Late Antiquity, medieval times, or the early modern period.[17] By making various other, personified voices speak in his place, the Church Father is acting on the rhetorico-'ethopoietic' assumption *par excellence*: 'self sells.'

While its indisputable impact has tended to go unnoticed in modern times (and the latter's study of literature), the practice of rhetorical *ethopoiía* – 'the making (*poiein*) of *ethos* by way of descriptive and actual speech (*sermocinatio*)' – decisively molded and dominated the Western literary tradition (*sensu lato*) from Antiquity to the early modern age, and remains a sustained, if latent influence in the present.[18]

"nescio" (*Confessions*, VIII.12.28–29), "nescio," "nesciebam" (VIII.12.30) – Augustine immediately tries (hence fails) to apply reason to the situation: "I started to ask myself eagerly whether it was common for children ['pueri'] to chant such words when they were playing a game of some kind. I could not recall ever having heard anything quite like it. [...] I understood it as nothing short of divine providence that I was being ordered to open the book and read the first passage I came across" (VIII.12.29). This course is induced by recalling an occurrence heard about (or read) that seems to quasi 'prefigure' (sc. with repeatable 'fulfillments,' here; generally thereto, cf. Küpper, *Discursive* Renovatio, pp. 89–90 with p. 174) Augustine's own case at hand: "I had heard ['audieram'] of Antony, how he had been challenged by a reading from the gospel which he happened to ['forte', sc. by chance] encounter, as if what he was reading was being spoken for himself ['tamquam sibi diceretur quod legebatur']" (*Confessions*, VIII.12.29) – *Scripture* itself acts as a 'speaker,' the word *kat' exochén* (for a Christian) is quasi personified. The basic structure of the passage that follows seems similarly formulaic (being likewise paronomastic, memorable): "'vade, vende [...] et veni, sequere me'" – the result of which is an 'instantaneous conversion': "et tali oraculo confestim ad te esse conversum" (*Confessions*, VIII.12.29).

17 On the concept of '*momentane Evidenz*,' here employed *mutatis mutandis*, see Hans Blumenberg "Wirklichkeitsbegriff und Möglichkeit des Romans." *Nachahmung und Illusion*, edited by Hans Robert Jauß, 2nd edition. Munich: Fink, 1983, pp. 9–27, passim, spec. pp. 10–12, 15, 26; for further references and applications, cf. DS Mayfield. *Artful Immorality – Variants of Cynicism: Machiavelli, Gracián, Diderot, Nietzsche*. Berlin: de Gruyter, 2015, pp. 48n., 92, spec. 92n., 256n.

18 This sentence is indebted to a formulation on the part of Prof. Eden, urging a reaccentuation and "foreground[ing]" of "the central place of ethopoetic construction in the literary tradition [...] as a way to account for the peculiar shape of at least some of its most well known texts" (email to the author, 26 June 2017). Generally, see Guido Naschert. "Ethopoeia." *Historisches Wörterbuch der Rhetorik*, vol. 2 [*Bie–Eul*], edited by Gert Ueding. Tübingen: Niemeyer, 1994, pp. 1512–1516, here p. 1515; cf. William Fortenbaugh, Christian Mouchel, and Franz-Hubert Robling. "Ethos," translated by Andrea Merger and Susan Nurmi-Schomers. Ibid., pp. 1516–1543, spec. p. 1541. As to medieval "exercise in prosopopœia," see Charles S. Baldwin associating (or equating) such with "imaginary adaptations" in his *Medieval Rhetoric and Poetic (to 1400): Interpreted from Representative Works*. Gloucester, MA: Peter Smith, 1959, pp. 141n., 215; referring to a letter by Sidonius Apollinaris, he gives "Ethicam dictionem" as "prosopopœia" (ibid., pp. 83, 83n.); and *"prosopopoeiae"* as "imaginary addresses" (*Renaissance Literary Theory and Practice: Classicism in the Rhetoric and Poetic of Italy, France, and England 1400–1600*, edited by Donald Lemen Clark. Gloucester: Peter Smith, 1959, p. 40). Scaliger handles *ethopoiía* under the header "EXPRESSIO PERSONARVM," praising Vergil for his "varia genera perſonarum" (Julius C. Scaliger. *Poetices Libri Septem: Faksimile-Neudruck der Ausgabe Leipzig von Lyon 1561*, edited by August Buck, 2ⁿᵈ edition. Stuttgart-Bad Cannstatt: frommann-holzboog, 1987, p. 83, III.ii); the most significant line for the present purpose occurs at the end of the section: "Humilem quoque perſonam, atque eius officium nõ fine Ethopœia, & Oeconomia" (ibid., p. 85, III.ii; the former term reappears in the Greek at p. 227, V.iii; as to "OECONOMIA," cf. pp. 103–104, III.xix). Scaliger then refers to "perſonæ fictæ" under the header "QVASI PERSONÆ," giving, *inter alia*, the following examples: "apud Maronem Fama: apud Ouidiũ Fames [...] apud Plautum Inopia, Luxuria, Lar, Arcturus. apud Æſchylum, Vis, Neceſsitas. apud Ariſtophanem, Fas, Nefáſque" (pp. 85, III.iii). As to *prosopopoiía* in conjunction with *ethopoiía* and *sermocinatio*, see Mary Carruthers on "[a] courtly French treatise on rhetoric (1463)" ("The Concept of *ductus*, or Journeying through a Work of Art." *Rhetoric Beyond Words: Delight and Persuasion in the Arts of the Middle Ages*, edited by Mary Carruthers. Cambridge: Cambridge University Press, 2013, pp. 190–213, here p. 205). Cf. Marvin T. Herrick. *Comic Theory in the Sixteenth Century*. Urbana: University of Illinois Press, 1964, pp. 132, 134. Charles O. McDonald speaks of "[t]he phenomenal popularity of Aphthonius in the English Renaissance," calling him "the mentor of practically every Renaissance schoolboy trained up in the arts of composition" – here with specific reference to *"ethopoeia"* (*The Rhetoric of Tragedy: Form in Stuart Drama*. Amherst: University of Massachusetts Press, 1966, pp. 75n., 124.; cf. pp. 75, 87). See Thomas O. Sloane and Walter Jost: "Ciceronian tactics drawn from judicial rhet[oric] seemed to fire the poets' imaginations [...]: arguing *in utramque partem* [...] became a kind of lawyerly embracing of contraries [...] reappearing in the argumentative [...] fabric of Tudor poetry and drama; *qualis sit*, or individuating a phenomenon by setting it within a thesis-to-hypothesis (or definite-to-indefinite-question), suffuses Boccaccian fiction and Sidneyan crit[icism]; *ethos* and *ethopoiesis* [...] pervade dialogues, mock encomia, and most discussions of courtliness. Schoolroom *imitatio* [...] brought fictiveness itself well within rhetorical exercises" ("Rhetoric and Poetry." *The Princeton Encyclopedia of Poetry & Poetics*, edited by Roland Greene et al, 4ᵗʰ edition. Princeton: Princeton University Press, 2012, pp. 1175–1181, here p. 1179). See the extensive sense of "ethopoeia" employed by McDonald (*Rhetoric of Tragedy*, pp. 18, 49, 165, 166 with 243, 173, 182, 190, 223, 234, 239, 257 with 258, 274, 289, 288–289 with 274 and 297, 291 with 195). While present in the title of Lorna Hutson's essay, *"Ethopoeia*, Source-Study and Legal History: A Post-Theoretical Approach to the Question of 'Character' in Shakespearean Drama" (*Post-Theory: New Directions in Criticism*, edited by Martin McQuillan et al. Edinburgh: Edinburgh University Press, 1999, pp. 139–160), it may remain unclear how the use of the term – "the historical legacy of Shakespeare's ethopoetic dramatic tradition," "the rhetorical persuasiveness of Shakespeare's *ethopoeia*" (pp. 145, 157) – ties in with Hutson's claims (not affected thereby); her references to progymnasmatic terms are problematic (pp. 140–141), possibly due to the manuscript used (cf. p. 158n.). Heinrich F. Plett stresses: "Die Prosopopoiie erlangt während des 16. Jahrhunderts in der Dichtung eine [...] [große] Popularität" (*"Theatrum Rhetoricum*: Schauspiel – Dichtung – Politik." *Renaissance-Rhetorik / Renaissance Rhetoric*, edited by Heinrich F. Plett. Berlin: de Gruyter, 1993, pp. 328–368, here p. 356; cf. p. 359). "Im Rhetorikunterricht der englischen Renaissance nehmen [...] Rollenübungen [sc. re *prosopopoiíai*] nach antikem Vorbild

Various forms of ventriloquism having featured prominently in the "*praeexercitamenta*," Heinrich Lausberg notes that it is particularly also in this fashion that *sermocinatio* "enters into poetry" (qua literature), so providing a nexus between history, drama, and rhetoric: "This complete merging of the practicing orator into the represented persona and into the social and historical situation brings the practice of [rhetorical] exercises into proximity with the theater."[19] Another link to the stage is provided by the rhetorical practice of 'vivid description' (*evidentia*) – producing 'a mimetic effect' of "simultaneity," 'eye-' or 'earwitnessing,' 'putting something before the eyes of someone.'[20] This rhetorical *desideratum* is evidently

---

einen so großen Raum ein, daß praktisch jeder Schüler zum Schauspieler-Dichter ausgebildet wird" (p. 355). For the *Progymnasmata*'s impact on German schooling practice, see Bernhard Asmuth. "Die Entwicklung des deutschen Schulaufsatzes aus der Rhetorik." *Rhetorik: Kritische Positionen zum Stand der Forschung*, edited by Heinrich F. Plett. Munich: Fink, 1977, pp. 276–292, spec. pp. 280–287. Asmuth inveighs against the elimination "der sich situationsgebunden gebenden Ethopoiie" in twentieth-century German schooling practice – itself a symptomatic effect of a "depragmatization," a widespread "undervaluation of partisan argumentation," and loss of a "relation and reference to the situation, the other, the person" (p. 286; trans. dsm).
19 Heinrich Lausberg. *Handbuch der literarischen Rhetorik: Eine Grundlegung der Literaturwissenschaft*, 4th edition. Stuttgart: Steiner, 2008, here (resp.): pp. 532–533, §1106 (cf. p. 543, §1131–1132); p. 548, §1146; and p. 549, §1149; trans. dsm (cf. p. 409, §823). For a précis of the *Rhetorica ad Herennium*'s terms in this regard (and references to the *Progymnasmata*), cf. McDonald, *Rhetoric of Tragedy*, pp. 44–46, spec. "*Sermocinatio*, or dialogue, introduces the problem of *decorum* in composing fitting dialogue for a character" (p. 45); "in all of these figures can be seen the close affinities of rhetorical teaching to the exigencies of dramatic composition, and in the majority of the figures the examples given are clearly based upon dramatic practices" (p. 46). See Oesterreich: "der schulrhetorische Übungsbetrieb [...] ['widmet'] der Prosopopoiie (*fictio personae*) besondere Aufmerksamkeit. Die Kunst der rhetorischen Persondarstellung wird hier durch die artifizielle Simulation von sozialen Charakteren [...] trainiert. Innerhalb dieser spielerisch inszenierten Schulübungen studiert der Redner [...] eine Vielzahl unterschiedlicher personaler Rollen und nähert sich darin dem Schauspieler an" ("Person," p. 863); cf. Mayfield, "Interplay," pp. 11, 11n.–12n., and passim. The devices of *ethopoiía, dialogismós, prosopopoiía* seem tailored to the *rhétor*'s *actio*, while also evincing a considerable affinity to the dramatic actor's performance (in all its physical aspects: face, gesture, movement, etc.). As to the nexus of '*hypókrisis*' (*actio*, here rendered "impersonating") and the preservation of *ethos* and *decorum* (cf. "accommodating ['tò eoikénai'] themselves to the rôles ['prosópois'] which they assume, so that what they say is not inappropriate") with regard to "dancing" and the "'exercises'" on the part of "the rhetoricians," see Lucian. "The Dance (Saltatio / ΠΕΡΙ ΟΡΧΗΣΕΩΣ)," edited and translated by Austin M. Harmon. *Lucian*, vol. 5. Cambridge: Harvard University Press, 1972, pp. 209–289, here pp. 268–269, §65; with Charles S. Baldwin. *Ancient Rhetoric and Poetic: Interpreted from Representative Works*. Gloucester: Peter Smith, 1959, p. 74n.
20 Lausberg, *Handbuch*, p. 400, §810; trans. dsm. Cf. "In antiquity, *prosopopoeiae* were school exercises in which writers took on the persona of a famous historical or mythological figure [...]. At times, [...] rhetorical and poetic theoreticians use prosopopoeia [...] more expansively to

indicate the vivid presentation of something absent or imaginary before the eye and ear" (Terry V. F. Brogan, Albert W. Halsall, and Jeffrey S. Sychterz. "Prosopopoeia." *The Princeton Encyclopedia of Poetry & Poetics*, pp. 1120–1121, here p. 1121). On *evidentia* generally, see Heinrich F. Plett. "EVIDENTIA: Zur Rhetorik der Präsenz in den *artes* der Frühen Neuzeit." *Norm und Poesie: Zur expliziten und impliziten Poetik in der lateinischen Literatur der Frühen Neuzeit*, edited by Beate Hintzen and Roswitha Simons. Berlin: de Gruyter, 2013, pp. 255–273, passim. Cf. these synonymous, affine terms: *'enárgeia,' 'hypotýposis,' 'demonstratio,' 'descriptio,' 'ékphrasis'*; *evidentia* is vital qua effect of *sermocinatio*, to which generally desirable rhetorico-theatrical end (see Mayfield, "Interplay," pp. 15–17, spec. pp. 16n.–17n.; with further references) the latter conduces significantly (as does ékphrasis); *evidentia* is particularly interactive. Cf. in "Ocular Demonstration ['Demonstratio'] [...] an event is so described in words ['ita verbis res exprimitur'] that the business ['negotium'] seems to be enacted ['geri'] and the subject to pass vividly before our eyes ['res ante oculos esse videatur']" (*Rhetorica ad Herennium*, edited and translated by Harry Caplan. Cambridge: Harvard University Press, 2004, IV.lv.68). The notes add the terms "ἐνάργεια [...] *evidentia, repraesentatio, sub oculos subiectio* [...] ὑποτύπωσις [...] *descriptio*" (p. 405n.). For a spec. application, Quintilian suggests: "A considerable contribution to the effect ['multum confert'] may be made by combining ['adiecta'] the true facts ['veris'] with a plausible picture of the scene ['credibilis rerum imago'], which, as it were, gives the impression ['videtur'] of bringing the audience ['perducere audientis'] face to face with the event ['in rem praesentem']" (*Institutio Oratoria*, 4.2.123); Quintilian here speaks of a "descriptio" (cf. "dilucida et significans descriptio," *Institutio*, 9.2.44, specified as "of places"; see *Rhetorica*, IV.xxxix.51 and 356n.). In the Latin, the sentence structure permits immediately 'juxtaposing' the terms performatively: "adiecta veris credibilis" (*Institutio*, 4.2.123). When treating it as a so-called 'figure of thought,' Quintilian echoes Cicero's definition of "*evidentia*" as "'putting something before our eyes ['sub oculos subiectio'],'" while mentioning the Greek term ("ὑποτύπωσις") also (*Institutio*, 9.2.40); he speaks of the "mode of vivid description ['in diatyposi']" as being typically hedged by formulae such as "'Imagine that you see ['credite vos intueri']'", or (like Cicero) by referring to 'the mind's eye' ("haec, quae non vidistis oculis, animis cernere potestis,'" *Institutio*, 9.2.41; with pp. 56n.–57n.). See: "In my mind's eye, Horatio" (William Shakespeare. *Hamlet*, edited by Harold Jenkins, 2nd edition. London: Thomson, 2003, I.ii.185). On the whole, the "Figure" is said to have "something particularly vivid ['manifestius'] about it" (*Institutio*, 9.2.43). For the quasi equivalent use of the terms *'tractatio,' 'diatýposis,' 'hypotýposis,'* see Scaliger, *Poetices*, p. 122, III.xxxiii; he links these to *'ethologίa'*: "Eſt autē Tractatio, quum rem ſub oculis ponemus, luculenta narratione perſequentes eas partes, quæ ἠθολογίαν maxime comprehendunt in perſonis: in locis autem notabiles quaſdam diſpoſitiones" (ibid.); to '*notatio*': "M. Gallio διατύπωσιν, perſonæ accuratam admodum ac feſtiuam poſuit in quarto, quam appellauit Notationem" (ibid.). Having handled *'hypo-'* resp. *'diatýposis,'* he turns to *'demonstratio,' 'descriptio,' 'effictio'* (with respect to *'prosopopoeia'*): "Deſcriptionem, quam M. Gallio definit, perſpicuam rei expoſitionem. Quæ verò minutius circa perſonam verſaretur, Effictionem. Non quòd fit ficta, id eſt falſa: ſed quaſi effigiationem. Effictio enim eſt pars fictionis in Proſopopœia" (ibid., pp. 122–123, III.xxxiii). A brief subchapter on "SERMOCINATIO" ensues, which Scaliger links to the preceding: "HVic adiuncta eſt Sermocinatio, quū certus attribuitur fermo perſonæ [...] Orationes enim quodam modo picturæ ſunt animorum. & qualis quiſque eſt, ita loquitur. & in obliquo" (p. 123, III.xxxv). The aforesaid nexus to *'diatýposis'* is reaffirmed for *'attributio,' 'prosopopoeia'*: "Attributio [...] fit quoties Rei aut Perſonæ attribuim rē, aut perſonam,

accomplished on the stage, seeing that – in terms of "mimesis" – "drama" features "the maximal degree of immediacy."[21]

Focusing on artful ventriloquism in application, the present *essai* takes up the exploratory approach detailed with regard to (auto)biography, extending it to other genres, specifically historiography, poetry, and philosophy (the latter two *sensu lato*).

Rhetorical economy (*"dispositio"*) signifies the expedient "selection and arrangement"[22] of the (verbalized) matter at hand: "it is not only what we say and how we say it that matters, but also in what sequence: Disposition is therefore essential ['opus ergo est et dispositione']."[23] The practice of *oikonomía* applies to

---

aut modum, aut orationem. Rei res, vt anno fteriltas, aeri tempeftas, nocti filentium, faxo afperitas" (p. 126, III.xlviii); '*prosopopoeia*' is given as "duplex": "Primus modus, vbi ficta perfona introducitur, vt Fama à Virgilio, & Fames ab Ouidio. [...] Alterum genus Profopopœiæ, vbi non perfona fingatur eo modo, fed orationis attributione. quę adeò pertinet ad διατύπωσιν, vt fuprà eius partem fecerimus Sermocinationem. [...] nánque fi attribuam Æneæ orationem, erit fermocinatio: propterea quòd vera perfona eft. quòd fi extra argumentum introducatur: veluti quum Æneas ait fefe à patre per fomniũ obiurgari: fanè eft Profopopœia. [...] præfertim fi rei mutæ fermo attribuatur [...] Eft & alius modus, quo non oratio, fed fenfus rei brutæ afignatur. ex re enim, quæ non eft perfona, fit perfona [...] quando alloquimur brutam rem, quæ non intelligit, quafi intelligat. [...] Quintilianus fcribit, oportere eius perfonæ cui attribuitur oratio, habitum defcribi: alioqui non effe Profopopœiam, fed διαλογισμόν. Mihi videtur omnis oratio effe διαλογισμός; Perfonæ verò habitum nequaquam pingi debere, fed orationem per fe fatis poffe ad perfonam illam declarandam" (ibid.). In concluding the subchapter, Scaliger notes the affinity of 'apostrophe' ('addressing those absent') in this context of 'attribution,' 'allocution': "Similes illis fuperioribus attributionibus funt alloquutiones, quæ ad abfentes diriguntur: qualis Æneæ ad Palinurum iam non exaudientem. & Apoftrophæ quædam" (ibid.).

21 Lausberg, *Handbuch*, p. 565, §1185; trans. dsm; cf. p. 560, §1171. Re Plato's *Republic*, George Grube notes that "any direct speech" is "counted as impersonation" (thus his translation of "μιμήσει"), and "[d]rama proceeds entirely by impersonation" (*The Greek and Roman Critics*. Indianapolis: Hackett, 1995, p. 51; cf. pp. 70n.–71n.); he adds: "the rhapsodes must have dramatized the speeches in recitation" (p. 51n.). With reference to Giambattista Vico, see Chaïm Perelman. *The Realm of Rhetoric*, translated by William Kluback, edited by Carroll C. Arnold. Notre Dame: University of Notre Dame Press, 1982, p. 176, §42; cf. p. 176n.
22 Heinrich Lausberg. *Elemente der literarischen Rhetorik*, 10th edition. Ismaning: Hueber, 1990, p. 27, §46; trans. dsm.
23 Quintilian, *Institutio*, 3.3.2. Cf. "Dispositio est ordo et distributio rerum" (*Rhetorica*, I.ii.3); "dispositio est per quam illa quae invenimus in ordinem redigimus" (III.ix.16; cf. pp. 184n.–185n.) – the guiding directive being expediency ("commode," "si commodum erit," III.ix.17). Cf. Quintilian, stating "that it is [...] not always expedient to be lucid ['nec dilucida semper sit utile exponere']" (*Institutio*, 4.2.32; cf. p. 236n.); regarding narrative arrangement, the orator likewise accentuates utility: "I prefer to narrate events in the order that is most advantageous ['eo malo narrare quo expedit']" (4.2.83). Any arrangement will be 'economical,' all *dispositio* being artful. On *"oeconomia"* in Quintilian, see ibid., 3.3.9 and p. 26n.; prior, and with respect to drama, the

all written and delivered genres: given a substratum heuristically encountered during the phase of *inventio* – whether factual and historical, or already based on a literary rendering, on (*ex tempore*) fabrication – no text or speech, nor any other work of art, could do without the procedures of selecting, assembling, arranging, organizing, framing, and displaying (in terms of 'layout') the material at hand in a manner deemed conducive to the respectively present case, the mode of treating it, and the desired effect: be it dissuading or accommodating, competitive and conflictual, pondering and assessing, or vituperative and laudatory (or again otherwise).[24] That it is always significant rhetorically into whose mouth words are being put – at what time, in which context and whose presence – marks a decisive nexus between *dispositio* and *sermocinatio*.[25]

---

rhétor states: "The old Latin poets [...] are also more careful ['diligentior'] about organization ['Oeconomia'] than most of the moderns, who have come to think that clever phrases (*sententiae*) are the only virtue in any work" (ibid., 1.8.8–9); cf. Herrick, *Comic Theory*, p. 102; Baldwin, *Ancient Rhetoric*, pp. 94–106, spec. 103n.

24 Cf. Grube, *Greek and Roman Critics*, p. 106: "Ammonius [...] quotes Theophrastus as saying that every speech has two aspects, the content and the effect upon the audience; the philosopher is mainly concerned with the first, the poet or rhetorician mainly with the second: they *choose* their words for effect and *arrange* them harmoniously."

25 Contrast Nicolaus ("The *Preliminary Exercises* of Nicolaus the Sophist," edited and translated by George A. Kennedy. *Progymnasmata*, pp. 129–172, here p. 166, §10.67), who does not seem to grant rhetoric's general polyfunctionality, or that of its devices; thereto, cf. Mayfield, "Interplay," pp. 5, 5n.–6n., 8n., 14n., 33n.; with further references. Rhetorical ventriloquism (in all its variants) cannot be restricted to a matter of *elocutio*, *ornatus*. On the efficacious placement of *sententiae*, Pierre Corneille's "Discours du poème dramatique" states: "il faut les placer judicieusement, et surtout les mettre en la bouche de gens qui ayent l'esprit sans embarras, et qui ne soient point emportés par la chaleur de l'action" (quoted in: Bernhard Asmuth. *Einführung in die Dramenanalyse*, 8th edition. Stuttgart: Metzler, 2016, pp. 166–167); while that is counseled and performed with a view to *docere*, other functionalizations are conceivable – and perhaps more prevalent. In a Theophrastan context, Jeffrey Rusten remarks that Menander's "philosophizing passages [...] are often given an ironic turn when put in the mouths of unsuitable characters" ("Preface. Introduction." *Theophrastus: Characters. Herodas: Mimes. Sophron and Other Mime Fragments*, edited by Jeffrey Rusten and Ian C. Cunningham. Cambridge: Harvard University Press, 2002, pp. 3–44, here p. 17); as to the "affinity" between the aforesaid philosopher and the poet, see Manfred Fuhrmann. *Die Dichtungstheorie der Antike: Aristoteles – Horaz – 'Longin,'* 2nd edition. Darmstadt: Wissenschaftliche Buchgesellschaft, 1992, p. 157; trans. dsm. Rusten also notes that "Lucian [...] shows a direct knowledge of the [Theophrastan] *Characters*" ("Introduction," p. 18). In a context of paradoxography, burlesque, and "cynicism," Ulrich Schulz-Buschhaus speaks of François Rabelais' "putting in the mouth of Panurge" an "encomium of creditors and debtors" (*Moralistik und Poetik*. Hamburg: LIT, 1997, p. 8; trans. dsm). In artful texts, inadvertency as to in whose mouth an utterance is put may lead to problematic views on what is supposed to be 'the text's meaning' or 'the author's intention.' Generally in

With respect to poetics, any writer (including philosophers) will select and (dialogically) situate specific characters, putting convenient words into their mouths – or (often at once) citing their apparently 'historical' counterparts in a manner advantageous to the respectively present purpose and context (this being the Platonic *praxis* generally), sometimes so as to speak specifically in the extratextual writer's stead (as received by the audience or reader).[26]

Concerning the intratextual economy, Lausberg adduces "the poet's conversation with the muse" as "a special variant" of *sermocinatio*; on the stage, or in autobiography, it may tend to take the form of a "monolog" or "soliloquy," and include a speaker's auto-*sermocinatio* – putting words into his own mouth (so to say) – for instance with a view to (imagining himself in, preparing for) a future situation.[27]

---

this respect (via specific applications), see DS Mayfield. "'Against the Dog only a Dog': Talking Canines Civilizing Cynicism in Cervantes' 'Coloquio de los perros' (With Tentative Remarks on the Discourse and Method of Animal Studies)." *Humanities* 6 (2017), pp. 1–39, here pp. 14n., 19, 19n., 22, 22n., 29, spec. 32n.–33n.; with further references. http://www.mdpi.com/2076-0787/6/2/28/pdf. Accessed 25 July 2018. See also below; and Mayfield, *Artful Immorality*, pp. 91n., 128, 182n., 184, 273. As to the Machiavellian (and Livian) practice, see Leo Strauss. *Thoughts on Machiavelli*. Chicago: University of Chicago Press, 1978, pp. 10, 42 and 137–167; using the metaphor "mouthpiece," as in p. 139; cf. Harvey C. Mansfield. *Machiavelli's Virtue*. Chicago: University of Chicago Press, 1996, pp. 132, 320n. On the nexus of *dispositio* and *actio*, cf. Cicero: "Aeschines […] thought that the same speech with a change of speaker would be a different thing ['qui orationem eamdem aliam esse putaret actore mutato']" ("On the Orator: Book III," edited and translated by Harris Rackham. *On the Orator: Book III*. Cambridge: Harvard University Press, 1942, pp. 1–185, here: III.lvi.213); similarly: "Multa fiunt eadem, sed aliter" (Quintilian, *Institutio*, 2.20.10). Cf. Karlheinz Stierle: "Wiederholung ist prinzipiell vom Wiederholten unterschieden" ("Was heißt Moralistik?" *Moralistik: Explorationen und Perspektiven*, edited by Rudolf Behrens and Maria Moog-Grünewald. Munich: Fink, 2010, pp. 1–22, here p. 2).

26 This phenomenon seems pervasive (and elusive); it may also apply to a spec. citational practice; cf. "'au nom du dieu! […] ne me parlez pas de cet-homme-là!'" (Voltaire ventriloquized, or quoted, in: Friedrich Nietzsche. *Nachgelassene Fragmente 1887–1889*: *Kritische Studienausgabe*, vol. 13, edited by Giorgio Colli and Mazzino Montinari, 2nd edition. Munich/Berlin: dtv/de Gruyter, 1999, p. 44, 11[95]347). It matters who is cited – when, in what context (and whose presence). Manfred Pfister notes that "das […] produzentenbezogene Phänomen der Verwendung einer Figur als 'Sprachrohr' für die Meinungen und Ansichten des Autors" frequently determines the process of reception (*Das Drama*: *Theorie und Analyse*, 11th edition. Fink: Munich, 2001, p. 149).

27 Lausberg, *Elemente*, p. 143, §433, and §432; trans. dsm. Rhetorically, such pertains predominantly to the deliberative genre: "Die Fingierung von Selbstgesprächen beruht auf der *coniectura animi*" (*Handbuch*, p. 410, §823) – i.e. vicariously putting oneself (anticipatingly, prudentially, deliberatively, purposively) in the position of an (and potentially any) *alter*. Cf. John T. Shawcross, referring to a poem by Thomas Wyatt ("Patience, though I have not"): "While the

From a poetico-hermeneutic perspective, the above procedure might also be taken to apply to an (extratextual) author anticipating his readership intratextually, (tacitly or explicitly) putting words into their mouths (*sermocinatio* functioning qua *subiectio*), so as to reply immediately on the page.[28] Dynamizing the

---

poet seems to address a personified Patience, it is clear that he is counselling himself" ("The Poet as Orator: One Phase of His Judicial Pose." *The Rhetoric of Renaissance Poetry: From Wyatt to Milton*, edited by Thomas O. Sloan[e] and Raymond B. Waddington. Berkeley: University of California Press, 1974, pp. 5–36, here p. 15). For predominantly dramatic realizations, cf. Plett, "*Theatrum Rhetoricum*," pp. 354, 356; generally in this respect, cf. Wilfried Barner. *Barockrhetorik: Untersuchung zu ihren geschichtlichen Grundlagen*, 2nd edition. Tübingen: Niemeyer, 2002, pp. 103–104 (spec. "Rollentrieb," p. 103; "Lust zur Rolle," "Spieltrieb," p. 104).

28 In Antiquity, the practice of declamations was crucial in this respect – performed (emphasizing *actio*, delivery) not only in schools, but also later in life; it is present in medieval scholastic disputations, and Renaissance Humanist dialogues; cf. Jan Bloemendal. "Rhetoric and Early Modern Latin Drama. The Two Tragedies by the 'Polish Pindar' Simon Simonides (1558–1629): *Castus Ioseph* and *Pentesilea*." *Rhetoric and Drama*, pp. 115–134, spec. pp. 115–117. https://www.degruyter.com/downloadpdf/books/9783110484663/9783110484663-006/9783110484663-006.xml. Accessed 25 July 2018; Martha Feldman. "The Castrato as a Rhetorical Figure." *Rhetoric and Drama*, pp. 71–96, here p. 75. https://www.degruyter.com/downloadpdf/books/9783110484663/9783110484663-004/9783110484663-004.xml. Accessed 25 July 2018; with Mayfield ("Interplay," pp. 23, 24n., 29, 29n.). See Nancy L. Christiansen: "examples for imitation came from all disciplines (poetry, history, philosophy, oratory, and scripture) and from all genres (*sententiae*, dialogues, epistles, verses, themes, and orations proper), all texts were treated as 'declamations'" ("Rhetoric as Character-Fashioning: The Implications of Delivery's 'Places' in the British Renaissance *Paideia*." *Rhetorica* 15 (1997), pp. 297–334, here p. 316). As to the aspect of anticipation qua linked to the *latter*, cf. Nicolaus, "Preliminary Exercises," p. 166, §10.66–67. In various formulations, the import of the latter is accentuated in the *Progymnasmata*: "Throughout the exercise [sc. of characterization] you will preserve what is distinctive and appropriate to the persons imagined as speaking and to the occasions" (Hermogenes. "The *Preliminary Exercises* Attributed to Hermogenes," edited and translated by George A. Kennedy. *Progymnasmata*, pp. 73–88, here p. 85, §9.21). "Speeches [...] need to fit the places and occasions [...]. We shall [...] give what is appropriate to each" (John of Sardis, and Sopatros. "Selections from the Commentary on the Progymnasmata of Aphthonius Attributed to John of Sardis, Including Fragments of the Treatise on Progymnasmata by Sopatros," edited and translated by George A. Kennedy. *Progymnasmata*, pp. 173–228, here p. 214, §11.196; cf. p. 217, §11.209). Similarly, Alberic stresses *decorum* in virtually every phrase concerning "*ethopoeia*" with respect to "letter writing" (Alberic of Monte Cassino. "Flowers of Rhetoric," translated by Joseph M. Miller. *Readings in Medieval Rhetoric*, edited by Joseph M. Miller et al. Bloomington: Indiana University Press, 1973, pp. 131–161, pp. 150–151, here p. 151, VII.1; cf. Lanham, "Writing Instruction," pp. 115–116, with p. 115n.). See Demetrius on the links to the epistolary genre: "the letter [...] is like one of the two sides to a dialogue" ("On Style," translated by Doreen C. Innes and William R. Roberts. *Aristotle: Poetics. Longinus: On the Sublime. Demetrius: On Style*, edited by William H. Fyfe et al. Cambridge: Harvard University Press, 1995, pp. 309–525, p. 481, §223) – a statement given to Artemon. "Like the dialogue, the letter should be strong in characterisation

discourse, Hans Blumenberg uses this technique in the following formulation: "Maybe someone [will] say."[29] One also encounters it as a sequentialized structuring device in Seneca (conspicuously with a view to *dispositio*): "Now some person [...] will say [...] Again, the objector mentioned above wonders at our saying [...] Again, this same objector wonders at our saying" ("Hoc aliquis [...] ait [...] Deinde idem admiratur, cum dicimus [...] Deinde idem admiratur, quod dicimus").[30]

['tò ethikòn']" (pp. 482–483, §227). Cf. "Humanists [...] taught letter-writing as if letters were a kind of conversation" (Thomas O. Sloane. "Rhetorical Education and Two-Sided Argument." *Renaissance-Rhetorik / Renaissance Rhetoric*, edited by Heinrich F. Plett. Berlin: de Gruyter, 1993, pp. 163–178, here p. 171). See Lanham, "Writing Instruction," pp. 110–111 (and George Kustas quoted therein, p. 110).
29 Hans Blumenberg. *Theorie der Unbegrifflichkeit*, edited by Anselm Haverkamp. Frankfurt a. M.: Suhrkamp, 2007, p. 38; trans. dsm.
30 L. Annaeus Seneca. *Epistles 66–92*, translated by Richard M. Gummere. Cambridge: Harvard University Press, 1920, LXXXI.11–12. The above may be seen as both fictionalizing an other for his present purposes, and simultaneously 'taking up and tying in with himself' (so to speak). One frequently encounters *sermocinationes* in the imagined objector, who is preventively inserted (also in direct speech) into a treatise or essay – a useful technique for stealing an opponent's thunder, and for dynamizing (what would otherwise seem) a monolog by adding other voices. Cf. Hermogenes, "*Preliminary Exercises*," p. 85, §9.20–21. With preventive purpose, Seneca puts this objection into Lucilius' mouth: "'Epicurus' inquis, 'dixit. Quid tibi cum alieno?'" (*Epistles 1–65*, translated by Richard M. Gummere. Cambridge: Harvard University Press, 1917, XII.11) – only to invalidate it; or rather, to anticipate and so defuse the conceivable objection, placed in the mouth of a protagonist equally functionalized. This dialogic rendering of the letter or essay has affinities to an 'internal debate' – the *persona* 'Seneca' might be said to be externalizing a notional 'Lucilius' (*prosopopoiía*), interacting with him by putting words into his mouth (*dialogismós*): "In secretum te meum admitto et te adhibito mecum exigo" (XXVII.1). In the above, the *sententia* had not been ascribed previously (as far as is assessable); hence Seneca synergizes its possible functionalizations: he first names an authority for a certain *dictum*, then appropriates it: "Quod verum est, meum est [...] quae optima sunt, esse communia" (XII.11). As suggested, it would probably not have been beyond the writer's *persona* (cultivated as 'Seneca') to have posited 'Lucilius' as a fictional addressee *tout court*, functionally standing in for his own *persona*; the diction often yields the impression of the sender of a message addressing himself; this circularity is then reproduced in (or by) the reader, who vicariously finds – or (deliberately) puts – himself in the position of the addressee and (if they are taken to be the same) the emitter of the message; such circuitousness seems particularly effectual in terms of auto-persuasion. Conversely, another writer might choose to reply implicitly to a friend (Michel de Montaigne to Étienne de La Boétie); or to a teacher, often tacitly (Aristotle to Plato). As to the aforesaid technique, see Blumenberg, noting an affine employment in René Descartes: "Wahrscheinlich war es einer der fiktiven Antwortbriefe, die von ihm in Umlauf gesetzt wurden, um auf gedachte oder indirekt übermittelte Einwände einzugehen" (*Höhlenausgänge*. 1989. Frankfurt a. M.: Suhrkamp, 1996, p. 450). In exploring a familiar, then current genre, the latter also serves for tying in with

With respect to '(famous) last words,' *sermocinationes* are often encountered (and likely the rule) qua attributing apposite, pregnant, laconic, prophetic utterances to the departing – as, emphatically, their 'last word.' Blumenberg's *Die Sorge geht über den Fluß* ends with the ensuing *sententia*, wryly put into the dying Martin Heidegger's mouth (hypothetically): *"Kein Grund mehr zur Sorge."*[31]

(and thus implicitly legitimizing) a resp. present utilization. The functions of *sermocinatio* are polyvalent, Protean.
31 Hans Blumenberg. *Die Sorge geht über den Fluß*. Frankfurt a. M.: Suhrkamp, 1987, p. 222. Approximately: 'no longer any grounds for caring' – the discursive implications can hardly be retained in translation. The section is entitled 'Ein noch unbestätigtes Schlusswort.' With respect to Blumenberg himself, Odo Marquard ties in therewith; cf. "Hans Blumenberg: Entlastung vom Absoluten." *Du: Die Zeitschrift für Kultur* 51 (1991), pp. 25–26, spec. p. 26. This *sermocinatio* (the philosopher putting apt last words in Heidegger's mouth) is itself a (partial) citation of a (putative) Roman epitaph (given the telling caption "DAS DASEIN"): abbreviated as "N F F N S N C," it is said to signify "NON FUI; FUI; NON SUM; NON CURO" (Blumenberg. *Begriffe in Geschichten*. Frankfurt a. M.: Suhrkamp, 1998, p. 29); as to a quotation serving as last words, cf. Blumenberg. *Goethe zum Beispiel*, edited by Manfred Sommer and Hans Blumenberg-Archiv. 1999. Berlin: Suhrkamp, 2014, p. 88; *Matthäuspassion*, 3rd edition. Frankfurt a. M.: Suhrkamp, 1991, pp. 225–230. In "Ein Dementi," and with respect to the 'future of reception,' Blumenberg gives his motives for inventing "ein angemessenes Sterbebettfazit" for Heidegger as 'not having wished to let him take his leave from Time and Being wordlessly' (*Die Verführbarkeit des Philosophen*, edited by Manfred Sommer. 2000. Frankfurt a. M.: Suhrkamp, 2005, p. 107); at once, Blumenberg notes that "Walter Bröcker" had (himself notified by Heidegger's wife) sent him the supposedly actual last words: "*Ich bleibe noch liegen*" – roughly 'I will stay in bed a while longer' (ibid.); also cited in a more assertive, quasi-non-temporal variant (as far as change or action in the future is concerned): "*Ich bleibe liegen*" (*Die Vollzähligkeit der Sterne*. 1997. Frankfurt a. M.: Suhrkamp, 2011, p. 224). Blumenberg expressly identifies himself as a "lover of 'last words,'" justifying his having previously 'crafted the apposite for lack of the factual ones,' and declaring his 'confidence that fiction will prevail over fact': "Trotzdem bin ich zuversichtlich, daß meine Fiktion – weil Fiktionen doch immer stärker sind als Fakten – überleben wird" (*Verführbarkeit*, p. 108; trans. dsm). See another of Blumenberg's characteristic statements to this effect: "Letzte Worte dürfen erfunden sein, wenn sie gut erfunden sind, da sie ohnehin zumeist erfunden werden müssen" (*Höhlenausgänge*, p. 386n.; cf. Mayfield, *Artful Immorality*, p. 42n.). For such legitimization as per the (effectuality of the) *aptum*, cf. Blumenberg. *Lebensthemen: Aus dem Nachlaß*. Stuttgart: Reclam, 1998, p. 152. With respect to Theodor Fontane, Blumenberg suggests a short poem on the former's part as his plausible 'last word': (*Vor allem Fontane. Glossen zu einem Klassiker*. Frankfurt a. M.: Insel, 2002, p. 38). Cf. also the short essay "Letzte Worte Wielands," which commences: "Not everyone gets the chance to die as he deserves. Death is simply the precise opposite of a chance. This has an effect on ['färbt auf (…) ab', sc. 'dyes'] the circumstances. Also on the last words, for which there still is time. Or on those, who have conveyed them to us" (*Goethe zum Beispiel*, p. 101; trans. dsm). Moreover, Blumenberg suggests: "'Ein Buch möchte ich noch fertig machen, das sollte mir vergönnt sein'. […] Als letztes Wort Edmund Husserls wäre das eines Gelehrten würdig" (Husserl quoted, and commented on, in: *Lebensthemen*, p. 136); cf. "Daß es

Referring to concepts treated in more detail in the extended digital version, the present *essai* offers instances of rhetorical ventriloquism as occur in various genres and discursive contexts. To facilitate the reader's tying in with the ensuing examples, the latter are drawn from what are likely to be more or less familiar sources and authors.[32] Moreover, they are emphatically comparatist – diachronic, trans-generic, interdisciplinary, diverse (contentwise, discursively) – precisely with a view to describing the functions and applications of various ventriloquistic devices in their specific context, as well as more generally and *de re*, the latter as 'universally' (in terms of the Aristotelian '*kathólou*') as possible.[33]

In historiographic genres, such as the Thucydidean, Sallustian, Livian, or Tacitean corpus, one encounters the nexus of *dispositio* and *sermocinatio* at every

---

eine 'unendliche Arbeit' sein würde, war nicht nur eine Phrase" (p. 137). With respect to Gottfried Benn, Blumenberg writes a short essay entitled "Letztes Wort des Zynikers" (pp. 170–172; here p. 170), which commences: "Letzte Worte spielen im Bestand des Überlieferten eine eigene Rolle. Der sie gesprochen hat, ist in absoluter Weise der Belangbarkeit für sie entzogen. Er erfährt nicht mehr und kann nicht mehr bestätigen, was ihm zugeschrieben wird. Der sie gehört hat oder haben will, ist in singulärer Weise für sie verantwortlich. Die Intimität der Situation, in der sie gesprochen oder geschrieben sind, verleiht Bedeutung auch dem, der dabei oder ihr Adressat war. Der Zeuge ist dem Bild dessen verpflichtet, der danach zu ihm nichts mehr gesagt hat" (p. 170; cf. Blumenberg. *Der Mann vom Mond*: *Über Ernst Jünger*, edited by Alexander Schmitz and Marcel Lepper. Frankfurt a. M.: Suhrkamp, 2007, p. 148). Similarly, the initial words of the essay entitled "Das eine letzte Wort": "Letzte Worte werden von den anderen überliefert, die sie gehört haben oder gehört haben wollen. Sie fallen sehr verschieden aus, sonst wäre es nicht interessant, sie zu berichten noch sie kennenzulernen" (p. 143). The editors of this posthumously published volume also grouped further essays with said theme in the resp. section ("IX. Letzte Worte," pp. 143–151) – among them a miniature entitled "Letztes Wort," giving that on the part of "Ernst Robert Curtius" (via Rolf Hochhuth, then Ernst Jünger) as "*Aufmachen!*"; Blumenberg's comment: "Kann man das ausdenken?" (p. 147). In the same essay, he refers to "Jünger" as a 'collector of last words' (cf. p. 149), which might also be thought to apply to Blumenberg's own practice. Generally, see Ahlrich Meyer. "Nachwort des Herausgebers." *Rigorismus der Wahrheit*: '*Moses der Ägypter' und weitere Texte zu Freud und Arendt*, edited by Ahlrich Meyer. Berlin: Suhrkamp, 2015, pp. 105–130, here p. 115. With respect to Johann W. Goethe's (supposed) "'*Mehr Licht*,'" see Jünger's quote, cited in Blumenberg, *Jünger*, p. 148; plus his appropriation thereof in *Höhlenausgänge*, p. 55.

32 Cf. Erving Goffman's statement, tying in with Georg Simmel's method: "The illustrative materials used in this study are of mixed status [...]. The justification for this approach [...] is that the illustrations together fit into a coherent framework that ties together bits of experience the reader has already had" (*The Presentation of Self in Everyday Life*. New York: Penguin, 1990, pp. 9–10).

33 Aristotle. "Poetics," translated by Stephen Halliwell. *Aristotle*: *Poetics*, pp. 27–141, here §9, 1451b.

turn.³⁴ Any historian will inevitably choose the specific material to be modeled from a vast corpus of contingent particularities – few of them based on his own experience, the far greater share gathered from various sources already extant, frequently amplified, varied, and reaccentuated by personified collectives, dead men revivified, attributed speeches and envisioned dialogues, verbally sketched appearances, studies in ethos (*prosopopoiía, eidolopoiía, dialogismós, charakterismós, ethopoiía*); moreover, he will be likely to aim at arranging actualities and pragmatic fabrications (such as conceivable speech acts or probable portrayals of

---

34 Cf. "Außer bei Lysias findet sich die E[thopoeia] besonders häufig in der rhetorisch beeinflußten *Historiographie*. Thukydides etwa setzt bewußt Reden und Charakterisierungen berühmter Politiker und Feldherren zur Darstellung von Geschichte ein" (Naschert, "Ethopoeia," p. 1514). In a Theophrastan context, Rusten speaks of "the famous sketches of historical figures in Sallust and Tacitus" ("Introduction," p. 19) as inspired by the rhetorical tradition of "Character sketching" – which he refers to as '*charakterismoí* or *ethologíai*' (p. 18; cf. Marcus Tullius Cicero. "Topics," edited and translated by Harry M. Hubbell. *On Invention. Best Kind of Orator. Topics*. Cambridge: Harvard University Press, 1949, pp. 375–459, here p. 446, xxi.83; Quintilian, *Institutio*, 1.9.3 and p. 210n.): *de re*, he must mean '*ethopoiíai*' – with '*charakterismós*' ('*effictio*') typically referring to the externals only. Rusten also notes that Christopher Gill "slights rhetorical influence" in this respect ("Introduction," p. 19n.; cf. Gill. "The Question of Character-Development: Plutarch and Tacitus." *The Classical Quarterly* 33 (1983), pp. 469–487, passim); in fact, the same holds true for the latter's other publication on the concept at hand (Gill. "Personhood and Personality: The Four-*personae* Theory in Cicero, *de Officiis* I." *Oxford Studies in Ancient Philosophy*, vol. VI, edited by Julia Annas. Oxford: Clarendon, 1988, pp. 169–199, passim; for a brief reference to rhetoric, cf. p. 194). As to the function of the Theophrastan *Characters*, Rusten notes (but cannot confirm) that a "suggested purpose is rhetorical instruction. There is no doubt that this is the use to which the work was eventually put; indeed it owes its very survival to its inclusion among the handbooks of the schools" ("Introduction," p. 22; cf. pp. 29, 33; see Grube, *Greek and Roman Critics*, p. 103). Contrast Gill's unrhetorical view on "Theophrastus' *Characters*," speaking of "the relative triviality of this work" ("Question," p. 469n.). On "Charakterzeichnung" in Horace, see Fuhrmann, *Dichtungstheorie*, p. 135; referring to Horace, "Ars Poetica," edited and translated by Henry R. Fairclough. *Satires. Epistles. Ars Poetica*. 1926. Cambridge: Harvard University Press, 2005, pp. 442–489, here pp. 462–465, v.153–178; cf. spec. "notanda sunt tibi mores," p. 462, v.156; "décor," v.157; "morabimur aptis," p. 464, v.178. Fuhrmann notes the nexus with "Hellenism, especially [...] Theophrastus, who [...] had given considerable attention to characterology" (*Dichtungstheorie*, p. 136; trans. dsm); as to a "Rhetorisierung der Poetik," he logs "die bedeutende Rolle [...] die [...] dem Konventionellen und Typischen zukommt. Die Kategorie der Angemessenheit, des Passenden und Schicklichen (prepon, harmotton; *decorum, aptum*) entstammte der Rhetorik" (p. 156). "Beide Bereiche, das Konventionelle und das Typische, scheinen in dem Aristoteles-Schüler Theophrast den für die hellenistische Zeit wichtigsten oder gar maßgeblichen Theoretiker gefunden haben" (p. 157). Cf. Baldwin: "Ancient poetic was [...] rhetoricated" (*Ancient Rhetoric*, p. 240); "most of the *Ars Poetica* applies equally to *ars rhetorica*" (p. 246, with p. 245).

character) in a plausible and appositely expedient manner, always being – in his way, and as a matter of course – 'economical with the facts.'[35]

In a procedural passage, Thucydides explicates the professional guidelines for the economy of *sermocinationes* within his historical narrative:

> As to the speeches that were made by different men [...] it has been difficult to recall with strict accuracy ['akríbeian'] the words actually spoken, both for me as regards that which I myself heard, and for those who from various other sources have brought me reports ['apangéllousin']. Therefore the speeches are given in the language in which, as it seemed to me, the several speakers would express, on the subjects under consideration, the sentiments most befitting the occasion ['perì ton aieì parónton tà déonta málist(a)'], though at the same time I have adhered as closely as possible to the general sense of what was actually said.[36]

The notion and practice of *dispositio* will per se signal that chronology does not tend to be the primary concern (even more so in other genres). In this respect, rhetorical economy is the *téchne*'s foremost task – especially with a view to employing it so effectually as to go unnoticed (*'celare artem'*). Moreover, any historian will seek to vary his subject matter and its treatment (*tractatio*) to avoid tedium, precisely by producing an intense and dynamic effect in the reader's experience

---

35 Hayden White refers to Jules Michelet's conception of "the historian" as "writing on behalf of the dead," and as "also writing *for* the dead" – as a "Prometheus," who "will bring to the dead a fire sufficiently intense to melt the ice in which their 'voices' have been 'frozen,' so that the dead will be able to 'speak once more' for themselves"; moreover, "[t]he historian must be able to hear and to understand 'words that were never spoken [...]'. The task of the historian, finally, is 'to make the silences of history speak[']" (*Metahistory: The Historical Imagination in Nineteenth-Century Europe*. Baltimore: Johns Hopkins University Press, 1975, pp. 158–159). In rhetorical terminology, the above formulations would primarily refer to *eidolopoiía*. White also mentions Karl Marx' putting words into the mouths of "[t]he French bourgeoisie" (cf. "has them say," p. 325) – a *sermocinatio* with a view to a collective (hence also a *prosopopoiía*). While diachronically and dependably central to historiography – as well as to White's own project *de re* – he does not seem to focus on such ventriloquistic processes, and in one instance explicitly recants their interpretive function: "The protagonist of *The Old Regime* was the old regime itself [...]. It is too strong to say that Tocqueville actually personified the old regime and made of it the Tragic hero of his story, but there is a certain Lear-like quality about its dilemma" (p. 215).
36 Thucydides. *History of the Peloponnesian War: Books I and II*, edited and translated by Charles Forster Smith. Cambridge: Harvard University Press, 1991, I.xxii.1. Cf. Jacob Burckhardt. *Griechische Kulturgeschichte III. Gesammelte Werke*, vol. VII. Darmstadt: Wissenschaftliche Buchgesellschaft, 1962, pp. 413–414; Wesley Trimpi. *Muses of One Mind: The Literary Analysis of Experience and Its Continuity*. Eugene: Wipf & Stock, 2009, p. 57n. Smith notes that Thucydides' "readers become spectators, as Plutarch expressed it" ("Introduction: Bibliography." *Thucydides: History of the Peloponnesian War*, vol. 1, pp. vii–xxiii, p. xvii): "He dramatises history" (p. xviii).

(*enárgeia*); to this end, he provides vivid descriptions of certain scenes, or puts (striking) words into the mouths of familiar, (supposedly) historical or mythological protagonists (*sermocinatio*) – brings the dead to life, in (and by) speech (*eidolopoiía*), drafts distinctive portrayals with a characterizing function (*ethopoiía*), personifies collectives or abstract entities (*prosopopoiía*).

Tacitus deploys the ventriloquistic technique most efficaciously – typically for terse sentences, and at crucial or climactic moments.[37] In a context relating the mutinies in the largely unsubdued area known as '*Germania*,' he presents them as worse than any "civil war" in the ensuing vivid description, which culminates in a distinctive *sermocinatio*:

> The yells, the wounds, and the blood were plain enough; the cause, invisible ['causa in occulto']: chance ruled supreme ['cuncta fors regit']. [...] No general or tribune was there to restrain: licence ['licentia'] was granted to the mob ['vulgo'], and it might glut its vengeance to the full ['satietas']. Before long, Germanicus marched into the camp. 'This is not a cure, but a calamity' ['non medicinam (...) sed cladem'], he said, with a burst of tears, and ordered the bodies to be cremated.[38]

The entire scene seems to be disposed like the climax and (cathartic) *dénouement* of a tragedy; the pathopoietic words here put in Germanicus' mouth are clearly functionalized with a view to *movere*.

One noted instance from Livy – being incomparably feckful also in generating myriad adaptations, reworkings, similarly floating in virtual cultural networks – is the 'rape of Lucretia,' her consequent suicide, and the establishing of the Roman Republic by Lucius Junius Brutus: initially, two short sentences are put into Sextus Tarquinius' mouth, prior to his violation of the archetypal Roman lady; they commence: "Tace, Lucretia."[39] The female protagonist is

---

[37] Baldwin notes that "*ethopœiæ*" (qua exercises) typically dealt with what "some [...] character of history or fiction ['must have said'] on a critical occasion" (*Ancient Rhetoric*, pp. 71–72; cf. p. 218) – here with emphasis on the latter phrase.

[38] Tacitus. "The Annals: Books I–III," translated by John Jackson. *The Histories: Books IV-V. The Annals: Books I-III*, vol. III, edited by Clifford H. Moore and John Jackson. Cambridge: Harvard University Press, 1931, pp. 225–643, I.xlix. The translation accentuates the centrality and effectuality of the *sermocinatio* by a proximate, alliterative paronomasia in the parallelism (adapted to the needs of an analytical language).

[39] Livy. *History of Rome: Books 1–2*, edited and translated by Benjamin O. Foster. Cambridge: Harvard University Press, 1988, I.lviii.2. "'Tace, Lucretia,' inquit; 'Sex. Tarquinius sum; ferrum in manu est; moriere, si emiseris vocem.'" As to the sustained intertextuality thereof, see Ian Donaldson. *The Rapes of Lucretia: A Myth and its Transformations*. Oxford: Oxford University Press, 1982, passim; as well as Pavel Sokolov's article in the present volume. On the concept of '(virtual) cultural networks,' see Joachim Küpper, *The Cultural Net: Early Modern Drama as a Paradigm*.

later given a longer sequence of direct speech, reporting Tarquin's physical transgression to her husband. From the descriptive narrative, Livy transitions into a plausible dialogic sequence: "to her husband's question, 'Is all well?' she replied, 'Far from it'" – the Latin being even more dynamic, with question and answer immediately succeeding one another in Livy's textual economy: "'Satin salvae?' 'Minime.'"[40] Needless to say, the writer was not present, nor does it seem likely that he had at his disposal documents giving a verbatim account of Lucretia's precise wording; yet such a quasi 'historicist' notion is unlikely to occur (irrespective of its irrefutability), seeing that momentaneous *evidentia* – effected by *descriptio* and the verbal highpoint of the *sermocinatio* – is so effectual that the recipient's *ratio* (whatever its valence otherwise) will here be suspended.

By contrast, Augustine treats this event delegatively, in that he refers to an unspecified orator: "A certain declaimer develops ['declamans ait'] this theme admirably ['Egregie'] and accurately ['veraciterque']: 'A wonderful tale ['Mirabile dictu']! There were two and only one committed adultery ['duo fuerunt, et adulterium unus admisit']."[41] Discursively, the Church Father requires this particular superstructure, his 'moral of the tale' – not Lucretia's direct speech (evoking her paganly inflected *ethos*, for which Augustine has no use). Since the declaimer is not known, while being all but tailored to the Christian *rhétor*'s purpose, the latter might as well have thought him up, using said *sententiae* as a pretext for the discursive needs in the economy of this particular context.[42] When words are being put into the mouth of what is deemed a deity at a given point in time (as per the respectively prevalent language regime), cases like these have a tendency to turn particularly problematic

---

Berlin: de Gruyter, 2018. https://www.degruyter.com/viewbooktoc/product/486166. Accessed 25 July 2018; "Rhetoric and the Cultural Net: Transnational Agencies of Culture." *Rhetoric and Drama*, pp. 151–175. https://www.degruyter.com/downloadpdf/books/9783110484663/9783110484663-008/9783110484663-008.xml. Accessed 25 July 2018; Mayfield, "Proceedings." *Rhetoric and Drama*, pp. 220–222. https://www.degruyter.com/downloadpdf/books/9783110484663/9783110484663-010/9783110484663-010.xml. Accessed 25 July 2018.
40 Livy, *History of Rome*, I.lviii.7.
41 Aurelius Augustine. *The City of God Against the Pagans*: *Books I–III*, translated by George E. McCracken. Cambridge: Harvard University Press, 1957, pp. 84–85, I.xix; with p. 84n. (concerning the declaimer).
42 Nor would it be beyond that *rhétor malgré soi* to be drawing on his own oratorical schooling, while discriminating between his rhetorical 'self' prior to, and after, the '*tolle lege*' (see above).

(qua 'speaking in the name of'). For lack of competence in that field, one may leave such aside, here.[43]

Being human, however, a scholar could seem qualified with respect to what is thought by some to be the other side, the Humanities – wherefore one might adduce these words, which John Milton aptly places in the mouth of his protagonist: "Better to reign in Hell than serve in Heaven!"[44] They are particularly pertinent here, since that assertion is a variation on a Homeric *sermocinatio*, which had long been floating in various cultural networks – the source context being the *Odyssey*'s hero meeting Achilles in Hades.[45] The latter is made to say:

---

43 Cf. *"Deum autem velle"* (Hans Blumenberg. *Die Genesis der kopernikanischen Welt: Typologie der frühen Wirkungen. Der Stillstand des Himmels und der Fortgang der Zeit*, vol. II, 3rd edition. Frankfurt a. M.: Suhrkamp, 1996, p. 406). This piece of writing is attributed to "Menippus the Cynic": "Epistles artificially composed as if by the gods ['apò tou ton theon prosópou']" (Diogenes Laertius. *Lives of Eminent Philosophers*, vol. II, edited and translated by Robert D. Hicks. 1925. Cambridge: Harvard University Press, 2005, pp. 104–105, VI.101). Similarly, when a writer or *rhétor* is said to speak for – to be the 'mouthpiece' of – another entity envisioned (vice versa, *de re*): "et Xenophontis voce Musas quasi locutas ferunt" (Marcus Tullius Cicero. "Orator," translated by Harry M. Hubbell. *Brutus. Orator*, edited by George L. Hendrickson and Harry M. Hubbell. Cambridge: Harvard University Press, 1962, pp. 295–509, here p. 350, xix.62). Cf. a *sermocinatio* of "God" in Seneca: "Puta itaque deum dicere" (*Moral Essays*, edited and translated by John W. Basore. Cambridge: Harvard University Press, 1928, p. 42, VI.3); at the outset: "the task is not difficult, – I shall be pleading the cause of the gods" (p. 3, I.1); plus the (quasi theodicy-like) setup or pretext: "You have asked me, Lucilius, why, if a Providence rules the world, it still happens that many evils befall good men" (ibid.). See Horace's *sermocinatio* for the goddess Juno concerning Troy and Rome (*Odes and Epodes*, edited and translated by Niall Rudd. Cambridge: Harvard University Press, 2012, III.3). Horace interrupts or ends his *sermocinatio* for Juno with the words (externalizing and personifying the Muse by addressing her): "non hoc iocosae conveniet lyrae; / quo, Musa, tendis? Desine pervicax / referre sermones deorum et / magna modis tenuare parvis" (III.3.69–72). See also Augustine's *prosopopoiía* treated above.

44 John Milton. *Paradise Lost: Authoritative Text. Sources and Backgrounds. Criticism*, edited by Gordon Teskey. New York: Norton, 2005, I.263.

45 For a figurative reapplication to (actual) political life, cf. Cicero's citation (or *sermocinatio*) of part of a letter by Atticus, (implicitly) equating Odysseus with Caesar, and the ghosts with the latter's followers (see the keyword "νέκυιαν"; Marcus Tullius Cicero. *Letters to Atticus*, edited and translated by David R. Shackleton Bailey. Cambridge: Harvard University Press, 1999, §177.IX.10; cf. p. 60n.); one might say that Atticus (as cited by Cicero) is inverting the procedure of *prosopopoiía* (resp. *eidolopoiía*), seeing that he quasi de-personifies (or 'ghostifies') human beings along the lines of a paradigmatic segment of a traditional, arch-familiar text.

Never try to reconcile me to death, glorious Odysseus. I should choose, so I might live on earth, to serve as the hireling of another, some landless man with hardly enough to live on, rather than to be lord over all the dead that have perished.[46]

While varied, the context remains similar, hence recognizable; but the Homeric *eidolopoiía* (Achilles being defunct at this point) has been transferred to an altogether different discursive setting in Milton.[47]

When inserted into a chiefly narrative context, likely ventriloquisms will often be realized as individual *sententiae* only – for instance, when Suetonius recounts Caesar's arrival in Africa: "No regard for religion ever turned him from any undertaking, or even delayed him. [...] Even when he had a fall as he disembarked, he gave the omen a favorable turn by crying: 'I hold thee fast, Africa' ['Teneo te', inquit, 'Africa']."[48] Given the context and its economy, the words put in Caesar's mouth here also serve an ethopoietic purpose.

From a metapoetical perspective, *sermocinationes* are at times embedded in anecdotal exchanges or dialogues. This typically occurs when (allegedly) historical figures meet, and celebrated or clever utterances are being put into their mouths for maximum effect (disposed with a view to an especially vivid immediacy, functioning as 'momentaneous evidence'); some may have already been floating in virtual cultural networks in certain variants, while others are crafted for, and disposed to suit, the particular (discursive) purpose at hand. In a context concisely exemplifying Spartan "terseness" ('laconism') – and also with an ethopoietic agenda – Plutarch attributes words to the respective parties:

---

46 Homer. *Odyssey*: Books 1–12, translated by Alan T. Murray and George E. Dimock, 2nd edition. Cambridge: Harvard University Press, 1998, XI.488–491.
47 For the reference, cf. Scott Ellege's note: "An ironic echo of *Odyssey* 11.489–91, where the shade of Achilles tells Odysseus that it is better to be a farmhand on earth than a king among the dead" (quoted in: John Milton. "Paradise Lost. Second Edition (1674)." *The Norton Anthology of English Literature*, vol. I, edited by Stephen Greenblatt, and Meyer H. Abrams. New York: Norton, 2006, pp. 1830–2055, here p. 1838n.) – whether or not there is 'irony' in play here would depend on the sense attached to that concept in this context. In Milton, the term *eidolopoiía* would arguably no longer be applicable, since Satan is not dead and cannot die (dogmatically speaking).
48 Suetonius. *Lives of the Caesars*: I–IV, translated by John C. Rolfe, edited by Keith R. Bradley, 3rd edition. Cambridge: Harvard University Press, 2001, I.lix. For an early modern refunctionalization of said fall in Pedro Calderón de la Barca, see Küpper, *Discursive* Renovatio, pp. 342–343, with n. "[V]eni•vidi•vici" – the most notorious words on Caesar's part – are not actually put in the victor's mouth in Suetonius, but "displayed among the show-pieces" of the triumph as "an inscription of but three words" – with this comment: "not indicating the events of the war [...], but the speed with which it was finished" (*Lives of the Caesars*, I.xxxvii.2).

when Philip wrote to them, 'If I invade Laconia, I shall turn you out,' they wrote back, 'If.' And when King Demetrius was annoyed and shouted, 'Have the Spartans sent only one envoy to *me*?' the envoy replied undismayed, 'One to one.'⁴⁹

In the second instance, a delegate – functionally standing in, and actually speaking for, a collective – demonstrates that the device of *prosopopoiía* might be replaced (with a view to verisimilitude, for instance) by referring to (an otherwise abstract political institution typically represented by) actual persons such as emissaries, ambassadors, etc.

In other genres, such as the Platonic or Lucianic dialogue, one frequently encounters protagonists that 'everyone knows' from similar renderings: these are familiar *personae* floating in the vast virtual networks of a culture's oral and written tradition, with characteristic sayings, dialogic anecdotes, or exemplary feats (at times rather loosely) attached to them (*dialogismoí, ethopoiíai*).⁵⁰ In such cases, there is a need to maintain a certain recognizability (as per the *aptum*), but also a considerable leeway in precisely this respect; hence a writer might produce the desired effects of both recognition (formally, an effect of repetition) and novelty (unfamiliarity) or variation in the recipients.⁵¹

---

49 Plutarch. *Moralia*, vol. 6, translated by William C. Helmbold. Cambridge: Harvard University Press, 2005, pp. 445, 511A. Cf. "the words of a Laconian, sparse and clear, differ from those of a man of Attica, which are voluble" (Aelius Theon. "The Exercises of Aelius Theon," edited and translated by George A. Kennedy. *Progymnasmata*, §8.116); "the words of a Laconian will be 'few and clear', and those of a man of Attica garrulous" (John of Sardis/Sopatros, "Selections," §11.196).
50 "Exemplum est alicuius facti et dicti praeteriti cum certi auctoris nomine propositio" (*Rhetorica*, IV.xlix.62). Cf. "A style without contrivance fits ethopoeias; for the speaker will say what is acknowledged universally in a scattered fashion, in short phrases and without connectives. And it ought to be wholly consistent with the character and the subject. Concise (*syntomos*): Vigorous, forceful; for that is the style of commonly accepted ideas and what each person knows" (John of Sardis/Sopatros, "Selections," §11.208,4; emphasis removed from "concise"). Cf. Gill, "Personhood," p. 181.
51 With respect to effectually using something '*xenikòn*,' see Aristotle, *Rhetoric*, 1404b. As to the *aptum* in the above respect, cf. Asmuth: "The ties between the poetics of drama and rhetoric are even closer with regard to the *characters* and their style of speaking. When Aristotle introduces *appropriateness* (πρέπον, [...] ἁρμόττον [...]) as a stylistic principle in his 'Rhetoric', he is thinking of diction as adequate to the situation and case at hand, but especially to the speaker's social status. Accordingly, the conceptions of his 'Poetics' concerning characters (Greek éthē, singular: éthos) in drama entirely adhere to the principle of appropriateness: the character of a dramatic persona is to be in accord with its social role, with the historical tradition, and with itself" (Bernhard Asmuth. "Drama," translated by DS Mayfield. *Rhetoric and Drama*, pp. 179–201, here p. 185. https://www.degruyter.com/downloadpdf/books/9783110484663/9783110484663-009/9783110484663-009.xml. Accessed 25 July 2018. On variation with a view to the audience, see Cicero: "Consequently it is necessary to choose ['est eligendum'] the style of oratory ['Genus (...) dicendi'] best calculated

This ties in with Aristotle's *Poetics*, stating that a well-known 'historical' or mythological character must be rendered according to the tradition – for the most part:

> Now, one cannot break up the transmitted stories (I mean, e.g., Clytemnestra's death at Orestes' hands, and Eriphyle's at Alcmaeon's), but the poet should be [rhetorically] inventive ['heurískein'] as well as making good use of traditional stories.[52]

To some degree of probability, a *persona*'s remodeling must proceed within certain limits set by custom, and be in keeping with what may be familiar to – hence deemed apposite by – a given audience regarding a particular (mythologico-historical) protagonist.[53] Aristotle habitually counsels to initially tie in with what 'everyone knows or might know' – with what is likely to be literally 'plausible' – since such evokes and effects a 'universal' common ground, on which to simultaneously draw and build for utmost impact: "With character, precisely as in the structure of events, one should always seek necessity or probability ['tò anankaion hè tò eikós']."[54]

The Aristophanic *Clouds* – staging 'Socrates' in a manner somewhat dissimilar from other renderings – may be the most notorious example in this respect:

---

to hold the attention of the audience ['quod maxime teneat eos qui audiant'], and not merely to give them pleasure ['delectet'] but also to do so without giving them too much of it ['sine satietate delectet']" ("On the Orator," III.xxiv.97) – i.e. 'variation without satiety for maximum efficiency'; the context being the *ornatus* (cf. III.xxv.99–100; Quintilian, *Institutio*, 4.2.118).

52 Aristotle, *Poetics*, 1453b. See also Joachim Küpper's article in the present volume. The fact that today many of the (mythological, historical) names given by Aristotle (perhaps spec. 'Eriphyle,' 'Alcmaeon') will be recognized only by specialists (in contrast to, say, 'Achilles' or 'Helen') may seem to prove the point the philosopher is making (see the note below).

53 This links to the rhetorical directive of always reckoning with, and adhering to, *decorum* (tò prépon) – meaning, suitability not only in subject matter, but also in terms of being credibly in accord with the common knowledge floating in virtual cultural networks at a given time. Cf. Wesley Trimpi, connecting *aequitas* and the *aptum*: "Equity gains its freedom from (written) statutes and poetry its freedom from (recorded) history by concentrating on qualitative issues. Equity seeks the proper relation between the individual controversy to be judged and the body of statutes to be applied to it, while poetry seeks the proper relation of given particular events, historical or imaginary, to a principle by means of which they may gain significance" (Wesley Trimpi. "Reason and the Classical Premises of Literary Decorum." *Independent Journal of Philosophy* 5/6 [1988], pp. 103–111, here p. 104).

54 Aristotle, *Poetics*, 1454a. Naturally, one might as well claim to be referring to a general consensus or common ground that does not obtain (or no longer); generally thereto, see Mayfield, *Artful Immorality*, pp. 80, 80n.–81n., 115, 187. Cf. "for this is already common knowledge, and there is nobody who does not agree ['homologei'], both from what he has been told ['akoe mathèn'] and from personal experience ['peíra']" (Dionysius of Halicarnassus. "Lysias [ΛΥΣΙΑΣ ΣΥΡΑΚΟΥΣΙΟΣ ΠΑΤΡΟΘΕΝ]," edited and translated by Stephen Usher. *Critical Essays*, vol. I. Cambridge: Harvard University Press, 1974, pp. 20–99, pp. 36–37, §10, here infinitized).

when contrasted with Plato's variously nuanced versions, the play evinces both a certain set of overlapping characteristics being attributed to the *persona* 'Socrates,' and a considerable scope as regards the tendency of the overall, ethopoietic 'image' conveyed. In a dialogic exchange with the would-be student Strepsiades, the latter asks: "tell me [...] what you're up to"; and the Aristophanic 'Socrates' replies: "I tread the air and scrutinize the sun."[55] With regard to the dramatist's poetics, these words represent a *sermocinatio* specially suited to the context and its economy.

Generally (and metapoetically) speaking, rhetorical ventriloquism may also serve as an (implicit) pretext for writing in the first place. With regard to Plato's delegated prolixity, Blumenberg wryly remarks: "Of course, only someone who lets Socrates speak is permitted to write that much" – while spiriting away his own philosophical *persona*.[56] Robert Branham suggests that one discern "Plato's

---

[55] Aristophanes. *Clouds*, edited and translated by Jeffrey Henderson. *Clouds. Wasps. Peace*. Cambridge: Harvard University Press, 1998, pp. 1–211, here v. 224–225.

[56] Hans Blumenberg. *Ein mögliches Selbstverständnis: Aus dem Nachlaß*. Stuttgart: Reclam, 1997, with the context: "Dialoge können nicht geschrieben, allenfalls nachgeschrieben werden, wie fiktiv auch immer. An der sokratischen Verweigerung des Schreibens rechtfertigt Plato den sokratischen Dialog: So viel darf eben nur schreiben, wer Sokrates reden läßt" (ibid.). To this extent, Plato – ostensively keeping silent about 'himself' – puts 'Socrates' (qua *persona*) into the notional (and semantic) position that would be labeled 'god' in other (usually religious) contexts. As to such silence with another accent, see Immanuel Kant, citing Bacon's "*Instauratio magna. Praefatio.* / *De nobis ipsis silemus: De re autem*" (*Kritik der reinen Vernunft. Werkausgabe*, vol. III, edited by Wilhelm Weischedel, 13th edition. Frankfurt a. M.: Suhrkamp, 1995, p. 7) – in other words: still letting the resp. prevalent 'god' speak (be it called '*res*,' or 'Reason,' or otherwise); see Blumenberg: "*De nobis ipsis silemus* [...]. Es ist ein Schlüsselwort der Epoche" (*Schriften zur Technik*, edited by Alexander Schmitz and Bernd Stiegler. Berlin: Suhrkamp, 2015, p. 74); "Ohne alle transzendentale Phraseologie wird fast zwanglos ihr identisches Ergebnis fällig, daß wir über uns schweigen: *De nobis ipsis silemus*" (*Beschreibung des Menschen*, edited by Manfred Sommer. Frankfurt a. M.: Suhrkamp, 2006, p. 15). Such silence (e.g. as a result of the state of transmission) may lead to attempts at personifying an author from the text. Sappho might be a particularly elucidating example. As to "the complex relation between face and voice in fragment 31" and "the mutual implication of speaking and not speaking in this poem," see Yopie Prins. "Sappho's Afterlife in Translation." *Re-Reading Sappho: Reception and Transmission*, edited by Ellen Greene. Berkeley, Los Angeles: University of California Press, 1996, pp. 36–67, p. 43; with "Sappho: Testimonia. Text," edited and translated by David A. Campbell. *Greek Lyric*, vol. I. Cambridge: Harvard University Press, 1990, pp. 2–205, here pp. 78–81, §31; Longinus, "On the Sublime," pp. 198–199, §10.2.; cf. Elizabeth D. Harvey. *Ventriloquized Voices: Feminist Theory and English Renaissance Texts*. London: Routledge, 1995, p. 124; "Ventriloquizing Sappho, or the Lesbian Muse." *Re-Reading Sappho*, pp. 79–104, here pp. 88–89. Prins notes: "Through [...] personification[,] Longinus is able to conflate poem and poet: Sappho *is* fragment 31" ("Sappho's Afterlife," pp. 49–50; generally, cf. pp. 42–43, 45–46, 53).

comic technique" in "presenting thinkers as personified expressions of their theories, as comic instantiations of their own dominant ideas."[57]

Many dialogues – such as Plato's *Symposium*, or Lucian's artful pieces – might be seen as virtually giving themselves to being put on stage, certain elaborate diegetic frameworks notwithstanding. Branham, also referring to Lucian's use of *prosopopoeia*, states:

> Where New Comic or classical tragic poets appear to have constructed their plays from the plot up, Lucian's procedure is just the opposite: he begins by selecting a recognizable voice or set of voices and then projects them into a provocative situation, whether in Hades, on Olympus, or in ancient Athens. Here his rhetorical training in imitating the masters serves him well. In fact, Lucian's protean ability for imitation and parody brings him into contact with every major genre from Homer through Theocritus.[58]

Plato and Lucian might be taken as expedient examples with a view to suggesting that the temporal distance to the 'actual life' of the historical individual is only of secondary import: once a recognizable *persona* is floating in the vast virtual networks of various (interwoven) cultures, it may take on – or relinquish en route – many different 'masks' or 'public images'; the latter suggest what will be deemed appropriate for that *persona* at a given point in time, and relatively regardless of genre (*de re*). Ventriloquistic techniques are of universal application, the same as the *rhetoriké téchne* on the whole – whether applied in historiography, drama, philosophical dialogue, or otherwise.

D. Laertius represents a *copia* in this regard: with rather few references to sources, and all but indiscriminately as to the emitting discourse or context, his *Lives* collect and assemble myriad instances as are likely to have been *sermocinationes* (stand-alone, embedded in *ethopoiíai*, part of dramatic works, etc.). Frequently

---

57 Robert B. Branham. *Unruly Eloquence: Lucian and the Comedy of Traditions*. Cambridge: Harvard University Press, 1989, p. 72.
58 Ibid., pp. 4–5. This reverses Aristotle's recommended procedure: "A plot is not unified, as some think, if built round an individual" (*Poetics*, 1451a); Halliwell glosses: "unity of 'hero' is not a sufficient (or even necessary) condition for unity of plot" (p. 57n.). This links to the accentuation of the '*kathólou*' in '*poíesis*' (*sensu lato*), as contrasted with the emphasis on "particulars" in "history" (1451b): "In comedy [...] the poets construct the plot on the basis of probability, and only then supply arbitrary names; they do not, like iambic poets, write about a particular person. But in tragedy they adhere to the actual names. The reason is that the possible seems plausible [...]. Yet even in some tragedies there are only one or two familiar names, while the rest are invented; and in certain plays no name is familiar[.] [...] adherence to the traditional plots of tragedy should not be sought at all costs. Indeed, to seek this is absurd, since even the familiar subjects are familiar only to a minority, yet nonetheless please everyone" (p. 57n.).

(or even typically), the reader of anecdotes is probably facing rhetorico-*enargic* fabrications crafted with a view to effecting strikingly vivid scenes, specifically by putting words into the mouths of particular *personae*. The *Lives* may thus be seen as a rhetorical arsenal of effectual attributions (*sermocinationes*) and characterizations (*ethopoiíai*) – a depot that might serve as a sort of 'checklist' as to what may be thought to have been aptly hence plausibly attached to certain supposedly historical figures. Multiple ascriptions of similar sayings or anecdotes to different protagonists point to overlaps in the 'personating' (typifying, characterizing) process – this being one of the necessary results of any 'image' floating in virtual cultural networks: once a rhetorical 'self' is found to 'sell,' it will inevitably be recycled, leading to further *sermocinationes* (a dynamics remaining fairly stable to this day).[59] The ensuing set of layered statements might serve as a sample:

> Sotion [...] says that he [sc. Anaxagoras] was indicted [...] on a charge of impiety ['asebeías'] [...] and that sentence of death was passed on Anaxagoras by default. When news was brought him that he was condemned and his sons were dead, his comment on the sentence was, 'Long ago nature condemned both my judges and myself to death'; and on his sons, 'I knew that my children were born to die'. Some, however, tell this story of Solon, and others of Xenophon.[60]

The latter signals that, metapoetically, the reader is here facing the characteristic floating of *sententiae* qua *sermocinationes*. As Blumenberg notes, Johann

---

[59] For Plotinus' (discursive) refunctionalization of a *dictum* on the part of the *Iliad*'s Agamemnon by 'putting it into the mouth of' the *Odyssey*'s hero, see Blumenberg, *Arbeit am Mythos*, pp. 87–88; in line with his overall thesis in that volume, the philosopher explicitly deems this "work on myth" (p. 88; trans. dsm). Cf. Harald Weinrich's formulation: "Sokrates [...], dem Plato die [äsopische] Fabel in den Mund legt" ("Thales und die thrakische Magd: allseitige Schadenfreude." *Das Komische*, edited by Wolfgang Preisendanz and Rainer Warning. Munich: Fink, 1976, pp. 435–437, here p. 435).

[60] D. Laertius, *Lives*, pp. 142–143, II.12–13. See Cicero: "the words Euripides has put into the mouth of Theseus ['a Theseo dicta'] [...]: [']this lesson from wise lips I learnt, / Within my Heart I pondered ills to come: [...] that [...] / No sudden care should rend me unprepared ['Ne me imparatum cura laceraret repens'][']. By the lesson which Theseus says he learnt form a wise man, Euripides means a lesson which he had learnt himself. For he had been a pupil of Anaxagoras, who, according to the story, said when he heard of his son's death, 'I knew that I had begotten a mortal ['Sciebam me genuisse mortalem']'. This saying shows that such events are cruel for those who have not reflected upon them" (Marcus Tullius Cicero. *Tusculan Disputations*, edited and translated by John E. King. Cambridge: Harvard University Press, 1945, III.xiv.29–30). For other variants, see Seneca's *sermocinatio* of 'Demetrius': "Do you ['immortal gods'] wish to take my children? – it was for you that I fathered them" (*Moral Essays*, p. 37, V.5); cf. "Good men lose their sons; why not, since sometimes they even slay them?" (p. 43, VI.2) – with the note referring to "Lucius Junius Brutus and Manlius Torquatus" (p. 42n.).

Wolfgang von Goethe refunctionalized the above aphorism, applying it to the (factual) demise of his own son: *"Non ignoravi me mortalem genuisse."*⁶¹

From a pragmatic perspective, D. Laertius' *Lives* demonstrate the degree to which the various forms of rhetorical ventriloquism are in fact effectual: its techniques conduce to producing a vivid, characteristic, and probable image of certain *personae* (*ethopoiía*, with respect to *eikós* and a view to *enárgeia*); and to crafting sayings (also in verbal exchanges) to be put into the mouth of these characters (*dialogismós*). So as to effect plausibility, attention is paid to remaining in accord with their *ethos* as generally understood, while a certain flexibility obtains as to what will be deemed apposite in terms of such attributions. Negotiating this tension in his textual economy – navigating with respect to the *aptum* – delineates the scope and leeway for the writer (dramatist, philosopher, orator, historian) as regards making his particular point (including where 'universal' by implication). The same as the overall *téchne*, the rhetorico-poetic device of *sermocinatio* is trans-generic in terms of application.⁶² Whereas the specific

---

61 Blumenberg, *Goethe zum Beispiel*, p. 225. See Goethe's refunctionalization of the statement vis-à-vis his own son (August) as related by Blumenberg: "auf die Nachricht, das einzige von ihm [sc. Goethe] bewirkte Leben sei erloschen, erwiderte er ohne Zweifel oder Verzweiflung, ausweichend in die lateinische Sprache, was zuerst von einem Griechen gesagt worden war, er habe gewußt, nur einen Sterblichen gezeugt zu haben: *Non ignoravi me mortalem genuisse*" (ibid.). Frequently, similar remarks ascribed or attributed to specific philosophers, or other *personae*, will actually derive from dramatic, dialogic, or comparable renderings – sometimes even explicitly, e.g. in D. Laertius: "Menippus in his *Sale of Diogenes* tells how, when he was captured and put up for sale, he was asked what he could do. He replied, 'Govern men ['andron árchein']'" (*Lives*, vol. II, pp. 30–31, VI.29); or, a case without direct speech: "Through watching a mouse running about, says Theophrastus in the Megarian dialogue [...], he [sc. 'Diogenes'] discovered the means of adapting himself to circumstances ['peristáseos']" (pp. 24–25, VI.22). As of early modern times, the source will often be novels; since the beginning of the twentieth century, they predictably derive from motion pictures – and from comparable forms of immediate, 'enargic' virtuality in the twenty-first. As to the 'floating of *sententiae*,' see the following phrases on the part of D. Laertius: "Sotion, however, [...] makes the Cynic address this remark to Plato himself" (p. 29, VI:26); "Others give this retort to Theodorus" (p. 45, VI.42); "But others attribute this remark to Diagoras of Melos" (p. 61, VI.59).

62 In a genealogical argument, David Sansone wishes to reverse dependences: "we are willing to believe, on the authority of Aristotle and others, that the earliest dramatists needed to learn from the earliest rhetoricians how to put persuasive words into the mouths of their characters. [...] on the contrary, it was the revolutionary innovation represented by the development of the drama that inspired the creation of rhetorical theory" (*Greek Drama and the Invention of Rhetoric*. Chichester: Wiley-Blackwell, 2012, p. 20). For Lysias' "comic characterization" ("*ethopoiia*") of an "*alazon*" and the staging of "an upside-down world (*mundus perversus*)," see Phillip Harding. "Comedy and Rhetoric." *Persuasion: Greek Rhetoric in Action*, edited by Ian Worthington. London: Routledge, 1994, pp. 196–221, spec. pp. 202–206, here pp. 202–203; he précises: "Lysias [...] used many of the

disposition (selection and placement, hence function) in a work with historical claims will typically be a highpoint or a climax (not least for reasons of variation in the textual economy), dialogic works featuring familiar *personae* consist of sequential, contextualized *sermocinationes* (with narrative elements reduced in keeping with generic conventions); in an equally metapoetic perspective, this ventriloquistic device proves especially expedient in drama, where the words have actually been put into various mouths, speech is dynamically enacted on the stage, and performed with a high degree of vivid immediacy and intensity.[63]

In (apparently) referential works, citations may take on a character similar to *sermocinationes*, specifically if the respective 'authority' is overtly or subtly recontextualized, overstated, misquoted, or fabricated altogether.[64] As Leo

---

techniques of the comic dramatist – exaggeration, incongruity, parody, absurdity, the impossible and, [...] as he makes his own character admit, he has masterfully taken the comic hero off the stage and put him in court" (p. 206). Cf. Mayfield, "Interplay," pp. 10n.–12n.; with further references.

[63] Such accommodates the audience's delight in, and gusto for, 'special effects' – and is thus conducive to effecting an unreflected persuadedness, an only apparently 'informed consent.' See Quintilian: "etiam credit facilius quae audienti iucunda sunt, et voluptate ad fidem ducitur" (*Institutio*, 4.2.119). Cf. Augustine's "*dilige et quod vis fac*" (as quoted in: Carolyn Hammond. "Timeline: Life of Augustine. The Wider Church and the Empire." *Confessions: Books 1–8*, pp. lx–lxv, here p. lxii); in Lawrence D. Green's words: "Once your auditor thinks you love him, you can tell him anything" ("Aristotle's *Rhetoric* and Renaissance Views of the Emotions." *Renaissance Rhetoric*, edited by Peter Mack. New York: St. Martin's Press, 1994, pp. 1–26, here p. 7); he gives a mediated version as "Ama, & dic quod vis" (ibid., p. 22n.; cf. Mayfield, "Interplay," pp. 18n.–19n.).

[64] Cf. "Thales is quoted verbatim by Seneca, although he left nothing written behind" (Hans Blumenberg. *Schiffbruch mit Zuschauer: Paradigmen einer Daseinsmetapher*. Frankfurt a. M.: Suhrkamp, 1979, p. 10n.; trans. dsm). See Grube's formulations (here as regards gleaning fragments to form a tentative notion of lost works): "Theophrastus is quoted as saying," "Ammonius [...] quotes Theophrastus as saying" (*Greek and Roman Critics*, p. 106); "a passage of Dionysius of Halicarnassus [...] quotes Theophrastus as saying" (p. 108); "attributes to Theophrastus a statement" (ibid.). Grube also cites "Gellius quot[ing] Varro as saying" (p. 163); these might as well be *sermocinationes*. Jorge Luis Borges often uses such devices, most notoriously in his "Pierre Menard, Author of the *Quixote*" ("Pierre Menard, Author of the *Quixote*," edited and translated by Andrew Hurley. *Collected Fictions*. New York: Penguin, 1998, pp. 88–95, passim). Mikhail Bakhtin stresses "the transmission and re-processing of another's word [...] the speaker introduces into the other's words his own intentions and highlights the context of those words in his own way" (*The Dialogic Imagination: Four Essays*, translated by Caryl Emerson and Michael Holquist. Austin: University of Texas Press, 2002, p. 355). "Rhetorical genres possess the most varied forms for transmitting another's speech, and for the most part these are intensely dialogized forms. Rhetoric relies heavily on the vivid re-accentuating of the words it transmits (often to the point of distorting them completely) [...]. Rhetorical genres provide rich material for studying a variety of forms for transmitting another's speech, the most varied means for formulating and framing such speech" (p. 354); "in the makeup of almost every utterance spoken by a social person [...] a

Strauss notes, Niccolò Machiavelli arguably outperformed all in the art of rhetorical ventriloquism: he often slightly alters traditional *dicta* by Livy or Tacitus (partly fictive, to begin with), but also *Scriptural* passages.[65] The manipulation of the source text or author is effective both in terms of the resulting statement, and with a view to readers able to discern the difference – hence that Machiavelli has, in point of fact, put words into the mouths of 'Livy,' 'Tacitus,' or the *Biblical* 'David,' while seemingly 'just' citing.[66] Whereas such changes are typically tacit,

---

significant number of words can be identified that are implicitly or explicitly admitted as someone else's, and that are transmitted by a variety of different means. Within the arena of almost every utterance an intense interaction and struggle between one's own and another's word is being waged, a process in which they oppose or dialogically interanimate each other" (ibid.).

65 Cf. Strauss, *Thoughts*, pp. 35–36, 42, 106–107, 137–167; spec. "Machiavelli's Livy is a character of Machiavelli" (p. 141); "Tacitus is less Machiavelli's model than his creation" (p. 165); see Mansfield, *Machiavelli's Virtue*, pp. 132, 320n.; Mayfield, *Artful Immorality*, pp. 83n., 91n. As to the refunctionalizations of *Scripture* and Tacitus, cf. Niccolò Machiavelli. *Il Principe*, edited by Giorgio Inglese. Turin: Einaudi, 1995, pp. 93–96, XIII; thereto, see Strauss, *Thoughts*, pp. 329n.–330n.; Mayfield, *Artful Immorality*, pp. 180–182). Cf. these formulations in Trimpi (infinitized here with a view to demonstrating universal applicability): "In referring to [...] [he] makes certain important, though inconspicuous, changes. [...] Each time [...] [he] cites this passage [...], he omits the qualifying phrase [...]. The omission is probably not accidental"; with context: "Plotinus has changed Plato's 'to become like God (ὁμοίωσις θεῷ)' [...] into 'to be god (θεὸν εἶναι)'" (*Muses*, p. 170).

66 It also applies to scenes dramatizing the exploits of the otherwise historical 'Cesare Borgia,' whom the factual author 'Machiavelli' is known to have met; in such cases, an intratextual 'Machiavelli' (with the *ethos* of a counselor) puts words into the mouth of his textual *persona* 'Cesare' so effectively that the ventriloquism might go unnoticed, and be taken at face value (sc. 'historically'). Cf. "Multum refert etiam quae sit persona suadentis" (Quintilian, *Institutio*, 3.8.48); *de re*, see this collocation: "auctoritate personarum" (10.1.97). Rhetorical ventriloquism is similarly utile in terms of this subtle device: "Hase de hablar a los presentes en los passados" (Baltasar Gracián. *Oráculo manual y arte de prudencia*, edited by Emilio Blanco, 9th ed. Madrid: Cátedra, 2011, p. 217, §210) – with the gloss: "referir la censura a un personaje de la historia" (p. 217n.); "Y es [...] el arbitrio empleado por los tacitistas [...] que se sirven de personajes de la antigüedad para verter sus juicios en sus libros" (ibid.); another statement is glossed: "que lo pone en boca de" etc. (ibid., p. 133n.). With regard to Shakespeare, see Julie Maxwell. "How the Renaissance (Mis)Used Sources: The Art of Misquotation." *How To Do Things with Shakespeare: New Approaches, New Essays*, edited by Laurie Maguire. Oxford: Blackwell, 2008, pp. 54–76, passim, spec. the central claims: "In scholarship, misquotation is vexing. In literature, it is an art" (p. 56); "Misquotation occurs in [...] verbal inexactness [...] quoting out of context, in ways that are recognizably transgressive: irreverent, self-serving, devious [...] 'The devil can cite scripture for his purpose' [...] *The Merchant of Venice* (1.3.98)" (p. 57–58); "Renaissance readers and writers [...] were taught to misquote creatively. Renaissance England was a quoting culture" (p. 58); "The New Testament is full of quotations from the Old, used mainly to justify arguments. So to quote or misquote the Bible, argumentatively, is to imitate its strategies" (p. 63); "Shakespeare's misquotations often economize" (p. 67); "Misquoting is an art" (p. 71).

the ensuing 'twisting of words' in a highly 'floatational,' frequently quoted and apparently recycled Ancient example makes a point of the distortion:

> when Aristotle observed that Isocrates succeeded in obtaining a distinguished set of pupils by means of [...] devoting his discourses to empty elegance of style ['ad inanem sermonis elegantiam'], he himself suddenly altered ['mutavit repente'] almost the whole of his own system of training, and quoted a line from *Philoctetes* with a slight modification ['paulo secus']: the hero in the tragedy said that it was a disgrace for him to keep silent and suffer the barbarians to speak, but Aristotle put it 'suffer Isocrates to speak'; and consequently he put the whole of his system of philosophy in a polished and brilliant form[.][67]

It will always be decisive, which words are being put into the mouth of whom, at what time, in which setting and whose presence – a matter of rhetorical *dispositio*; and ventriloquistically discrediting someone is not just a political, but also a literary and philosophical phenomenon.[68]

The polyphony constitutive of dialogues allows much leeway in the textual economy of *sermocinationes*.[69] It will be no accident that Plato perfected this

---

[67] Cicero, "On the Orator," III.xxxv.141; cf. 110n. See also: "Aristotle [...] under the stimulus of the fame of the rhetorician Isocrates, began like him to teach the young to speak and combine wisdom with eloquence ['prudentiam cum eloquentia iungere']" – with "dicere docere" adjoined in the Latin (*Tusculan Disputations*, I.iv.7); the gloss reads: "Isocrates, 'that old man eloquent' [...]. With reference to his rivalry with Isocrates[,] Aristotle made, it was said, constant use of the line, αἰσχρὸν σιωπᾶν, Ἰσοκράτην δ' ἐᾶν λέγειν" (pp. 8n.–9n.). Quintilian gives this version: "Isocrates' pupils distinguished themselves in every branch of study, and when he was an old man (and he lived to be 98), Aristotle began teaching rhetoric in afternoon lectures, often parodying (we are told ['ut traditur']) the well-known line ['versu (...) frequenter usus'] in the *Philoctetes*: [']Shame to keep quiet, and let Isocrates speak ['turpe esse tacere et Isocraten pati dicere'][']" (*Institutio*, 3.1.14; cf. p. 14n.).
[68] To say nothing of statements such as "The devil speaks in him" (William Shakespeare. *The Tempest*, edited by Virginia Mason Vaughan and Alden T. Vaughan, 3rd edition. London: Thomson, 2005, 5.1.129). Even so, an epideictic functionalization with a different tendency is also conceivable; in this respect, see the assorted words put into Lichtenberg's mouth by Blumenberg as an *hommage* ("'Wie geht's, sagte ein Blinder zu einem Lahmen. Wie Sie sehen, antwortete der Lahme.'" *Lichtenbergs Funkenflug der Vernunft: Eine Hommage*, edited by Jörg-Dieter Kogel et al. Frankfurt a. M.: Insel, 1992, pp. 21–23.). Ascribing an entire book to a particular authority might be seen as something like an editorial *sermocinatio*, with (potentially) far-reaching consequences in terms of (the history of) reception; a notorious case would be the *Rhetorica ad Herennium*; Harry Caplan states the needful: "The fact that the treatise appeared, from Jerome's time on, as a work by Cicero gave it a prestige which it enjoyed for over a thousand years" ("Introduction." *Rhetorica ad Herennium*, pp. vii–lviii, here p. vii–viii). See also *Of Eloquence: Studies in Ancient and Mediaeval Rhetoric*, edited by Anne King and Helen North. Ithaca, London: Cornell University Press, 1970, p. 2.
[69] Cf. Sloane: "humanist prose is [...] always many voiced" ("Rhetorical Education," p. 175). For Galileo Galilei's writings in this genre, several analyses on Blumenberg's part demonstrate a functional process of dialogic distribution (rhetorical *dispositio*); in one instance, the censor(s)

particular art of discourse, seeing that *dialogismós* is also a delegative device, enabling the distribution of otherwise (self-)contradictory statements, the enactment of argument *in utramque partem*; most importantly, it conduces to an effectual practice of *parrhesía* in permitting one's saying anything one cannot – or does not wish to – say in one's own name even so.[70]

---

had demanded that a certain formula be included in the text – and Galilei puts it into the mouth of Simplicio, the very protagonist who does not prevail in the dispute: "Anstoß sollte erregen, daß Galilei diese ärgerliche Formel dem Simplicio in den Mund legt, also der Figur des Dialoges, die am Ende Verlierer ist" (*Legitimität der Neuzeit*, 2nd edition. Frankfurt a. M.: Suhrkamp, 1999, p. 461; cf. pp. 64, 459; also: "Das Fernrohr und die Ohnmacht der Wahrheit." *Sidereus Nuncius: Nachricht von neuen Sternen*, edited by Hans Blumenberg, 2nd edition. Frankfurt a. M.: Suhrkamp, 2002, pp. 7–75, here p. 64). As to the formulations used to express the process of *sermocinatio* generally, see also: "läßt Galilei den Salviati sagen" (Blumenberg, *Legitimität*, p. 465); "[Giordano] Bruno läßt seinen Teofilo sagen" ("Einleitung: Das Universum eines Ketzers." *Das Aschermittwochsmahl*, edited by Hans Blumenberg. 1969. Frankfurt a. M.: Insel, 1981, pp. 9–61, here p. 42); later also in literary adaptations of the former's *persona*: "Der Ausspruch, den Brecht Galilei hier in den Mund legt" (*Legitimität*, p. 463). In an epistolary context, cf. "Lambert läßt seinen Korrespondenzpartner schreiben" (Blumenberg. *Die Genesis der kopernikanischen Welt: Der kopernikanische Komparativ. Die kopernikanische Optik*, vol. III, 3rd edition. Frankfurt a. M.: Suhrkamp, 1996, p. 647); including a ventriloquized reaction: "Das ist nun wieder ein Punkt, an dem Lambert seinen Korrespondenzpartner empört und verwirrt reagieren lassen kann" (p. 650); "läßt Lambert seinen fiktiven Partner resigniert fragen" (p. 652). For further variants of describing the act of ventriloquism, cf. "Cicero [...] makes Appius Caecus and Clodius [...] address ['adloquitur'] Clodia" (Quintilian, *Institutio*, 3.8.54). "Cicero has Antonius suggest" (Christiansen, "Rhetoric as Character-Fashioning," p. 307). See Gill's formulation (infinitized): "Cicero [...] engages in debate [...] with imagined spokesmen" ("Personhood," p. 198). Blumenberg notes: "J[ünger] läßt [...] den Bruder Otho [...] sagen" (*Schriften zur Literatur: 1945–1958*, edited by Alexander Schmitz and Bernd Stiegler. Berlin: Suhrkamp, 2017, p. 28; cf. Blumenberg, *Jünger*, p. 12) – such a metapoetical formulation presupposes an (extratextual) author. Cf. also the phrase indicating the recipient of the *sermocinatio* in place of the ('unknown') emitter: "Hercules [...] dem ein unbekannter Tragiker [...] jene [...] Worte geliehen hat" (Rudolf Hirzel. "Der Selbstmord." *Archiv für Religionswissenschaft* 11 [1908], pp. 75–104, 243–284, 417–476, here p. 284n.).

70 Generally thereto, see DS Mayfield, "Otherwise: Rhetorical Techniques of Contradiction (With Remarks on Quintilian, Augustine, Machiavelli, Shakespeare, Gracián)." *Contradiction Studies*, edited by Gisela Febel, Cordula Nolte, and Ingo H. Warnke. Wiesbaden: Springer, forthcoming. Cf. the ventriloquistic variant found in Emporius: "There is a third kind of *ethopoeia*, which is introduced only on account of the thing to be done; [...] this approach is called the attorney's (*pragmaticus*)" – with the glosses adding: "Emporius means by this creating an imaginary agent for a desired action" ("Concerning Ethopoeia," translated by Joseph M. Miller. *Readings in Medieval Rhetoric*, edited by Joseph M. Miller et al. Bloomington: Indiana University Press, 1973, pp. 33–36, here pp. 35, 35n.). The orator continues: "It is brought in once in a great while so that a certain attitude will not appear at all or will appear very vaguely" (p. 35) – with his example implying a mode of indirection as the function of this device, where one artfully delegates responsibility,

Performing its constitutive vicariousness in the meta-rhetorical play *Words made viſible*, Samuel Shaw's personified *Sermocination* may have the last word:

> *Sermo.* I am that Figure, Sir, by whom men recite the words of another in their diſcourſe. I am that Author of that ingenious Art of *Quotation*, whereby men may ſpeak as much *Hereſie, Blaſphemy, Treaſon*, as they will, and yet not be guilty of any theſe. The Author of that pleaſant Divertiſement of *Tale-bearing, Detraction, Miſpriſſion* and *Miſrepreſentation*: the Author of that profitable Trade of *revealing ſecrets* and *betraying Counſels*. I have taught the *Teachers* themſelves to ſteal a whole Gooſe, feathers and all; and yet this is not felony but a large Quotation; and ſo that paſſes for *Sermonizing*, which is nothing but *Sermocination*. [...] more men live and act *Sermocination* than ſpeak it; ſeeing with other mens eyes, *acting by other mens policy, and flaunting with other mens wit and money*.[71]

---

or deflects attention to another (hence away from oneself). As to delegation in an affine sense, see Mayfield, "Talking Canines," pp. 13n., 22n., spec. as regards Ilse Nolting-Hauff's remark with respect to Cervantes (cf. "Pikaresker Roman und menippeische Satire." *Die Pluralität der Welten: Aspekte der Renaissance in der Romania*, edited by Wolf-Dieter Stempel and Karlheinz Stierle. Munich: Fink, 1987, pp. 181–200, here p. 194).

71 Samuel Shaw. *Words Made Visible: Or Grammar and Rhetorick Accommodated to the Lives and Manners of Men. Represented in a Country School for the Entertainment and Edification of the Spectators*. London (at the Flying-Horse near St. Dunstans Church in Fleetstreet): Daniel Major, 1679, p. 170. In this witty, parrhesiastic, and highly political school play, the *persona* of *Sermocination* is preceded by *Apoſiopeſis* (pp. 168–169; with reference to the Jesuits, p. 168); and followed by *Proſopope* (pp. 170–171) and *Sarcaſm* (pp. 172–176). The former gives the ensuing exposition of itself – featuring another anti-Catholic invective, here by way of paronomastic punning on the early modern English spelling of *prosopopoiía*: "I am that *Figure*, Sir, whereby men act ſome other perſon living or dead. I need not take much pains to diſcover to you, what ſucceſs my pains have had. The very laſt ſyllable in my name is greater than all the names of the Monarchs upon Earth; and I have given him the power to be ſo, by teaching him to act the perſon of one that died ſixteen hundred years ago. I raiſe the dead as familiarly as any *Conjurer*: I make the vileſt *Uſurper* upon earth to paſs for a *Reformer*, the falſeſt *Traytors* to be eſteem'd as faithful *Counſellors*, a meer *Aſs* to paſs for a *Lion*, and a Carrion *Crow* for a *Peacock*; and all this without any change of natures at all" (p. 171); when asked whether its name not rather be "*Hypocriſie*," *Proſopope* replies with an accentuation of pervasive representative action and life by proxy in human affairs similar to *Sermocination*'s aforesaid statement, thereby linking the two figures via the vicarious: "Men call me ſo ſometimes, Sir, but alaſs that name is too narrow for my nature. For in one word, all men act over again the lives of other men, and whatever is done in the World is done by *Proſopope*" (ibid.). For an analysis of this school play staging and enacting rhetorical figures themselves, see Brian Vickers. "Some Reflections on the Rhetoric Textbook." *Renaissance Rhetoric*, pp. 81–102, spec. pp. 92–98; on *prosopopoiía* in Shaw, see Vickers, p. 94; Christiansen, "Rhetoric as Character-Fashioning," p. 332.

Notes on Contributors

Toni Bernhart studied German literature, history of theater, and geography at the University of Vienna, and completed his PhD thesis on color semantics in Hans Henny Jahnn at the Humboldt-Universität zu Berlin in 2001. From 2013 to 2015, he was a fellow of the DramaNet project; afterwards, he earned a grant from the Deutsche Forschungsgemeinschaft (DFG) for his project "Quantitative Criticism," based at the University of Stuttgart. He completed his habilitation thesis entitled *Volk – Schauspiel – Antivolksstück: Genese einer kulturgeschichtlichen Formation* in 2017 and is currently preparing its publication. Bernhart's main research interests comprise German folk theatre as well as quantitative methods in interpretation theory. He edited the morality plays by Johannes Ulrich von Federspiel, *Hirlanda* (1999), and Johann Herbst, *Das Laaser Spiel vom Eigenen Gericht* (2010). Further publications include works on Goethe, Alexander von Humboldt, Arthur Schnitzler, and Christoph Schlingensief. In addition, Bernhart is a playwright and stage director.

Ekaterina Boltunova is an Associate Professor at the Faculty of Humanities, National Research University/Higher School of Economics, Moscow. In 2017–2018, she was a Visiting Professor at the University of Illinois at Chicago; in 2008–2009, she taught as a Fulbright Scholar at Columbia University. She also gave lectures at Yale University (2017), Smith College (2017), Amherst College (2017), and the University of Illinois, Urbana-Champaign (2009), and was a participant of multiple international research projects. Her research interests include the cultural and political history of the Russian empire and the USSR; topography and the semiotics of power; the imperial discourse of war; historical memory; and Soviet and post-Soviet reception of the imperial space. She is the author of *Peter the Great's Guards as a Military Corporation* (2011, in Russian); "Reception of Imperial and Tsarist Spheres of Authority in Russia, 1990s–2010s." *Ab Imperio* 2 (2016), pp. 261–309; "Russian Officer Corps and Military Efficiency: 1800–1914." *Kritika: Explorations in Russian and Eurasian History* 16 (2015), pp. 413–422; "Imperial Throne Halls and Discourse of Power in the Topography of Early Modern Russia (late 17th – 18th centuries)." *The Emperor's House: Palaces from Augustus to the Age of Absolutism*, edited by Michael Featherstone (2015), pp. 341–352; and numerous other articles.

Gautam Chakrabarti is a researcher with the ERC sub-project "Learning 'the Moscow Rules': Theatre Artists from Postcolonial India in the Eastern Bloc, 1950–80," at the Centre for Global Theatre History, Ludwig-Maximilians-Universität München. He is also an Assistant Lecturer in "Berlin and German Studies" at the Freie Universität Berlin (FUB). He has previously taught South Asian Studies at the Humboldt-Universität zu Berlin and English and Comparative Literature at the FUB, where he was a Dahlem Research School HONORS Postdoctoral Fellow (2014–2015) with the project "'Non-Committal Involvements': Literary Detectives and Cold Warriors across Eurasia." In 2016, he was a Global Humanities Junior Research and Teaching Fellow at the Hebrew University of Jerusalem. He also finished, with Prof. J. Küpper at the FUB, his PhD on "Familiarising the Exotic: Introducing European Drama in Early Modern India" (2011–2014); this dissertation is currently in preparation as a book manuscript. He has studied and taught English Literature and Cultural Studies in various universities in India, and has also researched, taught and/or lectured in Finland, Russia, the Baltic States, Poland, Israel, South Africa, and Brazil (2006–). He was a Visiting Lecturer at universities and institutes in

St. Petersburg, Russia (Winter 2008/2009). His primary research interests are in comparative literary-cultural history and world literature.

Kirsten Dickhaut is a Professor of Romance Literatures at the University of Stuttgart. Her main fields of research are intermediality, drama in early modern times, and magic/sorcery/witchcraft. Her recent publications include: Kirsten Dickhaut, editor. *Art of deception: Kunst der Täuschung. Über Status und Bedeutung von ästhetischer und dämonischer Illusion in der Frühen Neuzeit (1400–1700) in Italien und Frankreich* (2016) as well as "*Plaire et instruire ou comment Molière présente les valeurs religieuses dans L'École des femmes.*" *Le fait religieux dans les littératures française et québécoise: Présences, résurgences et oublis*, edited by Gilles Dupuis, Klaus-Dieter Ertler, Alessandra Ferraro, and Yvonne Völkl (2017), pp. 61–84.

Susanne Friede is a Professor of Romance Literatures at the Department of Romance Studies at the University of Klagenfurt, Austria. She serves as joint editor of the *Literaturwissenschaftliches Jahrbuch* (2015–) and is head of the Austrian-wide interdisciplinary research project "The Exercise of Judgement in the Early Modern Period" (2017–). Her further research areas include anticlassicisms in the Cinquecento (in the framework of a project funded, since 2018, by the German Research Foundation, DFG, and the Austrian Science Fund, FWF); French Grail literature of the twelfth and thirteenth centuries; troubadour poetry of the thirteenth century; European cultural journals; and the relationship between literature and ethnography in France and Italy (1840–1910). Her most recent publications comprise a monograph about the Italian novel at the dawn of the 20th century, *Der italienische Roman der Jahrhundertwende* (2015), as well as *Autorschaft und Autorität in den romanischen Literaturen des Mittelalters*, a volume on authorship and authority in the Middle Ages jointly edited with M. Schwarze (2015).

Gaia Gubbini is a researcher at Freie Universität Berlin. She earned the degree of Doctor Europaeus in Romance philology at the University of Siena before she became a research fellow at the École Pratique des Hautes Études in Paris in 2012, and an Alexander von Humboldt fellow at FUB in 2013. Continuing her work at Freie Universität, she joint "DramaNet" and was subsequently awarded funding by the Fritz Thyssen Stiftung for her research project "Vulnus amoris: A Trajectory in Medieval Romance Literature" (2016–). Gubbini has published on medieval literatures in Langue d'oc, ancient French, and ancient Italian, exploring their links to Latin philosophical and medical treatises. Her research themes also include troubadour poetry and the senses, the relationship between body and spirit as well as the role of *imaginatio* in medieval romance literature, the idea of love in Dante and Petrarch, as well as Arthurian myths in ancient French literature. She has recently published the edited volume *Body and Spirit in the Middle Ages: Literature, Philosophy, Medicine* (Berlin: de Gruyter, 2018) and is currently working on a habilitation thesis ("second book") entitled *Proust's Inner Self and the Western Tradition: Novelty and Continuity*.

Blair Hoxby is a Professor at the Department of English at Stanford University. He writes on the literature and culture of England, France, Italy, and Spain from 1500 to 1800, recently with a view to the theory and practice of tragedy during that period. Apart from numerous articles, Hoxby has recently published a book-length study entitled *What Was Tragedy?: Theory and the*

Early Modern Canon (2015), which offers an examination of early modern tragedy that is free from Romantic notions of the tragic. Hoxby is also the author of *Mammon's Music: Literature and Economics in the Age of Miton* (2002), an analysis of the commercial revolution in the seventeenth century in its effects on the literature of the time. Hoxby also writes on the poetry and prose of John Milton and John Dryden, and their Augustan heirs.

Julia Ivanova is an Associate Professor at the School of Philology and a leading research fellow at the Poletayev Institute for Theoretical and Historical Studies in the Humanities at the National Research University/Higher School of Economics, Moscow. She has written on Neo-Latin humanist literature, Counterreformation political thought, and Renaissance medicine. Her more recent publications are dedicated to the history of method in the early modern humanities, Prospero Alpini's idea of Egyptian medicine, and Giambattista Vico's juridical thought.

Janina Janke is a researching artist, theater director and stage designer. After an apprenticeship as a carpenter, she studied European ethnography and philosophy in Munich, and then stage design at the Berlin University of the Arts. In 2006 she co-founded the artist collective OPER DYNAMO WEST. Since then, her work has taken place in dialogue with particular buildings and spaces in Berlin and abroad, such as the *Zoologischer Bahnhof* Berlin, Le Corbusier's *Unités d'habitation* in Berlin and Marseille, and the UN headquarters in Vienna, Nairobi, New York City, and Geneva. Janke conceives and realizes spatial interventions, experimental stagings and artistic research projects, all at the intersection of art, architecture, and science. Her work seeks to make the aesthetic, social, and narrative structures of urban spaces acoustically, visually, and scenically palpable. In 2008/09, Janina Janke was a fellow of the Graduate School of the Arts and Sciences of the Berlin University of the Arts; in 2009, she was awarded a project fellowship at the Akademie Schloss Solitude. In 2010, she was a fellow of the German Academy in Rome, Casa Baldi. From 2011 to 2015, she participated in "andere räume – knowledge through art," a long-term research project of artists and scientists supported by the *Austrian Science Fund* (FWF). In 2012/13, she was Artist in Residence of the United Nations; in 2014, a fellow of the Cité internationale des arts in Paris; in 2015, an artist in residence at Quartier 21 – MuseumsQuartier Vienna.

Olga Kuptsova is a Professor at the National Research University/Higher School of Economics, Moscow, as well as a Senior Researcher at the Russian State Institute for Art Studies; in addition, she has been a Visiting Professor at the Maison des sciences de l'homme, Paris. Her publications include: *From the History of Soviet Theater Criticism, 1917–1926* (1984); *Essays on Russian Theatrical Culture* (2003); *The Life of the Estate Myth: Lost and Found Paradise* (2008); "Le théâtre à Moscou: voie sans issue ou periode de transition." *Revue russe* (2000), pp. 35–43; "Meyerhold et la France, lettres des années 1920–1930." *Les voyages du théâtre: Russie–France* (2001), edited by Hélène Henry, pp. 101–118; "Theaterspiele in Garten und Parkanlagen russischer Landsitze um 1800: Versuch einer Typologie." *Die Gartenkunst*, edited by A. Ananieva, G. Grünig, and A. Veselova (2013), pp. 173–180.

Joachim Küpper is a Professor of Comparative Literature and Romance Literatures at Freie Universität Berlin, Germany. He has published widely on literary, historiographical, and philosophical texts from Homer to the twentieth century. In addition, his research focuses on literary theory and aesthetics. His most recent publication is a book dealing with a network theory of cultural dynamics (*The Cultural Net*, 2018). In the course of his career, he was awarded the Heinz Maier-Leibnitz prize as well as the Leibniz prize of the Deutsche Forschungsgemeinschaft. In 2010, he received an Advanced Grant from the European Research Council, Brussels. Küpper was the Principal Investigator of the ERC project "Early Modern European Drama and the Cultural Net (DramaNet)" and the founding director of the Dahlem Humanities Center, Berlin. Currently, he serves as the director of the international network "Principles of Cultural Dynamics." He is a member of the Göttingen Academy of Sciences, the German National Academy of Sciences as well as the American Academy of Arts and Sciences. For many years, he has been a Visiting Associate Professor at the Johns Hopkins University and an invited Director of research ("Directeur de recherche invité") at the École des Hautes Etudes en Sciences Sociales (EHESS), Paris. His publications include: *Discursive* Renovatio *in Lope de Vega and Calderón* (Berlin/Boston, MA: de Gruyter, 2017; Open Access); Petrarca: *Das Schweigen der Veritas und die Worte des Dichters* (Berlin/New York, NY: de Gruyter, 2002); *The Cultural Net: Early Modern Drama as a Paradigm* (Berlin/Boston, MA: de Gruyter, 2018; Open Access); "The Traditional Cosmos and the New World," *Modern Language Notes* 118 (2003), pp. 363–392.

DS Mayfield studied American, English, and Spanish Literature at Würzburg University, and Comparative Literature in Berlin and Cambridge (UK). An alumnus of the Friedrich Schlegel Graduate School at Freie Universität Berlin, he became a member of the DramaNet project, working on early modern drama (Rojas, Machiavelli, Shakespeare), with Blumenberg as a theoretical framework. In 2015, he was a Global Humanities Junior Research and Teaching Fellow at Johns Hopkins University. He has edited a volume on *Rhetoric and Drama* (Berlin: de Gruyter, 2017; Open Access) and published a monograph with the title *Artful Immorality – Variants of Cynicism: Machiavelli, Gracián, Diderot, Nietzsche* (Berlin: de Gruyter, 2015).

Jan Mosch was a member of the DramaNet research project at Freie Universität Berlin (2013–2016) and is currently finalizing his PhD thesis, exploring how the "scribbling age" (Robert Burton) that defined post-Reformation culture shaped the uneasy negotiation of heteronomy and individual agency in tragedies by Shakespeare and Racine. As a junior lecturer, he has taught classes in British literature, particularly contemporary fiction. He serves as a theatrical reviewer for the Yearbook of the German Shakespeare Association (2012–) and is joint editor of a volume that explores the conceptualization of culture as a (virtual) network through case studies of the dynamic dissemination of early modern drama: *Poetics and Politics: Net Structures and Agencies in Early Modern Drama* (Berlin: de Gruyter, 2018; Open Access).

Elena Penskaya is a Professor of Russian and European Literature at the National Research University/Higher School of Economics, Moscow. At the HSE, she holds the position of Head of the School of Philology and serves as a Principal Investigator in the Theater Studies Laboratory. From 2010–2011, Prof. Penskaya was a Visiting Professor at the Sorbonne; in 2016, she lectured as a Visiting Professor at the Humboldt Universität zu Berlin. She is the Executive Editor of the *Education Studies Quarterly* (HSE) and a member of the editorial board of the *International Encyclopedia of Literary Museums*. Her research is dedicated to the crossroads of West-European and Russian historical, cultural, and literary contexts from the 19th through the

21st centuries. Her further scholarly interests comprise intellectual history, Russian and West-European literature and drama, and comparative studies. Her most recent books are on the Russian entertainment culture of the Silver Age (1908–1918), the anti-formalist campaign of the 1930s, the era of 'removal,' as well as Russian formalism and modern humanitarian knowledge.

Natalia Sarana is completing her PhD studies at the Department of Russian Literature, School of Philology, Higher School of Economics (Moscow). She earned an M.A. in Comparative Literature from HSE in 2014 and a B.A. in Journalism in 2012. Sarana has also studied at the University of Cambridge as a Visiting PhD student, and, as an exchange student, at the University of Essex (M.A. level) and at the University of Westminster (undergraduate level). She has published on Leo Tolstoy and Aleksey Pisemsky, and her research interests include Anglo-Russian literary relations in the 1850–1890s as well as the European novel, and drama, of formation.

Pavel Sokolov is an Associate Professor at the School of Philosophy and leading research fellow at the Poletayev Institute for Theoretical and Historical Studies in the Humanities at the National Research University/Higher School of Economics, Moscow. He has published on Late scholasticism, early modern Biblical hermeneutics, and political thought. His more recent publications deal with eighteenth-century Dutch medicine, the reception of Thomas Hobbes's political ideas in the Netherlands, and Giambattista Vico's conception of heroism.

Index

Accius 38
Addison, Joseph 104, 105, 143
Aeschylus 38
Afanasyev, Alexander 117
Ahndoril, Alexandra 123
Alighieri, Dante 42, 55, 129
Ammirato, Scipione 77
Appian 38
Aristophanes 183
Aristotle 4, 9, 28, 38, 50, 59, 61, 83
Arulenus Rusticus 78
Augustine 52, 74, 160, 179
Augustus 73
Aurobindo, Sri 129

Bacon, Francis 109
Bakhtin, Mikhail 43
Baldissone, Giusi 70
Balzac, Honoré de 32, 34, 36, 37
Banerjee, Reverend Krishna Mohan 146
Barnes, Julian 16
Barthes, Roland 3, 32
Batyushkov, Fyodor 112
Beaumarchais, Pierre-Augustin Caron de 116
Beaumont, Francis 103, 105
Bede the Venerable (Beda Venerabilis) 43
Belcari, Feo 68
Belinsky, Vissarion 117
Benserade, Isaac 98
Bethune, John Elliot Drinkwater 132, 145
Blackburn, Stuart 144
Blumenberg, Hans 173, 184, 186
Boccaccio, Giovanni 62, 71, 151
Boccalini, Traiano 81
Bodel, Jean 42
Boethius 50
Bracciolini, Poggio 62, 64
Bradley, Andrew C 41
Brandt, Geeraardt 72
Branham, Robert 184
Byron, Lord George Gordon 129
Bysack, Gour Dass 132, 135, 139

Calcidius 53
Campanella, Tomaso 98
Casanova, Pascale 140
Catherine II (Empress of Russia) 86
Cats, Jacob 75
Cervantes, Miguel de 15, 38, 114, 118, 119
Chastelain, George 58
Chateaubriand, François-René de 34
Chatterjee, Bankim Chandra 129
Chaudhuri, Amit 132, 133, 134
Chrétien de Troyes 44, 58
Cicero 38, 76
Cixous, Hélène 141
Coleridge, Samuel Taylor 139
Colevelt, Jacob Janszoon 81
Conches, William of 50, 53
Corbiau, Gérard 97
Corneille, Pierre 97, 99

Dalmia, Vasudha 144
Dal, Vladimir 113
Dancourt, Florent Carton 116
Datta, Michael Madhusudan 129
Davenant, William 103
Davis, Jessica M. 102
Defoe, Daniel 3
De la Court, Pieter and Johan 78
Dennis, John 104
Dharwadker, Vinay 145
Diderot, Denis 34
Diogenes Laertius 185, 187
Diomedes 38
Dionysius of Halicarnassus 7
Donatus 38
Dryden, John 39, 103, 105, 110, 143

Ennius 38
Eriksson, Stig A. 123
Euripides 38
Evanthius 38

Fassman, David 88
Fatouville, Nolant de 116

Favart, Charles Simon 116
Fielding, Henry 106, 110
Flaubert, Gustave 32, 37
Foley, John Miles 12
Frappier, Jean 45, 46
Fuqua, Antoine 56

Gay, John 104, 105, 110
Geertz, Clifford 11, 97, 144
Geoffrey of Monmouth 44
Goethe, Johann Wolfgang von 128, 140, 187
Gogol, Nikolai 117
Goldoni, Carlo 119
Golitsyn, Vasily V. 89
Gozzi, Carlo 119
Greenblatt, Stephen 92, 96
Grigoryev, Apollon 116
Grotius, Hugo 83
Gruter, Jan 73
Gupta, Kshetra 136, 144

Harsdörffer, Georg Philipp 143
Hastaba, Ellen 153
Hegel, Georg Wilhelm Friedrich 41
Heidegger, Martin 174
Herder, Johann Gottfried 40, 147
Hobbes, Thomas 78, 109
Hoffman Baruch, Elaine 124
Hogarth, William 107
Homer 129, 180
Hooft, Pieter Corneliszoon 72
Horace 38
Huet, Busken 81
Hutcheon, Linda 12

Jonson, Ben 14

Kantorowicz, Ernst 97
Karatygin, Pyotr 116
Kashin, Nikolai 112
Kelly, Henry Ansgar 50
Kewes, Paulina 13
Khlodovsky, Ruf I. 62, 64
Knight, Alan E. 57
Konrad, Eva-Maria 4
Konstan, David 12
Konst, Jan W. H. 83

Kotlyarevsky, Ivan 119
Kraus, Christina 73

Lausberg, Heinrich 167, 171
Le Goff, Jacques 53, 54
Lesage, Alain-René 116
Leuker, Tobias 58
Lipsius, Justus 74
Livy 1, 7, 38, 73, 74, 76, 78, 79, 80, 85, 178, 189
Locke, John 109
Lope de Vega, Félix 39, 118
Lucian of Samosata 6, 182, 185
Lully, Jean-Baptiste 98
Luzhenovsky, Nikolay 113

Macaulay, Thomas Babington 131
Machiavelli, Niccolò 60, 62, 64, 79, 80, 83
Macpherson, James 147
Macrobius 51, 53, 54
Mahabharata 137
Malory, Sir Thomas 56
Manuzio, Aldo 69
Marabito, Raffaele 151
Marivaux, Pierre de 116
Marx, Karl 32
Mayer, Jean-Christophe 2
McTavish, Rebecca 135
Mellish, Joseph 139
Meyerhold, Vsevolod 118, 120
Michler, Werner 147
Milton, John 104, 180
Minucius Felix 63
Mochalov, Pavel 115, 116
Molière 97, 114, 117, 119
Montaigne, Michel de 74
Morello, Ruth 1
Moretti, Franco 126
Morgann, Maurice 40
Mukhopadhyay, Bhudev 136
Müller, Adam 40
Musset, Alfred de 116, 117
Mysovskaya, Anna 117, 119

Naevius 38
Nandy, Ashis 134
Nennius 43
Neuyes of Neuye 75

Oatley, Keith 12
Ostrovsky, Alexander 112, 122
Otway, Thomas 110
Ovid 74, 76

Pacuvius 38
Patouillet, Jules 112, 117
Paul the Deacon 11
Perrault, Charles 111
Pers, Dirck Pieterzoon 75
Person, Raymond F. 12
Peterson, Indira Viswanathan 146
Petrarca, Francesco 151
Phillips, Arthur 17
Phillips-Court, Kristin 68
Phrynicus 38
Piksanov, Nikolai 112
Pipkin, Amanda 75
Plato 33, 53, 61, 182, 184, 190
Plutarch 181
Pontano, Gioviano 63
Potemkin, Grigory A. 91
Prandoni, Marco 72
Propp, Vladimir 126
Pufendorf, Samuel 78
Pushkin, Alexander 116

Raaflaub, Kurt A. 12
Racine, Jean 39
Richardson, Captain David 131
Richardson, Samuel 35, 36
Richelieu, Cardinal Armand Jean de Plessis 96
Ricoeur, Paul 2
Ritchie, Guy 56
Rowe, Nicholas 40, 110
Rucellai, Giovanni di Bernardo 38
Russo, Luigi 70
Rymer, Thomas 39

Salisbury, John of 51
Sallust 175
Sastri, Sivanath 131
Sastri, Vedanayaka 146
Schiller, Friedrich 10, 114, 116, 139
Schlegel, Friedrich 40
Schliemann, Heinrich 7

Scholl, Margaret 122
Scriblerus Secundus 107, 110
Seneca the Younger 78
Shakespeare, William 2, 10, 11, 13, 14, 17, 18, 37, 38, 39, 41, 96, 105, 110, 114, 115, 118, 131
Shaw, Samuel 192
Shchepkin, Mikhail 119
Shubin, Fedor 87, 89
Sidney, Sir Philip 4, 8
Skinner, Quentin 78
Skvortsova, Ekaterina 88
Sophocles 123
Spanier, Markus 155
Steele, Richard 143
Stein, Alexander 112
Stow, John 1, 8
Strauss, Leo 189
Suetonius 39, 181
Swift, Jonathan 110

Tacitus 38, 73, 74, 75, 77, 78, 80, 81, 175, 178, 189
Tasso, Torquato 143
Thoma, Ernst 158
Thomson, James 110
Thucydides 175
Tieck, Ludwig 111
Toffanin, Giuseppe 74
Trissino, Gian Giorgio 38
Tscholl, Werner 157

Valla, Lorenzo 60
Varneke, Boris 112
Vdovin, Gennady 89
Veinberg, Pyotr 119
Veltman, Alexander 116
Vergil, Polydore 1, 7
Verkaik, Jan W. 81
Veselovsky, Alexey 117
Vico, Giambattista 84
Vidyasagar, Ishwar Chandra 135
Villiers, George, Duke of Buckingham 103, 110
Vinsauf, Geoffrey of 51
Virgil 143

von Birken, Sigmund 143
Vondel, Joost van den 38, 75, 80, 81, 83, 85

Wace 44, 58
Walpole, Horace 89
Walter, Philippe 44

White, Hayden 5, 11, 16
White, Henrietta Sophia 135
White, T. H. 56
William Davenant 11

Zimmer Bradley, Marion 56
Zimmermann, Everett 18

www.ingramcontent.com/pod-product-compliance
Lightning Source LLC
Chambersburg PA
CBHW021730220426
43662CB00008B/787